Getting It Done

Getting It Done

Postagreement Negotiation and International Regimes

edited by Bertram I. Spector and I. William Zartman

UNITED STATES INSTITUTE OF PEACE PRESS
Washington, D.C.

The views expressed in this book are those of the authors alone. They do not necessarily reflect views of the United States Institute of Peace.

UNITED STATES INSTITUTE OF PEACE
1200 17th Street NW, Suite 200
Washington, DC 20036-3011

First published 2003

Printed in the United States of America

The paper used in this publication meets the minimum requirements of American National Standards for Information Science—Permanence of Paper for Printed Library Materials, ANSI Z39.48-1984.

Library of Congress Cataloging-in-Publication Data
Getting it done : postagreement negotiation and international regimes / edited
  by Bertram I. Spector and I. William Zartman.
       p. cm.
    Includes bibliographical references and index.
     ISBN 1-929223-43-9 (cloth : alk. paper) — ISBN 1-929223-42-0 (paper :
alk. paper)
     1. International law. 2. Treaties. 3. International cooperation. 4. Negotia-
tion. I. Spector, Bertram I. (Bertram Irwin), 1949– II. Zartman, I. William.

KZ1321.G48 2003
341—dc21   2003047767

*To our parents, Samuel and Rose, and Ira and Edythe,
who taught us to get it done,
and to our wives, Judith and Danièle,
who helped us to see it through*

Contents

Foreword

Getting It Done is a theoretically ambitious volume whose conclusions have a very practical import. At the conceptual level, the editors and authors explore the intersection of negotiation theory and regime theory so as to explain how international regimes—multilateral entities such as NAFTA and NATO that abide by a particular set of rules and principles—evolve through a process of continual negotiation. This is an exploration into unchartered territory. Previously, most scholars have assumed that once the ink was dry on an agreement to set up a regime, the signatories would comply with its terms and the regime would prosper—or they would not comply and the regime would likely founder. Betram Spector, William Zartman, and their fellow authors, however, make the important point that reaching an agreement is a stage in a negotiation, not the end of the process. A regime, they argue, is in a constant process of renegotiation throughout its life as the interests and power of its members shift and as changes occur in the nature of the problem—pollution or the practice of torture, for instance—that the regime addresses.

The theoretical implications of this novel approach are substantial, and should stimulate rich discussion among academics who specialize in the inner workings of international organizations. But the implications have a practical relevance, too. After all, if Spector, Zartman, and the contributors are right, then those who work in the trenches of international regimes should view their activities in a new light. They are not just administrators—trying to ensure that the members comply with the regime's rules—and not just representatives—trying to find a way to work within the regime's constraints while promoting the interests of the member-states. They are also negotiators, working to redefine both goals and the means to achieve those goals. Moreover, their negotiations are likely to take place on at least two different levels: at the level of the regime itself, and at the national level, where different groups compete to set the agenda for participation in the regime. The number of people affected is by no means negligible. In addition to those who staff the hundreds of different international organizations, there are the national representatives who fill the standing committees and general assemblies, the policymakers who establish the guidelines within which the representatives operate, the nongovernmental organizations and industry groups that press for stricter and better enforced rules, or who argue for exemptions from those rules, and the media that can turn an issue into national and international headlines or bury it in the back pages.

This practical aspect of Spector and Zartman's analysis means that, although *Getting It Done*'s readership may be drawn chiefly from the worlds of academe and scholarship, its ultimate influence should extend more widely. The transmission of ideas between the academic and the practitioner and policymaking communities is seldom straightforward and rarely instantaneous. Yet new ideas and approaches do move from one community to the other, and can do so surprisingly quickly, especially in the United States, where scholars often enlist in the service of one or another administration, and where policymakers frequently retire to the sylvan shades of academe to heal bureaucratic wounds or compose their memoirs.

Throughout its existence, the United States Institute of Peace has sought to facilitate the flow of important new insights about international conflict from one community to the other. To borrow the title of a book published by the Institute and written by former Institute fellow Alexander George (himself both a distinguished scholar and an influential adviser to policymakers), much of our work involves *bridging the gap* between these worlds. Some work sponsored by the Institute has flowed swiftly into the deliberations of official Washington; the influence of other Institute-supported studies has percolated more slowly and subtly. The single most important criterion from the Institute's point of view is not the speed of transmission but the value placed by one or both communities on the ideas conveyed.

In addition to meeting the high standards of quality that the Institute demands, *Getting It Done* offers a new perspective on a subject to which the Institute has appropriately devoted significant attention: negotiation. The range of books published by the Institute on negotiation is considerable, extending from broad conceptual analyses such as Raymond Cohen's *Negotiating Across Cultures* and John Paul Lederach's *Building Peace*, to assessments of particular negotiations such as Helena Cobban's *Israeli–Syrian Peace Talks* and my own *Exiting Indochina*, to explorations of the negotiating style of individual nations. In this latter category, the Institute has published or is about to publish book-length analyses of the negotiating behavior of China, Russia, Japan, North Korea, Germany, France, and the United States. These volumes are part of the Institute's ongoing Cross-Cultural Negotiation Project, which aims to reduce conflict by making negotiations more productive through enhancing awareness of the impact of culture on negotiating styles.

Getting it Done differs from these other volumes in several respects, especially in its conceptual ambition and in focusing attention not on bilateral encounters between nation-states but on multilateral arenas in which states are by no means the only players. That said, *Getting It Done* is published by the Institute for the same overarching reason as its other titles on negotiating theory and practice: to contribute first-rate research and generate potentially valuable ideas on how best to make international negotiation more productive in the service of fostering collaboration and conflict resolution among nations and communities

Richard H. Solomon, President
United States Institute of Peace

Acknowledgments

The editors would like to extend their great thanks to the United States Institute of Peace and to the International Institute for Applied Systems Analysis for their support and assistance for this project. We are grateful as well to Volker Rittberger, Fen Osler Hampson, Nazli Choucri, Dean Pruitt, and several anonymous reviewers for their many useful insights and critiques. The contributions of Ronnie Hjorth and Hugo Maria Schally to the early stages of the project are also appreciated. Our sincere thanks go to Nigel Quinney for his intelligent editing of the text.

Contributors

Bertram I. Spector is executive director of the Center for Negotiation Analysis, technical director of Management Systems International, Inc., and editor-in-chief of *International Negotiation: A Journal of Theory and Practice*. From 1993 to 1995, he was a fellow at the Foreign Policy Institute, Nitze School of Advanced International Studies, the Johns Hopkins University. Spector served as leader of the Processes of International Negotiation (PIN) Project at the International Institute for Applied Systems Analysis in Austria from 1990 to 1993. He is coeditor of *Negotiating International Regimes* and has published articles on negotiating with villains, negotiation readiness, water diplomacy and environmental security, and corruption in developing countries in the *Journal of Conflict Resolution, Negotiation Journal, American Behavioral Scientist,* and the *Annals of the American Academy of Political and Social Science.* He consults with governments and civil society organizations in Eastern Europe, the former Soviet Union, and Africa on governance, democracy, and conflict issues and has conducted studies for the U.S. government, the United States Institute of Peace, Battelle-Pacific Northwest Laboratories, the United Nations/New York, the Austrian government, and the Swedish Council on the Planning and Coordination of Research. Spector obtained his Ph.D. from New York University.

I. William Zartman is Jacob Blaustein Distinguished Professor of International Organization and Conflict Resolution at the School of Advanced International Studies of the Johns Hopkins University, where he directs the Conflict Management Program. He holds a doctorate from Yale University and an honorary doctorate from the Catholic University of Louvain. He is a former distinguished fellow of the United

States Institute of Peace, an Olin Professor at the U.S. Naval Academy, and Halévy Professor at the Institute of Political Studies in Paris. He is editor of *Peacemaking in International Conflict, Preventive Negotiations, Power and Negotiation,* and *The 50% Solution,* among others, and author of *Cowardly Lions: Missed Opportunities to Prevent Deadly Conflict and State Collapse* and *Ripe for Resolution,* among others. He is a member of the Carter Center's International Council for Conflict Resolution and of the Processes of International Negotiation (PIN) Project of the International Institute for Applied Systems Analysis in Austria.

◆　◆　◆

Pamela S. Chasek is an assistant professor of government and director of international studies at Manhattan College in New York City. She is also cofounder and editor of the International Institute for Sustainable Development's *Earth Negotiations Bulletin,* a reporting service on UN environment and development negotiations. She has been a consultant to the United Nations Environment Programme, the United Nations Development Programme, and the United Nations Department for Economic and Social Affairs. Chasek is the author of numerous articles and publications on international environmental politics and negotiation, including *Earth Negotiations: Analyzing Thirty Years of Environmental Diplomacy; Global Environmental Politics,* 3d edition, with Gareth Porter and Janet Welsh Brown; and *The Global Environment in the Twenty-first Century: Prospects for International Cooperation.* She holds a Ph.D. from the Paul H. Nitze School of Advanced International Studies at the Johns Hopkins University and was a Young Scientist at the International Institute for Applied Systems Analysis in Austria.

Anna Korula has fifteen years' experience in the area of human rights, including several years as an active negotiator and mediator. She is currently in Liberia, where she is consulting on human rights implementation, as well as on reintegration and reconciliation, especially with reference to the protection of child soldiers. Korula has previously worked for the United Nations as a human rights officer and civil affairs officer in peacebuilding missions in Croatia, Bosnia, and East Timor. She has also served as a research scholar at the International Institute for Applied Systems Analysis in Austria and has conducted research at universities in the United Kingdom, Germany, and the United States. She received her M.A. from Webster University, St. Louis.

Janie Leatherman is associate professor of international relations in the Department of Politics and Government at Illinois State University and codirector of Peace and Conflict Resolution Studies. She has written extensively on early warning and conflict prevention and the OSCE, including the books *Breaking Cycles of Violence* (lead author) and *From Cold War to Democratic Peace,* as well as a number of articles and book chapters. Leatherman has consulted with national and international organizations on conflict early warning and prevention, including the South Balkans Working Group (the Council on Foreign Relations, New York), Catholic Relief Services, Search for Common Ground, the U.S. War Crimes Ambassador, United States Agency for International Development, and the United Nations University. She has received grants and fellowships from the Social Science Research Council, the United States Institute of Peace, the Swedish government, the International Studies Association, Fulbright-Hayes, and the American Scandinavian Foundation. Leatherman has previously held appointments at the University of Notre Dame and Macalester College. She received her Ph.D. from the Graduate School of International Studies, University of Denver, in 1991.

Gunnar Sjöstedt is a senior research fellow at the Swedish Institute of International Affairs, where he directs programs on international environmental and trade regimes, international negotiations, and psychological operations and strategic intelligence. He has conducted extensive analysis of the transformation of the GATT into the WTO and the postagreement negotiations that sustain that trade regime. As a member of the Processes of International Negotiation (PIN) Project at the International Institute for Applied Systems Analysis (Austria), Sjöstedt has edited several books, including *International Economic Negotiation* (2000), *International Environmental Negotiation* (1993), *Containing the Atom: International Negotiations on Nuclear Security and Safety* (2002), *Negotiating International Regimes: Lessons Learned from the UN Conference on Environment and Development* (1994), and *Transboundary Risk Management* (2001).

Lynn Wagner is currently serving as an issue cluster expert for sustainable development, forests, and deserts on the International Institute for Sustainable Development's linkages website. Eight years of watching UN environmental negotiations as a writer for the *Earth Negotiations Bulletin* have led her to apply her primary research interest—the relationship between negotiation process and outcome—to the expanding field of international environmental negotiations. She has written and coauthored several articles, including "Negotiations in the UN Commission on Sustainable Development: Coalitions, Processes, and Outcomes" and the forthcoming "A Commission Will Lead Them? The UN Commission on Sustainable Development and UNCED Follow-Up." Wagner received her Ph.D. from the Johns Hopkins School of Advanced International Studies and was a Young Scientist at the International Institute for Applied Systems Analysis in Austria.

Getting It Done

Regimes and Negotiaion
An Introduction

Bertram I. Spector and I. William Zartman

MANY OF TODAY'S economic, environmental, and security problems are managed by international regimes. From the World Trade Organization (WTO) and the North Atlantic Free Trade Area (NAFTA), the Mediterranean Action Plan and the Conventions on Climate Change and on the Protection of the Ozone Layer, to the United Nations and the Organization for Security and Cooperation in Europe (OSCE), regimes establish global or regional guidelines for behavior. As "social institutions consisting of agreed upon principles, norms, rules, procedures and programs that govern the interactions of actors in specific issue areas" (Levy, Young, and Zürn 1995, 274), regimes are commonly understood to provide governance, order, and structure to international problem solving.

Over the past two decades, the research agenda on regimes has focused primarily on why regimes are formed and how well states have complied with the agreements establishing them, but analysts have bypassed the important questions of regime sustainability: how regimes operate, adapt, transform, and remain vital to the interests of their stakeholders. Problems are not static and neither are their solutions, and the power and interests of regime signatories are also fluid. International actors do not merely comply or not with regime rules and norms; they adjust those rules and norms over time to fit their changing interests and changing approaches to problem solving. To be viable over the long term, regimes have to evolve and that evolution is accomplished through a process of continuous negotiation. Regimes are born through negotiation processes, and they evolve through *postagreement* negotiation processes.

The intersection of regime theory and negotiation theory is the focus of this book. If regimes are an approach used by international actors to resolve mutually troublesome problems, postagreement negotiation is the process that keeps those regimes vital and alive, renewing and revising them as knowledge, problems, interests, norms, and expectations change. Negotiations within regimes deal with conflicts that continue or emerge between the regime parties' interests, uncertainties that are clarified over time by advances in science or changing situations, and problems that remain unresolved or that emerge in the course of attempts at resolution. Negotiations must also deal with the pedestrian tasks of harmonizing the regime's principles and norms with practical ways of implementing them; when broadly stated and widely accepted goals and ideals meet with a harsher reality, negotiation is a vehicle for adjusting the differences and getting things accomplished. Regimes are thus not final legislation but ongoing normative processes, and to treat them as hard law by focusing on compliance is both to miss their reality and to mistake their nature.

Getting it done—the process describing how regime goals are achieved—is the theme throughout the volume. We want to understand the dynamics of how regimes work to accomplish their objectives. "Getting to the table" (Stein 1990), "getting to yes" (Fisher and Ury 1981), and "getting past no" (Ury 1991) all seek one common result: getting it done. Problems typically are not solved by the negotiated agreement that forms the regime itself. Certainly, much has been accomplished by the time diplomats are able to shake hands on a basic text establishing a regime, but almost always, more still needs to be done to get it done.

The governments back home have to ratify and accept the agreements, and domestic stakeholders have to be convinced that they will benefit by accepting the potential costs and risks of implementation. Laws must be changed, rules and standards modified, and, sometimes, lifestyles adjusted to accommodate the "common good" represented in the negotiated regime. At the international level, new approaches that stimulate the effective implementation of the regime must be put into motion. This could mean the development of new structures and institutions, or the looser development of commonly accepted norms and principles that will monitor, enforce, verify, and generally govern the new agreement. In the process of doing all this, the nature of the target and the course to it shift. New appreciations of problems develop, along with new understandings of the appropriate paths to deal with them. New forces aggregate as courses and costs become clearer: Domestic interests crystallize as applied implications become apparent, international coalitions shift as interests are reinterpreted, opposing forces organize as programs become clearer, and the parties involved find new sources of power in the pursuit of their goals.

All of the activities that take place subsequent to "getting to yes" can be categorized as a broad process of regime evolution and re-creation that has as its goal the resolution or management of the problems that initially prompted negotiations. But these "getting it done" activities have another important attribute in common: they are all negotiation processes—negotiations that occur on the domestic as well as the international level. In these postagreement negotiations, new actors are involved, as well as new issues, new interests, new venues, new strategies, and new solutions. These negotiations can in many ways be considered even more critical than the initial negotiations, for it is success or failure in these postagreement processes that actually produces resolution or management of the original problem.

This book does not merely provide a more accurate or dynamic account of international regimes. It explains why international regimes have difficulty in achieving stability and hence why the image of legislation-then-compliance is misleading. To achieve stability, a regime must solve the initial problem, conform to the power and interests of the significant parties, fit the norms and meet the expectations of the participants, and so overcome the opposition that rises with progress in regime building. But in international affairs, much more than in domestic legislation, problems are fluid, the parties are sovereign states with their own interests and levels of power, participation is based on trust and satisfaction rather than a legal system, and norms and expectations need to be settled on a global level rather than just within a single state with a limited population.

The study of negotiation in general has increasingly come to emphasize that negotiation is not completed when the initial agreement is signed. Instead, its intended effect requires continuing attention to implementation and postsettlement monitoring. In the case of regimes, this lesson takes a different form: the negotiations themselves need to be repeated as circumstances evolve, uncertainties are clarified, and the interests and power of the parties undergo changes as a result. Some regimes, such as the new Law of the Sea, achieve stability after lengthy initial and then postagreement negotiations. The Conference on Security and Cooperation in Europe (analyzed in detail in chapter 5 of this volume) achieved such stability until the problem changed with the end of the Cold War. Changing from a conference to an organization, the new OSCE is still looking for a stable formula and continues its postagreement negotiations. The ozone depletion regime (treated extensively in chapter 6) has moved through postagreement negotiations toward a stable formula, only to be challenged by a crystallizing opposition at a crucial turning point.

The current argument builds on the body of work already available on regimes while correcting it. Not only a clearer understanding of regimes but also simply the passage of time makes this possible. Earlier studies focused on the formation of regimes during a particular era, the Cold War. As a result, researchers debated the impact on state behavior of the new phenomenon, the regime, and concentrated on its holding power, the issue of compliance. They also addressed the role of the dominant state, or hegemon, in regime formation. These three topics—impact, compliance, hegemon—framed the questions of the moment. But the passage of time has shown regimes to be something else than singly legislated objects of compliance, and the choice of the parties to be something beyond merely exit or loyalty (Hirschman 1970). Participants—and their analysts—have found their voice in recursive negotiations that repeatedly alter the course of regimes, and the ongoing history—rather than the founding moment—of regimes supports this new understanding.

The first three chapters of the book provide a theoretical framework of the international regimes–negotiation nexus that expands and corrects the conventional understanding of the subject. I. William Zartman's chapter is an unconventional portrayal of regime formation and evolution, structured around six propositions that link postagreement negotiation inextricably with the dynamics of regimes. Focus must be given to the regime process, which can be characterized by conflict and coordination, uncertainty, recursive negotiations over treaty formation and problem-solving applications, the absolute costs of participation, and continual re-creation. Bertram I. Spector's chapter focuses on the negotiation aspects of regime dynamics by dissecting the postagreement negotiation process into its domestic and international

dimensions and comparing its pre- and postagreement stages analytically. In doing so, it presents an analysis of regimes as life courses, rather
than a single event, that can be understood and explained behaviorally.
The chapter by Gunnar Sjöstedt posits that negotiation over changing
conceptions of consensual knowledge is the dynamic that sustains
regimes and keeps them relevant over time. By focusing on basic norms
and principles, rather than the more common treatment of regimes as
rules, it emphasizes the fundamental element in regime formation
without which the rules have no footing and so offers a framework for
explaining the course and direction of regimes in movement.

The four regimes that are analyzed in the following chapters—the
Mediterranean Action Plan, the OSCE, the ozone depletion regime,
and the torture regime—illustrate this theoretical framework. They
depict widely differing negotiation circumstances that have resulted in
a broad range of regime dynamics. The four regimes were chosen out
of a number of potential cases across a span of issues so large and so
broad that it would be difficult to find a representative selection. A
number of criteria governed the selection, although doubtless other
cases would meet the same requirements as well.

First, the project looked for a split between global and regional examples, mainly because, although many regimes begin in one region
and spread around the world, the dynamics of regional issues tend to
be both older and less studied. We selected Europe as the region because of the number and development of its institutions of cooperation. Second, we picked cases for their longevity, a characteristic necessary for the observation of an ongoing negotiation process. The two
regional cases date from 1974–75, the global cases from 1987–89.
Third, to achieve breadth we chose cases from several issue areas.
One area of concentration is environmental protection, since it is an
issue of growing attention in regime building; the other two issues are
human rights and security, representing a newer and an older area of
institutional cooperation. More specifically, the regime on security and
cooperation in Europe and the ozone depletion regime were selected
because of their prominence among the regimes frequently studied,

and the other cases were selected for the opposite reason, to counterbalance well-known cases with cases less well studied. Four cases do not make a proof, of course, but they do provide an illustration of the larger conceptual points, offering enough anchorage for them to be discussed and retested before ultimately being utilized by analysts and practitioners.

The case studies not only look at the goals, achievements, and institutional structures of each regime but demonstrate how these regimes get their work done and how they refine and adjust their courses through negotiation. They examine the negotiation processes by which these regimes are governed, operate, and evolve. In many ways, the initiating preagreement negotiations were a useful prelude to subsequent negotiations and help to explain the progression of the regime. But so many new issues, actors, and conditions usually emerge in the postagreement negotiation theaters that the themes of the prelude do not always anticipate the middle movements, let alone the finale (if such exists). Sometimes the negotiations have been successful in helping the regime evolve effectively; sometimes the negotiations were faulty and the regime's goals were not achieved.

Regimes in continual motion are the theme of the concluding chapter. The usual pattern begins with elaboration through negotiation and then moves through corrective amendment toward more detailed measures of implementation and down to the "puzzle phase" of application (Kuhn 1962). While some regime-building efforts follow such a smooth path, most of them undergo major changes in course as they encounter new interests and resistance, encounter domestic reactions, and absorb exogenous impacts. It is the struggle between these pressures and system-maintenance efforts to stay the course that characterize the recursive negotiation of international regimes. We then draw lessons across the case studies to help refine the theoretical framework. We conclude with recommendations that can help enhance future regime processes, with a particular focus on improving interaction between the international and domestic levels of negotiations.

References

Fisher, Roger, and William Ury. 1981. *Getting to Yes.* Boston: Houghton-Mifflin.

Hirschman, A. O. 1970. *Exit, Voice, and Loyalty: Responses to Decline in Firms, Organizations, and States.* Cambridge, Mass.: Harvard University Press.

Kuhn, Thomas. 1962. *The Structure of Scientific Revolutions.* Chicago: University of Chicago Press.

Levy, Marc, Oran Young, and Michael Zürn. 1995. "The Study of International Regimes." *European Journal of International Relations* 1 (3): 267–330.

Stein, Janice, ed. 1990. *Getting to the Table.* Baltimore: Johns Hopkins University Press.

Ury, William. 1991. *Getting Past No.* New York: Bantam.

Part I
Framework

1

Negotiating the Rapids

The Dynamics of Regime Formation

I. William Zartman

INTERNATIONAL REGIMES are continuous two-dimensional negotiations among sovereign states for the purpose of resolving a problem of coordination under conditions of uncertainty. This characterization contains a number of important propositions, some pointing out new aspects of regimes and others building on many aspects of previous studies. The main thrust of this chapter is to correct the image of a regime as something that is decided through a process but that then remains relatively fixed, inviting analysis of ratification, compliance, and effectiveness. It is a profound misunderstanding of the regime-building process to believe that it is merely a matter of legislation and compliance. Regime building is ongoing negotiation.

Instead of the static picture, we propose to substitute an image of regimes as continually in evolution through negotiation: negotiations on an initial agreement followed by postagreement negotiations, with parties sporadically negotiating both with other parties to the regime and within their own domestic and intraparty levels. In the process, we will explain, over these first three chapters, why the nature of regimes makes stable guidelines for agreement (formula) and implementation (details) difficult to attain, and what effect the dynamic nature of regimes has on analysis and practice.

This more dynamic image of regimes is expressed in a number of propositions, stated here, which will be developed in the course of the following analysis:

◆ *Proposition 1:* Regimes are recursive, two-dimensional (vertical, horizontal, and sometimes diagonal) negotiations for the purpose of interstate problem solving, rather than two-level negotiations over a treaty ratification.

◆ *Proposition 2:* Regimes govern the behavior of parties (member-states and their citizens) by imposing an agenda for combat as well as by providing justifying norms and limiting constraints.

◆ *Proposition 3:* Parties continually seek to adjust regime rules and party behaviors to fit their approach to the problem rather than simply complying (or not complying) with regimes.

◆ *Proposition 4:* Disparities among parties in power, interests, costs, and benefits perform the motor role in moving regime negotiations through their recursive iterations.

◆ *Proposition 5:* Recursive regime negotiations repeatedly focus on the question of absolute costs under uncertainty ("Will we cost ourselves unnecessarily now and forever to forestall the uncertain threat of future costs?") rather than either on uncertainty of cooperation or on relative gains.

◆ *Proposition 6:* The stability of a regime is a function of the degree of certainty of information about the transaction problem, the degree of divergence of the participating states' interests, and the degree of harmony of current norms and expectations. The greater the capacity of a regime's negotiated formula to resolve the transaction problem, to meet participating states' interests, to fit current norms and establish coherent expectations, and so to overcome opposition to it, the more stable the regime. The inherently fluid nature of problems, power, interests, norms, and expectations involved in international regimes makes such stability rare, requiring repeated (recursive) negotiations to stabilize the formula that meets these criteria.

Despite the insightful work conducted over the past decade and a half on international regimes (Rittberger and Mayer 1993; Hasenclever, Mayer, and Rittberger 1997), the approaches used have obscured important aspects of the nature of regimes. Regime studies have focused much of their attention on the conditions leading to regime creation but little on the process of creation itself.[1] Once a regime is created, it has generally been examined to determine its effectiveness in terms of the parties' compliance with its provisions rather than in terms of its evolution in dealing with the subject problem (Hasenclever, Mayer, and Rittberger 1997, 2, 42–43; Chayes and Chayes 1993; Young 1994; Victor, Raustiala, and Skolnikoff 1998). The regime is studied as essentially an intergovernmental compact, with little consideration of its effects on the ground and on its own evolving nature. Using these criteria, it is hard to evaluate the success of regimes since they are judged statically but in reality constitute a moving target, like checking the speed of a train by using a single snapshot.

These characteristics of the current study of regimes miss the basic nature of a regime as a living thing, established in response to a problem of cooperation under conditions of uncertainty and evolving—indeed, expanding and contracting—as part of a continual re-creation process.[2] The dominant method in that repeated creation is negotiation, a process that is too little considered in the study of regimes. Most of the regime literature focuses on *why* states cooperate and neglects *how* states cooperate in conceptual terms. The neglect of the regime-building process goes hand in hand with the general neglect of conceptual study of multilateral negotiation. While it is hard to understand why regime studies have paid so little attention to negotiations to create regimes, it is perhaps more understandable that they have missed the dynamic character of regimes once created, because much of this evolution has occurred in the two decades since the original defining work on the subject (Krasner 1983).[3] Now, two decades later, it is possible to propose a different approach to the understanding of regimes because the moving picture of history has imposed a more dynamic subject than originally presented.

This chapter integrates the negotiation process into the study of regimes as the framework for renewed attention to the subject, including an examination of regimes in evolution. It will first examine the general nature of regimes in international relations and then lay out six analytical assumptions about the process of regime building, examine the four factors involved in regime evolution that meet in the negotiation process, explain the challenge of building a stable regime, and finally address the question of dynamic stability and evaluation.

Regimes in International Relations

As a result of the inattention to the processes of regime creation and evolution, uncertainty persists about the nature of international regimes. "Regime" is one of those concepts—from "power" all the way to "love" and including "integration," regime's predecessor concept—where "we all know what it means" but a solid working definition and process understanding are still being sought. In the case of regimes, the confusion arises from lack of clarity about the relation between regimes and the processes that maintain them.[4]

The 1983 definition of "regime"—"principles, norms, rules and decision-making procedures around which actor expectations converge in a given issue area" (Krasner 1983, 1)—is usually cited, but the debate has moved on to the particular empirical objects to which the term properly applies. Regimes can cover many forms, scopes, and degrees of formality, and regime building may be a component of an evolving regime. It is hard to analyze the process of regime formation without a better idea of the point at which the process can be called a regime. And so scholarship has turned to other interesting topics, leaving the ongoing process of regime building to fend for itself.

Partly to overcome these problems and partly attracted by the fad-value of a new term, recent discussion of the subject has moved from "regimes" to "governance," resulting, however, in wider spaces of imprecision. "Governance," directly derived from the Greek term for "rudder," refers to a widespread process of political steering, and international governance can take place through many types of interaction —from war to the America's Cup—that most people would agree to place outside regimes. However, the shift to governance has one merit for our purposes: it draws attention to an ongoing process of steering rather than a one-time event. That aspect is the major focus of this study, for which the term "regimes" will be retained.

A regime is a living organism par excellence, and its stability is unlikely to be a steady-state endpoint. Indeed, the concept of "regime" was devised to meet the need for something (even) looser and less rigid than "international law" or "international organization." It would subvert the idea of regime to analyze it as "arriving" when it achieved legal or organizational status. Instead, regimes persist *as* regimes by maintaining their flexibility, their ability to change in response to the varying needs for coordination and problem solving that gave them birth, and their adaptability to the shifting constellations of power and interests among their members.

Unlike other types of negotiated agreements, regimes are ongoing agreements moving through time. Compliance is therefore an inappropriate or at least incomplete notion because regimes and their treaties continue to evolve. Regimes cannot be understood as complying with their initial documents, any more than individuals "comply" with the conditions of their birth or nations "comply" with their constitutions. At the same time, regimes are not simply the international manifestation of an agreement but must be understood to involve the actions of member-states in interpreting, applying, avoiding, and responding to the terms of the initial agreement and its subsequent variations. Since regimes are behaviors as well as rules and regulations, they involve the actions of parties to stay within but also to get around the rules. All this involves negotiation.

In one image, regimes are watercourses flowing through time and space. Neither just the source nor the surface, they involve the entire body of water from its upper manifestations as international agreements to its deep-level effects on local politics (and local and national politics' effects on the surface). What is going on in the water and how the water reacts with the bottom are important for understanding movement on the surface and in the flow over time. Similarly, to pursue the metaphor, obstacles to the course such as dams, shallows, and bends are important to an understanding of the flow. Too often, only their surface manifestations (the regime agreement) have been studied, and the slowly growing literature on local regime-related activities (the bottom) has not been used to relate the bottom to the surface. The Brundtland Commission's exhortation to "Think globally, act locally," for example, has implications for analysis that have not been pursued. It takes an understanding of resistance along the bottom to understand why the forward flow of the regime is slowed, and without this, there is often an unwarranted optimism—seen also in the earlier analysis of integration—over the creation of the superficial agreement. Thus the definition in Proposition 1: Regimes are recursive, two-dimensional (vertical, horizontal, and sometimes diagonal) negotiations for the purpose of interstate problem solving, rather than two-level negotiations over a treaty ratification.

Some of the ambiguity can be brought under control by defining basic concepts more clearly. Regimes are instruments of *inter*national cooperation that fall short of *supra*national organization, instruments of coordinated and collectively self-managed interdependence. Coordination and management are required to secure information, "organize negotiation processes, set standards, perform allocative functions, monitor compliance, reduce conflict and resolve disputes" (Eden and Hampson 1990, 6). Thus, a regime is more than simply "rules, norms, regulations and behaviors" (Krasner 1983); it is the institutionalized effort to shape, monitor, and support these outputs, with the understanding that that institutionalization remains inter- and not supranational. Since specific encounters mark the formalization of the evolving regime, characteristics of the multilateral negotiation and domestic political processes govern the building of regimes.

More broadly, with regard to international relations theory, this analysis is placed squarely in the sparsely inhabited territory between neorealism and neoliberalism. In part this is because neither school is fully adequate to the subject, since "realism" focuses on explanations of conflict and cannot handle cooperation, whereas "liberalism" explains cooperation and cannot handle conflict. Yet regimes involve both and so are not the exclusive domain of either approach. The original question of regime analysis—basically empirical but with important theoretical implications—was: Do regimes shape state behavior, or do states simply do what they can and want (as, according to Thucydides, the realist Athenians maintained)? Only when taken as caricatures are the answers mutually exclusive.

We hold that regimes do matter and that states (that is, decision makers acting in the name of states) do modify their behavior because of their and others' engagements within regimes, including behavior designed to reduce the amount of behavior regimes modify. Regimes matter as opportunities, as constraints, and as a political arena or battlefield. Parties do try to do what they can and will try hardest when they perceive that vital interests are involved, but what they can do is constrained by their relations with other states acting in their own interests in regimes (and elsewhere). The polar positions—that regimes do not

exist or that they exist as corporate actors that actually do things—
seem so far beyond simple common sense and empirical evidence as to
be not worth debate. What continues to be of concern is how states
behave within and toward their collective conventions, whether tacit
or explicit. And that question can be answered only by considering
regimes as two-dimensional, dynamic processes. Thus Proposition 2:
Regimes govern the behavior of parties (member-states and their citizens) by imposing an agenda for combat as well as by providing justifying norms and limiting constraints.

While the main focus of this work is on regimes as rules in evolution through negotiation, it is important here to underscore what this
approach does not imply. In stressing their evolutionary nature, we do
not remove from regimes their institutional or constraining nature, any
more than the frequent revision of a tax code deprives it of its authority at tax-collection time, or the evolving and amended nature of a
constitution removes its capacity to govern the political process. States
behave within a regime as it stands between negotiations, although
that behavior will include local negotiations over implementation. In
other words, there may be some fluidity and even contestation within
the regime, but there is no vacuum.

Assumptions for Analysis

Several assumptions are necessary to start the analysis. First, we
assume that (1) regimes are a problem-solving effort, impelled by a felt
need for some order—norms, rules, regulations, and expectations—in
existing interactions, because the cost of disorder and transaction inef-
ficiencies impedes the achievement of the purposes for which the transactions were instituted. Regimes grow out of interdependencies and
interactions; they do not initiate them but they do further and expand
them. Recognizing the initiation of a regime as a response to a problem
addresses several questions. It facilitates analysis of the causal question:
Regime initiation is caused by states responding to conflicts in the
conduct of transactions. In this, they are motivated by and use power,
interests, norms, and values. It also facilitates an evaluation of regimes

and their stability, since they have a purpose to accomplish. This question will be addressed at the end of this essay.

Furthermore, we assume that (2) states initiate formal cooperation when they feel their interests need organized coordination (Morgenthau 1960, 183; Lipson 1991). The formalizing event is often preceded by preparatory and partial negotiations. Sometimes the incremental process begins bilaterally and even outside government channels, and the main round of negotiations serves to collect and coordinate these diverse efforts around a coherent formula. Formalization is not likely to be an imperceptible rise on a featureless trend toward a regime. It is a response to a problem, triggered by an exogenous challenge or an endogenous breakdown in current attempts at self-regulation—a relatively sharp escalation in the feeling of need. Such intensified feelings may be spontaneous or may be directed by particular parties whose power and/or interests are affected. The result is an explicit attempt to create a regime through multilateral negotiation. This step represents an important threshold in the formation of a regime and should be recognized as the point of formal regime creation, ending the informal phase. (In contrast, some attempts at self-regulation never leave the informal phase and therefore never crystallize as regimes.)

We can therefore assume that (3) the process of regime building is, at least on the part of some of the parties, intended to establish rules, regulations, norms, and expectations governing the given issue area. The formal process starts with agreement negotiations and continues with recursive postagreement negotiations. Regimes do not build themselves, although in seeking to build a regime, policy agents may start a process that takes on a dynamic of its own and is larger than their simple policy goals and efforts. The role of spontaneity in regime building will be addressed below.

As a result, we assume that (4) some of the parties are interested in preventing formation of a regime or at least in limiting the attainment of the goals of others. Thus, concomitantly if not symmetrically, progress toward regime formation arouses a counterprocess. Indeed, we can hypothesize that this opposition will grow with the evolution of the regime: The more the integration, the more the opposition, until a point in the regime-building process at which stability is reached. A loose regime does not provide much cause for opposition (except against the foreshadow of its expansion), but as it expands, constrains, and formalizes, it arouses more opposition, even as it may attract more supporters. But the fluid nature of the type of problem international regimes handle and the high degree of uncertainty involved mean that even when apparent stability is reached, in terms of parties' power and interests, new information and new forms of the problem are likely to call that stability into question.

Therefore, we can assume that (5) any momentary process of regime building has its own interactional dynamic, whose outcome will lie somewhere between the extreme positions, although not necessarily in the middle or on the side of progress (as sometimes assumed). Thus, regime building is marked by periodic confrontations between proponents and opponents as the former seek to advance the process and the latter to retard, evade, or undo it. These confrontations typically take the form of negotiations, and they result in a new status quo in the evolution of the regime. In this way, regime building is neither a one-shot affair nor a smoothly flowing evolution, but a series of negotiations large and small taking place within an independently evolving context.

Finally, (6) the outcome of these negotiations is often built up inductively, cobbled together out of the most pressing pieces, or sectorally, addressing only the squeaky-wheel aspect of the problem rather than its whole structure. Some order may grow out of the transactions themselves, either as behavioral patterns or as implicit attempts at self-regulation (such as the social practice of driving on one side of the road), but there are few if any known cases where such spontaneous order has fully succeeded (cf. Camazine et al. 2001). In fact, spontaneity is a less likely characteristic of regulation than of accentuated calls for greater, explicit efforts at regulation.

More likely than a single spontaneous pattern of regulation are multiple, competing attempts that undermine one another, increasing the need for order. Also more likely than collective self-regulation are individual units' attempts at regulating themselves and then perhaps others, again creating competitive patterns (such as the spreading local efforts to establish standardized time areas in the United States before the national time zones were created). On the international level, such attempts often begin regionally before spreading around the globe; for that reason, regional attempts make up half the cases examined in this volume.

The process is an incremental one, in which parts are put together by trial and error into a momentary, unstable resting place preparatory to further movement. Definitions are often avoided in favor of lists of covered activities, which are only later joined under a definitional umbrella. Areas of attention are identified and combined to form the scope of the agreement. A package is constructed out of either a core coalition of key interests or a diverse coalition of disparate interests. Then the agreement is expanded, to the extent possible, either to extend the coverage or to fill in the holes. Commitments are outlined and then strengthened against resistance to weaken them. Negotiations on environmental regimes have characteristically begun with statements of intent, codes of conduct, or differential obligations, exceptions, and reservations, which are then gradually turned into binding obligations. Private watch groups monitoring behavior replace signatories' engagements or international organizational constraints, until new norms have been introduced far enough to constitute comprehensive expectations, rules, and regulations. The salient formulating—but not necessarily initial—negotiations lay out the basic formula, and the subsequent postagreement negotiations fill in and revise the details.

Attempts have been made to categorize the disorder of this incremental process into various models, so that alternative ways of forming regimes can be evaluated and utilized (Benedick et al. 1991). The models are scarcely watertight and tend to spill over into each other as the incremental process seeks its own path on each occasion. The taxonomic difficulty is not posed only by unruly reality; it also stems from the many dimensions along which models could be constructed. These include the scope of coverage, stringency of obligation, inclusiveness of the parties, degree of institutionalization, provisions for extension, quantity of resources, and means of enforcement, among others.

Regimes begin in some specific form and evolve under the impact of various stimuli, according to a number of different patterns. They include (1) a universal and comprehensive treaty, which is then subjected to overall review and revision from time to time, as in the Law of the Sea (Sebenius 1984; Friedheim 1993); (2) a framework agreement of general principles, followed by specific protocols applying the principles to narrower component issues, as in the Ozone Treaty sequence from Vienna to Montreal to London (Benedick 1991), analyzed by Pamela Chasek in chapter 6 of this book; (3) an action plan of loose goals, followed by the negotiation of implementing treaties that gradually tighten the obligations, as in the Mediterranean Action Plan (Haas 1990; Chasek, Wagner, and Zartman 1996), as analyzed by Lynn Wagner in chapter 4 of this book;[5] (4) a basic trade-off between two opposing blocs and principles that then turns into an organization for their pursuit, as in the Conference and then Organization for Security and Cooperation in Europe (CSCE/OSCE), discussed by Janie Leatherman in chapter 5 of this work; (5) an agreement to hold a periodic review conference, intercalated with monitoring and specific regulatory sessions, as in the World Administrative Radio Conference (Fliess 1987); (6) a small core agreement, expanded gradually to include related issues in order to maintain its coherence, as in the acid rain agreements; (7) a process-oriented convention on implementation measures tied to levels of scientific information and policy coordination but without commitments, followed by interim negotiations, like the Climate Change Convention (Patterson and Grubb 1992; Bodansky 1993); (8) a weak and ineffective attempt to handle a recognized problem whose initial inadequacies in turn become the goad to a tighter and more effective agreement, such as the Whaling Convention of 1946 or the 1954 Convention for the Prevention of Pollution of the Sea by Oil, which turned into a ban on whaling by the International Whaling Commission in 1985 and the Maritime Pollution (MARPOL) Convention of 1973, respectively; (9) international standards with self-selected national exemptions, as in the regimes against torture analyzed by Anna Korula in chapter 7 of this work; (10) a cluster of small sectoral agreements, joined together in later negotiations to cover the entire issue area, also as in the acid rain agreements; (11) a growing network of bilateral agreements rationalized into a multilateral ensemble, as in the transboundary air pollution agreements among European countries that gave rise to consolidated controls in 1979, 1984–85, 1988, and 1991 (Scapple 1996); (12) a limited-party agreement, expanded by new adherents to complete the coverage, as in the Chemical Weapons Agreement (Floweree and Aberle 1993) or the Uruguay Round process (Winham 1990);[6] (13) statements of principles giving rise to a regional convention, which is then extended globally while the parties continue to search for an effective formula, as in the African and then world ban in the Basel Convention on dumping toxic wastes.

In reality, these ideal types are softened, combined, or complemented by one another when regimes are established and as they evolve. Nonetheless, it is clear that each form in this latitudinal taxonomy opens up its own longitudinal taxonomy of evolutionary possibilities. We do not have enough experience as yet to know which of these forms is best, what "best" means, or what their individual implications are. It does not seem that any particular type provides the best way to stability. Since different issues pose different problems and different challenges for cooperation, different types and patterns of regimes will be appropriate as paths for negotiations.

Factors in Regime Evolution

The process of regime formation does not stop with adoption of a founding agreement. Negotiation continues as regimes evolve, since loopholes need to be tightened or loosened, new members brought in or old ones dropped, obligations strengthened or lifted, ambiguities removed or provided, coverage extended or reduced, and so on. Because of the change and uncertainty inherent in the subject, the initial form of the regime is unlikely simply to solve the problem. But even if it did, to the satisfaction of some of the parties at the moment, those parties, and other or potential parties, would continue to return to the negotiating table to revise, reduce, expand, and/or correct the form of the regime in place. The effort is a learning process, and if some parties do not want to learn, the need to do so is forced on them by the learning of others. Negotiation continues in order to deal with the problem, both to shape the ongoing process of cooperation and to revisit and rectify engagements originally included or excluded. The idea of an ultimate instrument governed thereafter by *pacta servanda sunt* is a notion of a bygone era.

But negotiation is not only a multilateral exercise among the signatories; it is also an exercise in reentry, application, implementation, and response between the upper and lower levels of the regime "watercourse." Negotiators or their domestic colleagues return home to sell, mend, and enforce the results of their negotiations, and they return to the next round of negotiations with the results of their implementation, including new instructions and inputs and new awareness of the regime's imperfections. This vertical contact with the "lower level" does not concern ratification alone (Putnam 1988; Evans, Jacobson, and Putnam 1993). As the stream flows on, a rolling wave from the bottom stirs up new material and carries it to the surface, affecting its force and flow.

Four factors are simultaneously involved in regime evolution, coming together from time to time in renegotiations.[7] One is *system maintenance,* or the inertial tendency of a regime to persist as constructed at any moment. Parties become engaged and committed to a relationship and seek to maintain it, even incurring momentary losses as a result. Frequently they negotiate to maintain the relationship against threats of loss resulting from its discontinuance, even though its maintenance may have visible costs and the costs of discontinuance may be only hypothetical (Stein and Pauly 1993). Regime maintenance may be the consequence of sunk costs, with sunk costs interpreted in terms of nonmaterial commitment as well as of finances. System-maintenance tendencies as commitments to past engagements or investments will find themselves confronted by new situations with their own costs and interests, and the continued operation of the relationship will enter as an element into the cost and interest calculations in responding to the new challenges. The inertia of an established regime can outweigh worsened relations between the parties resulting from conflicting interests in a new situation (Rittberger and Zürn 1990), although of course conflicts over important issues can destroy an established regime. For example, the elephant issue under the Convention on International Trade in Endangered Species is a case of system maintenance in which the protection rules were reaffirmed in 1991 above all for the purpose of continuing the regime rather than for dealing with the particular problem.

There is a danger in identifying this factor in such a way that it reifies the relationship itself as an actor. It is on the parties as actors that the exigencies of system maintenance operate, pressing for continued cooperation rather than working in both negative and positive directions as in the other factors discussed below. System maintenance is reflected in the fact that the regime continues between negotiations, whatever the pressures of the other factors. Again, Proposition 2: Regimes govern the behavior of parties (member-states and their citizens) by imposing an agenda for combat as well as by providing justifying norms and limiting constraints.

The second factor is the *adjustment* of the basic formula and implementing details of the regime's initial instrument, with the parties continually reviewing the effectiveness of problem solving, coverage of issues, intensity of obligations, thoroughness of information, and degree of monitoring. Parties seek to maintain, gain, or regain through negotiations what was gained, not gained, or lost in past negotiations. Some try to close loopholes, while others seek to reopen them; some find the degree of commitment inadequate for the effective working of the system, while others find it constraining and onerous; and so on. States refuse or limit their cooperation under the agreement if the loopholes provide unequal (relative) gains to others or if obligations outweigh the perceived (absolute) gains for the cooperating parties (Grieco 1990, 35; cf. Grieco 1988). It is simply wrong and even ideological to claim that the comparison of gains is necessarily interparty or intraparty; it is either or both depending on the vagaries of the case. Thus, the successive Ozone Treaty negotiations involved a continual review of obligations and membership in order to recognize and reduce a common danger. In sum, Proposition 3: Parties continually seek to adjust regime rules and party behaviors to fit their approach to the problem rather than simply complying (or not complying) with regimes.

The third factor involves a *cybernetic* series of learning loops tying domestic to international governance (Faure and Kolb 1994). After negotiations, regimes return to the domestic scene of the participating states for the next round of action. Such action involves implementation by domestic agencies, including further debate and negotiations within governmental institutions, but it also involves further pressures by domestic NGOs for and against the newly established regime (Susskind 1995). Obviously, the two strands are joined, as NGOs pressure legislatures, lobby executives, and test the courts. In a broad sense, this interaction too is negotiation, with its associated pressures and security points. Its output is both a set of implementations of the previous international negotiations and also a set of inputs into the next round, where it rejoins the momentary results of the two previously discussed processes.

The ingredients of the domestic process are multiple and diverse, varying according to the individual states' agendas. They can include elections—critical or continuing; intergroup encounters among the crucial sectors of society, business, science, and public interest groups; and the competing attempts of various sides in the debate over the regime to mobilize their followers. Ultimately, the nature of the domestic interaction is contained and shaped by the nature of the polity itself. Defensive participation in the Mediterranean Action Plan (MAP) led the Algerian government to create positions in environmental science and maritime pollution whose holders under the subsequent regime constituted a specialized interest group that enabled the country to play a more positive role in subsequent negotiations (Haas 1990; Chasek, Wagner, and Zartman 1996).

A particularly important element of the domestic aspect of regime building concerns the development of norms that underwrite the negotiation of rules. While this aspect will be developed in some detail by Gunnar Sjöstedt in chapter 3, it is important to point out here the need for harmony between domestic norms and international negotiations, as well as the dismantling effect that the absence of such harmony can have on regime implementation. The effect is two-directional, of course; consensual norms on the international level can affect domestic thinking and knowledge. There is no formula for calculating which causal arrow is stronger.

While the domestic dimension of regimes has been noted occasionally, and the two-level structure of regime negotiations has been subject to some analysis (Putnam 1988; Evans, Jacobson, and Putnam 1993), the domestic dimension has not been studied as a constituent part of the process of regime evolution. Specifically, two-level negotiations have been considered as necessary for ratification and therefore as ending with the initial agreement, whereas the present analysis sees the domestic reaction and interaction as an integral component of regime evolution as well as initiation. In sum, Proposition 1: Regimes are recursive, two-dimensional (vertical, horizontal, and sometimes diagonal) negotiations for the purpose of interstate problem solving, rather than two-level negotiations over a treaty ratification.

Finally, to all these endogenous factors must be added an *exogenous factor*, involving accidents, unforeseen challenges, new information, other regimes, and other external inputs and changes (Myers 1995). As noted, regime building begins with a problem, generally caused by exogenous factors, and the subsequent trajectory of the regime can be deflected and accelerated by further events of the same nature. The ozone negotiations were impelled by periodic injections of new scientific information; the regional and global negotiations and declarations surrounding the Basel Convention on Hazardous Wastes were similarly driven in spurts by incidents of environmental damage involving hazardous wastes; the evolving European security regime was shaken and reshaped above all by the Bosnian crisis.

Exogenous challenges can also come from other regimes. Competing efforts to deal with aspects of the same problem in overlapping geographic or functional areas occur at the intersection of various regime systems as networks and systems of negotiated regulation come into shape (Kremenyuk 2002; Chasek 1994). European regimes to deal with acid rain and maritime pollution impinged on global acid rain negotiations and on the Mediterranean Action Plan, respectively; the United

Nations, NATO, WEU, and OSCE all influenced one another's evolution as they competed for the same functions. As regimes grow, they run up against other growing regimes and the two, like two meeting streams, become involved in the complex and contradictory processes of maintaining their own separate integrity and taking each other's jurisdiction into account. A current example of two regimes' meeting each other is found in the environmentalists' attacks on the North American Free Trade regime, where boundary or turf wars are taking place over the ownership of political or issue space, not unlike the wars that have marked international relations over geographic boundaries.

At given points in the evolution of the regime, these four processes bring the parties back to multilateral negotiations to formalize the regime's evolution. Sometimes this formal encounter is mandated by the agreement, as a review process or periodic meeting of the contracting parties; sometimes it is necessitated by the second element, need for adjustment, or the third, domestic inputs, or the fourth, exogenous events; sometimes it is unspecified and therefore needs a clarion call (as provided by Malta in the Law of the Sea) or a convenient anniversary (as seized upon twenty years after the United Nations Conference on the Human Environment [UNCHE] in Stockholm to call to order the United Nations Conference on Environment and Development [UNCED] in Rio). The ability of the regime to deal with change can be provided in the regime itself or invented as changes and challenges arise. Both impose strains on the regime: the first can tax the regime beyond its ability to respond, while the second involves two actions (invention and then application of the response) and thus poses a greater challenge to negotiations (Levy, Young, and Zürn 1994, 9).

The outcome of the negotiations is determined by the power and interests of the parties to the encounter at the time of the negotiations, within the context of the evolving regime. Since the encounter is one of problem solving under uncertainty, power is conceived of in relation to either the problem or the solution. Always a concept both crucial and elusive (Zartman 1997; Zartman and Rubin 2000), "power" can be characterized here as the actions taken to block or form a regime, based on the degree of necessity of a party to the regime or coalition in formation (veto power) (Porter and Brown 1995, esp. 104). So conceived, power can be turned into measurable indices, based on a party's contribution either to the problem (for example, its degree of consumption or of pollution) or to the solution (for example, as a contributor to a fund). Similarly, interest is best characterized in terms of the costs of the problem and its solution, tempered again by the element of uncertainty. This element, too, can be refined into a measurable index, calculating the ratio of preventive cost to the cost of danger, modified by their probabilities. Such a calculation would of course be heuristic at best, since the very nature of the problem is the uncertainty of the probabilities. These indices will not be calculated here, but their ingredients will be a qualitative part of the case analyses. In sum, Proposition 4: Disparities among parties in power, interests, costs, and benefits perform the motor role in moving regime negotiations through their recursive iterations.

The mixture of power and interests among the parties translates into different roles they can play. Dynamic stability is achieved through an appropriate balance of roles. A limited list of role strategies from which parties can choose can be identified inductively, although there is not yet a clear conceptual dimension (other than metaphorical) to the list (Sjöstedt 1993; cf. Sprinz and Vaahtoranta 1994).[8] Parties can drive, conduct, defend, brake, derail, ride, or leave. *Drivers* try to organize participation to produce an agreement that is consonant with their interests.[9] *Conductors* also seek to produce an agreement but from a neutral position, with no interest axe of their own to grind.[10] *Defenders* are single-issue players, concerned with incorporating a particular measure or position in the agreement rather than with the overall success of the negotiations. *Brakers* are the opposing or modifying resistance, brought into action by the progress being made on either the broad regime or specific issues. *Derailers* are out to destroy the regime, not merely to soften its provisions or slow it down. *Riders* are filler, with no strong interests of their own and so available to act as followers. *Leavers* pursue an exit policy, either partially through individual exceptions and derogations or wholly through withdrawal from the negotiations and the regime.

Conducting and driving are the strategies that best fit regime formation. These strategies depend on a procedural or substantive leader that agglomerates parties into agreement. While pursuing its own interests, each party is brought to play its own score in the right way to bring a harmonious result. The conductor could be a sovereign state with its own interest-related agenda subordinated to getting a generally satisfactory agreement. But the multilateral nature of negotiations weighs in favor of a more disinterested leader to provide order to the proceedings. Thus many environmental and other regime conferences give a prominent role to a secretary general, conference chair, secretariat, or other organizing agency as a key to the effective creation of integrative outcomes (Boyer 1996). States more often choose a driver's over a conductor's strategy, for many reasons. Often, no state is powerful enough to be hegemonic, interests are usually defensive and partial rather than global, and potential leaders are above all regional and interest group players and so are tainted. In this situation, the procedural conductor is actually welcome, since it allows parties to pursue their interests more effectively, facilitating agreement. The impact of a procedural or conductor role is important, since it underscores an effective alternative to the allegedly necessary role of hegemon. All of these roles are available, to be used by various parties at various times, although a party's adoption of one role—driver or conductor, for example—colors its ability to shift to another role later on.

Thus, the evolutionary process of which the negotiations are a part has both a synchronic and a diachronic dimension. The particular outcome represents the results of the encounter of the moment, but it is also a stage in the battle over the evolution of the regime as it moves from encounter to encounter between parties and from constellation to constellation of power and interests. Rather than being a tabula rasa, the agenda is set by the condition of the regime at the time of negotiations, whether this refers to the initial pressing problem or to the later reiterations. Thus, "where you go depends on where you're coming from" (see Munton and Castle 1992, and Cutler and Zacher 1992). Their evolving nature makes regimes temporary, contested, unstable, and continuously expandable and perfectible rather than overarching and deductive, as an optimal formula should be in a negotiated agreement (Zartman and Berman 1982).

For those trying to move the process forward, instability is a vulnerable but creative characteristic of negotiations for an environmental regime; the temporary formula should be so constructed that it calls for its own improvement and moves the process along—one that "falls forward" as a temporary solution that, constructively, cannot last in its momentary form (Scapple 1996). However, for opponents, that same instability is an opportunity to impede, to renegotiate later for a looser agreement, or to fall backward toward less or different forms of regulation. Thus, the regime formation process is anything but linear. It goes up and down from negotiation to negotiation, constellation to constellation, the dynamics—perhaps better, the kinetics—of the synchronic encounter determining the points that mark the diachronic evolution.

Thus, the evolution of the regime at any given point is a function of system maintenance (M), adjustment (A), cybernetic (C), and exogenous (E) factors.[11] Symbolically,

$$R = f(+M \pm A \pm C \pm E)$$

While the first factor works to maintain the regime, the other three factors can work in either direction, to strengthen or weaken it or to alter its direction, according to the conjuncture of power, interests, and values of the parties in their recursive negotiations. These components are developed further in the following chapter, by Bertram Spector.

Obstacles to Stability

Within the standard definition of negotiation as the process by which conflicting positions are combined to form a common decision, the negotiators seek to produce a *formula for agreement on the resolution of the problem*, which is then translated into acceptable implementing details (Zartman and Berman 1982). Multilateral decision making is an exercise in managing complexity, since it is characterized by such a large number of interacting variables that there is no dominant pattern or dimension (Klir 1985). Parties entering multilateral negotiations make a conceptual scan of the complexity and then refine it into a cognitive model constructed out of the interrelated elements of simplification, structuring, and direction (Zartman 1994). *Simplification* means reducing the number of elements to the most important (which will vary by party interests, costs and benefits, and situation), *structuring* means giving these elements some priority and relation to one another, and *direction* means moving these components toward an intended policy goal, usually located along a spectrum depending on the importance of a particular issue outcome or a general agreement to the interests of the party. When to this characteristic complexity the element of uncertainty is added, regime evolution takes on an additional dimension of complexity that provides it with identifiable features and implications.

A formula has particular importance in regime building, especially when understood as a shared sense of justice or terms of trade (Young 1994; Brams and Taylor 1996; Zartman et al. 1996). A sense of rules, regulations, expectations, and behaviors must rest on agreement on broad principles of fair allocation in the given issue area. The uncertainty of the problem and its costs, as well as of the costs of managing it, means that that agreement on relevant principles of justice is likely to be loose, contentious, tentative, and fluctuating. Yet the nature of the principle of justice is the basic subject of the formula, which in turn allows Homans' maxim—"The more items at stake can be divided into goods valued more by one party than they cost to the other[s] and goods valued more to the other party than they cost to the first, the greater the chances of successful outcome" (Homans 1961, 62)—to be played out to the fullest, and Homans' maxim is the key to any negotiation.

Two types of processes are involved in the multilateral negotiation of regimes, coalition and consensuation. *Coalition* is the more usual way of thinking about multilateral negotiation, relating both to parties and to issues. Coalition among many parties is often used as the theme for analyzing multilateral negotiation (Olson 1965; Snidal 1985; Lax and Sebenius 1991; Dupont 1994; Hampson 1995; Crump and Zartman 2003) and gives rise to a limited number of strategies. Parties seek to aggregate other groups and parties into a coalition large enough to win, or to divide opposing groups into smaller parts so as to absorb or merely weaken them, or to confront other groups to defeat them or work out a deal with them. Although coalitions are usually conceived of as international groupings of states, transnational cooperation across states is a growing characteristic of multilateral negotiation. Transnational coalitions of scientists, technologists, and business constitute one type of coalition whose members mobilize their resources—knowledge, skill, and money—to raise public consciousness or strike a deal with political leaders accountable to constituent groups.

But coalitions can be made among issues as well, in order to reduce their complexity and make them manageable. Issue coalitions have their own tactics. Fractioning, packaging, linkages, and trade-offs—the basic devices of the negotiation process—are all ways of making coalitions among issues, interests, and positions. Two categories of trade-offs are available. One is the standard notion of substantive exchanges, where one party's concession on one item is traded for another's concession on another item, including new items not previously on the agenda used as side-payments. The move from the Tokyo to the Uruguay Round of negotiations within the General Agreement on Tariffs and Trade (GATT) involved bringing into the GATT regime new issues that had previously been excluded and that allowed for the basic trade-off of the Uruguay Round (Winham 1986, 2002). Trade-offs can also be made within the same item, by trading breadth for depth in regulation. In many cases a regime began with relatively strict coverage of a relatively small number of items, often achieved through a small number of steep steps, and was later expanded to cover a larger number of items. The opposite approach is relatively broad coverage through loose restrictions or gentle steps. Each approach has problems that require recursive negotiations to deal with: the first can lead to incoherence and imperceptible results, whereas the second invites generalized resistance and tends to "fall backward" to less effectiveness.

Other trade-offs are procedural, buying agreement with special treatment through such devices as exceptions and inducements.

Exceptions to the agreement can help establish a principle but temporarily weaken its effectiveness. Later, the incipient regime can be consolidated by negotiating away the exceptions, possibly against other trade-offs in new circumstances. Or, as the reverse of the exception, restrictions can be traded for inducements, which are then tapered off as compliance proceeds on its own and becomes it own inducement. Many environmental negotiations have turned to compensation as a way of establishing trade-offs across the North-South divide. Indeed, the entire structure of UNCED is based on a massive trade-off designed to bridge the North-South gap between environment and development. Compensation can provide an immediate transfer of resources but has an air of bribery; it must be so structured that individual parties are not able to enjoy its benefits as a public good while opting out of its obligations.

The other type of negotiation process is *consensuation,* where the limits of the parties' positions are ascertained beforehand and then a proposal tabled that falls within those limits and achieves acceptance without bargaining. Consensus is the largest coalition, a coalition of the whole that is characteristic of multilateral negotiation, and is based on a decision rule under which, essentially, abstention is an affirmative rather than a negative vote. Multilateral agreements are arrived at by consensus when a coalition formed by a significant but unspecified number of parties is in favor and the rest do not oppose. Parties not in agreement can abstain without blocking the outcome, and parties opposing can be left out as long as their number does not become significant. Strategies of incremental participation and agreement then become possible (Zartman 1987, chap. 10). At the same time, the significant number requirement means that lowest-common-denominator (LCD) agreements without teeth are common.

The absence of such a consensus on the basic trade-off has, for example, kept the metaregime on environmental matters advanced at Rio in 1992 from making clear and unambiguous progress: Whether environmental matters should be governed by a principle of compensation (for delayed development) or equity (for incurred investments) or equality among all parties is still an unresolved question, in regard both to the general environmental debate and to the various sub-regimes in formation—global warming, ozone depletion, desertification, among others—that derive from it.

The basic reason why regimes are ongoing negotiations and cannot resolve their problem of coordination once and for all is that the problem is characterized by ignorance and uncertainty. While any negotiated outcome involves contingent agreements to handle future events, regimes characteristically confront high levels of uncertainty about the nature and magnitude of the problem with which they are concerned. More than other multilateral negotiations, negotiations over regimes are rule-making exercises rather than one-time redistributions of tangible goods. Their main goal is to harmonize national legislation and establish rules for the ongoing allocation of costs and benefits against changes and challenges of undetermined nature and magnitude (Scharpf 1989, 12; Zartman 1994, 6). The parameters of the problem become clearer or take on new forms as time goes on, necessitating meetings of the parties from time to time to reconsider their previous decisions.

This uncertainty is not the frequently discussed "veil" that is said to favor fairness as a fallback solution (Rawls 1971). Whereas the veil of ignorance obscures preferences equally for competing options, the ignorance in regime decisions obscures the uncertainties of future costs and gains, but not the reality of the present costs of problem solving. The parties have to calculate the likely cost of the engagements they make against the uncertainty of the costs of the problem they are seeking to alleviate. Against these costs they must also calculate benefits, both from the status quo and from possible changes, although costs weigh more heavily in their calculations; as indicated in prospect theory, parties tend to be more risk averse concerning gains than losses, and therefore future opportunities need to be very sure if they are to outweigh investments in the status quo (Farnham 1994). The fall-back solution in this case is conservative inaction or LCD compromises rather than liberal fairness, making regime adjustment negotiations a slow, careful process (Brams and Kilgour 1999). In sum, Proposition 5: Recursive regime negotiations repeatedly focus on the question of absolute costs under uncertainty ("Will we cost ourselves unnecessarily now and forever to forestall the uncertain threat of future costs?") rather than on either uncertainty of cooperation or relative gains.

In considering these calculations, debates over relative gains or relative compliance as the key issue are misplaced. Of course, every absolute loss or gain has its relative or externally comparative dimensions, just as every relative gain or loss starts as an absolute (that is, an internally relative) increment; the standard terms are misleading. But states establishing policy on global warming or deep sea mining or human rights or pollution are concerned first and foremost with the costs to them of abatement and prevention to meet dangers and opportunities whose very existence is unproven, not with the comparison of their costs against someone else's or the chances of someone else's noncompliance. These latter two elements are of course not irrelevant or unrelated, but they are not the primary focus of policymaking. The primary concern is absolute costs, or absolute costs relative to one's own uncertain gains.

Such uncertainty exacerbates the problem of finding mutually agreeable solutions, reinforcing the change in the nature of the problem. The question is not so much one of fearing defection from a salient solution but rather one of multiple equilibriums, a problem common to both Prisoners' Dilemma and Battle of the Sexes in the game-theoretic terms in which the regime debate is often couched (Hasenclever, Mayer, and Rittberger 1997, 104–113). Often these equilibriums are not polar opposites but matters of degree—for example, as in differences in constraints, quotas, or restrictions (Wolf 1997). But they reflect tenaciously held positions since parties' uncertainty over the need for or benefit from constraints increases their reluctance to take on the costs necessary to adopt them. Since knowledge and other givens affecting cost calculations are continually changing, multilateral policymaking through negotiation needs to recur from time to time.

The final reason why regimes are recursive negotiations with great difficulties in achieving stable, long-term formulas relates to the nature of regimes as normative constructs. Just as regime building rests on the coordination of many states' interests and power under uncertainty, so it also depends on the presence of supportive norms and coordinated expectations around the world. The task is sizable and elusive for several reasons. On the one hand, its very magnitude is a challenge. Bilateral or even regional negotiations have their problems in finding a normative base for the international contracts they create, but their terrain of action extends to only a few states. The problems of developing a consensus simultaneously in the United States, Canada, and Mexico on the benefits of free trade and circulation as the basis for implementing the North American Free Trade Agreement (NAFTA) stand as an example. But global regimes must rest on a much broader consensus involving nearly two hundred countries, though obviously the importance of each country's contribution to that consensus varies, just as do the power and interests of the parties.

On the other hand, norms are a circular matter in regime building. Regimes themselves are norms, principles, and expectations, as well as rules and regulations, a point that Sjöstedt develops in a subsequent chapter. But they also rest on an existing structure of norms and expectations, just as they affect that structure by their negotiation and implementation. If the regime brings in new norms that conflict with preexisting values and expectations, some education, debate, and publicity will be required before it begins to be accepted and then implemented domestically, whatever the diplomats may decide among themselves. The most striking example, on the regional level, is the enormous campaign that accompanied the conversions from national currencies to the euro in the participating European Union member-states. An equally telling case is the education and change of mentalities required for the notion of global warming and associated remedial measures to take hold in the public consciousness as a basis for acceptance and implementation of the Climate Change Convention and its protocols. One-time (or even several-time) negotiation of new regime norms is not sufficient when these norms and expectations clash with existing beliefs.

To put it positively, the challenge to regime builders is to devise a formula that will coordinate the parties' efforts to handle a threatening danger of uncertain costs and magnitude, in such a way that possible (but unforeseeable) future changes in their interests and relative power and in the nature of the danger remain satisfied by the formula, and a concordance is established between ambient norms and expectations and those contained in the regime. While flexibility would appear to be the answer, the appearance is deceiving. On one side, too much flexibility frequently is the result of an inability to agree on effective precision, resulting in a weak regime that does not solve the initial problem. On the other, when flexibility is appropriate it must be flexibility in the right direction, re-posing the problem of uncertainty and change. In other words, getting it done requires getting it right. Thus, Proposition 6: The stability of a regime is a function of the degree of certainty of information about the transaction problem, the degree of divergence of the participating states' interests, and the degree of harmony of current norms and expectations. The greater the capacity of a regime's negotiated formula to resolve the transaction problem, to meet participating states' interests, to fit current norms and establish coherent expectations, and so to overcome opposition to it, the more stable the regime. The inherently fluid nature of problems, power, interests, norms, and expectations involved in international regimes makes such stability rare, requiring repeated (recursive) negotiations to stabilize the formula that meets these criteria.

Dynamic Stability and Evaluation

This chapter has developed a number of propositions, working hypotheses that should be useful in guiding research into new angles on regimes.[12] These propositions are not causal hypotheses. In part, such hypotheses must follow from further research, but in addition the regime process does not lend itself to causal modeling. The evolution of regimes through multilateral negotiations continues over time, stayed and deflected by the changing effects of surface, deep-level, and exogenous pressures and events. The effects that such influences have on the basic uncertainty of the problem and on the cost calculations of the parties are unpredictable, and the parameters for analysis under varying situations remain to be identified.

These discussions have shown that negotiations make a difference, and that regime analysis without taking that fact into account is at best incomplete. How do negotiations make a difference? In continually (or recursively) providing an alternative to compliance or withdrawal by giving an opportunity to adjust the course of the regime. It is in not taking account of the third alternative that analyses of compliance distort the reality of the choices available to practitioners of regimes,[13] and they have done so by arguing only over whether regimes matter to states without asking whether states matter to regimes. Iklé's (1964) work at the foundation of negotiation analysis made the fundamental observation that negotiation is a threefold choice between acceptance, rejection, or improvement, equivalent in regard to regimes to compliance, withdrawal, and negotiation. Hirschman (1970) has shown that voice is one of the three situational responses of an actor, along with exit (withdrawal) and loyalty (compliance). Negotiation matters because it enables the parties to avoid the stark choice between compliance and withdrawal by engaging in recursive negotiations to adjust the efforts to solve the initial or evolving problem and to bring to those problem-solving efforts the feedback from domestic reactions.

How, then, can regime building be evaluated if it is a fluid and ongoing process? And how can regimes stabilize expectations if they are constantly renegotiated (Hasenclever, Mayer, and Rittberger 1997, 185)? In all the terms of this discussion there is a certain dynamic. It assumes three dimensions: that regimes move backward and forward according to the power and interest constellations of the moment, that they reverberate up and down in tying local to national and global effects, and that they spread sideways to meet a felt need for order in a given issue area. Together, they produce the dynamic stability discussed above, whereby a regime meets the needs for which it was created by growing to the maximum relevant membership and by eliminating the conflict in the concerned issue area. Thus, it is not necessarily by greater and greater regulation, or more and more members, or even tighter and tighter regulations, or—above all—more and more complex institutionalization that the success or evolution of the regime can be judged, but by its coverage and harmonization of its chosen subject. Regime formation—as, in turn, the negotiations that punctuate it—is above all a conflict management device and, as such, a collective security engagement.

It is against these two components that a regime's effectiveness and evolution must be judged. On one hand, the regime should aim to include all the parties to the conflict—as in a collective security agreement—rather than—as in a collective defense agreement—pitting itself against some relevant but excluded parties. At one stage, it can be judged positively if it includes most of the relevant members, even at the cost of exceptions from the full coverage of the agreement; later, it must be judged according to its effective coverage and the removal of those exceptions. The same phased progress should be used to evaluate compensation and other inducements. On the other hand, it should aim to solve the initial problem, eliminating transactional conflict among the parties and between the parties and the regime's goals. This includes providing ways of continuing to manage and eliminate new instances of conflict in the issue area and providing supports for the conflict management system—setting standards, monitoring practices, gathering information. It is thus the nature of the issue or regulated activity that is the measure of success, not some external criterion, and that measure may actually vary as time goes on, rather than requiring an ever more integrated response.

If this is close to notions of regime resiliency (Powell 1994), it steps back from that criterion by recognizing that robustness or staying power does not lie in the existence of the regime itself but comes from the continuing efforts of committed parties to keep the regime resilient. Regimes are not quite in permanent flux (Kratochwil 1989; Neufeld 1993), but they face frequent challenge and periodic adjustment, like any other norm. They remain strong if their adherents are able to beat back challenges, and they change when challenge becomes overwhelming. That change may result in their being discarded in times of issue realignment, but it more frequently results in regime readjustment. That is the process this study addresses.

Notes

1. Only Young (1989a) and Young and Osherenko (1993) place importance on the bargaining process in regime formation.

2. The one author who recognized this evolutionary nature was, not surprisingly, Oran Young, the same author who brought negotiations into the process of regime creation; see Young 1983, 105–107. "International regimes do not become static constructs even after they are fully articulated. Rather they undergo continuous transformation in response to their own inner dynamics as well as to changes in their political, economic and social environments. In this connection, I use the term 'transformation.'" Here the term used is "evolution," which includes both minor tinkering and major alterations, a distinction that Young understandably finds difficult and that is not required, at least for present purposes. The following analysis carries further some of the ideas initiated in Young 1983 and 1989a.

3. It could quite well be argued that regimes have been around for a long time and many studies of them as ongoing negotiations could well have informed the study of regimes. Cf. Preeg 1970; Malgren 1973; and Winham 1977a, 1977b on economic regimes, none of which were noted in the original work on regimes; and, in the subsequent period, Winham 1986 on GATT; Sjöstedt 1993 on environmental regimes; Spector, Sjöstedt, and Zartman 1994 on UNCED; and Zartman 1994 and Hampson 1994 on multilateral negotiations.

4. For a discussion of another case of polysemy, referring to both product and process, on the word "thought," see Geertz 1983, 147–148. Similarly, Ruggie discusses regimes as a consummatory rather than a merely instrumental value, relating to Weber's distinction between value- and purpose-rationality, although it might seem that the distinction could run either way; Ruggie 1983, 196, referring to Weber 1978, 24–26.

5. Regime patterns (2) and (3) are often referred to as the transformational approach; see Lang 1989; Dunnoff 1995; and Young, Demko, and Ramakrishna 1996.

6. Sometimes called a strategic construction approach; see Downs, Rocke, and Barsoom 1997; Barrett 1994; and Zartman 1987, 292.

7. Two of these were foreshadowed by processes identified by Young (1983, 106–113) as part of regime transformation: "internal contradictions" are similar to the present second factor of regime adjustment, and "exogenous forces" are similar to our fourth, exogenous, factor. Young's other process, "shifts in the underlying structure of power," is reflected in the inputs of power, interests, and values that are involved in any negotiation. It is the addition of the other two factors, system maintenance and cybernetic loops, that distinguishes the two approaches.

8. Roles are related to but quite different from Young's (1989a, 1991) discussions of leadership. Roles are a typology that allows classification, with implications but not causal hypotheses. Leadership discussions are based on a tautological hypothesis ("Institutional bargaining is likely to succeed when *effective* leadership emerges . . . [and] fail in the absence of such leadership" [Young 1989a, 373, emphasis added]) and do not break into any clear typology, other than effective/ineffective.

9. Young (1991, 288) discusses these as structural leaders.

10. Young (1989a, 373) calls these brokers or entrepreneurs.

11. Unlike in his earlier discussion (1983, 110), Young (1989a, 371–372) assigns a positive direction to the effects of exogenous shocks "for the most part." The original discussion seems more convincing, although the differences may lie in the difference between broader and more ambiguous exogenous "forces" (1983, 110) and narrower and more specific exogenous "shocks or crises" (1989a, 371).

12. I am grateful to John Odell for triggering some key ideas in this conclusion.

13. Hayashi (1999) has elegantly shown that parties will bolt peace-keeping obligations when the costs of compliance are higher than the costs of bolting.

References

Barrett, Scott. 1994. "Self-Enforcing International Environmental Agreements." *Oxford Economic Papers* 36: 878–894.

———. 1998. "On the Theory and Diplomacy of Environmental Treaty-Making." *Environmental and Resource Economics* 11 (3–4): 317–333.

Benedick, Richard. 1991. *Ozone Diplomacy.* Cambridge, Mass.: Harvard University Press.

Benedick, Richard, et al. 1991. *Greenhouse Warming: Negotiating a Global Regime.* Washington, D.C.: World Resources Institute.

Bodansky, Daniel. 1993. "The United Nations Convention on Climate Change: A Commentary." *Yale Journal of International Law* 18: 451–558.

Boyer, Brook. 1996. "Positional Bargaining and Coalition Structures in International Environmental Organization." Ph.D. diss., Graduate School in International Relations, Geneva.

Brams, Steven, and D. Marc Kilgour. 1999. "Fallback Bargaining." Paper presented to the International Studies Association, Washington, D.C.

Brams, Steven, and Alan Taylor. 1996. *Fair Division.* Cambridge: Cambridge University Press.

Camazine, Scott, et al. 2001. *Self-Organization in Biological Systems.* Princeton, N.J.: Princeton University Press.

Chasek, Pamela. 1994. "The Negotiating System of Environment and Development." In *Negotiating an Environmental Regime: Lessons from UNCED,* ed. Bertram I. Spector, Gunnar Sjöstedt, and I. William Zartman. London: Graham and Trottman.

Chasek, Pamela, Lynn Wagner, and I. William Zartman. 1996. "Le Maghreb dans les negociations internationales de l'environnement." In *L'Environnement maghrébin en danger,* ed. Abdullatif Bencherifa and Wil Swearingen. Rabat: Éditions Université Mohammed V, Faculté des Sciences Sociales. Also in *North African Environment at Risk,* ed. Wil Swearingen and Abdullatif Bencherifa. Boulder, Colo.: Westview.

Chayes, Abram, and Antonia H. Chayes. 1993. "On Compliance." *International Organization* 47 (2): 175–206.

Crump, Larry, and I. William Zartman, eds. 2003. *Multilateral Negotiations.* Special issues of *International Negotiation* 8 (1) and (2).

Cutler, Claire, and Mark Zacher, eds. 1992. *Canadian Foreign Policy and International Economic Regimes.* Vancouver: UBC Press.

Downs, George, David Rocke, and Peter Barsoom. 1997. "Designing Multilaterals." Mimeo.

Dunnoff, Jeffrey. 1995. "Toward the Transformation of International Environmental Law." *Harvard Environmental Law Review* 19: 241–311.

Dupont, Christophe. 1994. "Coalition Theory." In *International Multilateral Negotiations,* ed. I. William Zartman. San Francisco: Jossey-Bass.

Eden, Lorraine, and Fen Osler Hampson. 1990. "Clubs Are Trumps: Towards a Taxonomy of International Regimes." Carleton University Center for International Trade and Investment Policy Studies paper 90-02.

Evans, Robert, Harold K. Jacobson, and Robert Putnam, eds. 1993. *Double-Edged Diplomacy.* Berkeley: University of California Press.

Farnhan, Barbara, ed. 1994. *Avoiding Losses/Taking Risks.* Ann Arbor: University of Michigan Press.

Faure, Guy-Olivier, and Deborah Kolb. 1994. "Organizational Theory." In *International Multilateral Negotiations,* ed. I. William Zartman. San Francisco: Jossey-Bass.

Fliess, Barbara. 1987. "The World Administrative Radio Conference 1979." In *Positive Sum: Improving North-South Negotiations,* ed. I. William Zartman. New Brunswick, N.J.: Transaction.

Floweree, Charles, and Rickie Aberle. 1993. "The Chemical Weapons Ban Negotiations." School of Advanced International Studies (SAIS) Case Studies, SAIS, Washington, D.C.

Friedheim, Robert. 1993. *Negotiating the New Ocean Regime.* Columbia, S.C.: University of South Carolina Press.

Gardner, Richard. 1992. *Negotiating Survival.* New York: Council on Foreign Relations.

Geertz, Clifford. 1983. *Local Knowledge: Further Essays in Interpretive Anthropology.* New York: Basic Books.

Grieco, Joseph. 1988. "Anarchy and the Limits of Cooperation." *International Organization* 32 (3): 485–508.

———. 1990. *Cooperation among Nations.* Ithaca, N.Y.: Cornell University Press.

Haas, Peter. 1990. *Saving the Mediterranean.* New York: Columbia University Press.

Hampson, Fen Osler. 1995. *Multilateral Negotiation.* Baltimore: Johns Hopkins University Press.

Hasenclever, Andreas, Peter Mayer, and Volker Rittberger. 1997. *Theories of International Regimes.* New York: Cambridge University Press.

Hayashi, Hikaru. 1999. "Game Theoretic Model of Peacekeeping." Paper presented to the annual meeting of the American Political Science Association, Atlanta.

Hirschman, Albert O. 1970. *Exit, Voice, and Loyalty: Responses to Decline in Firms, Organizations, and States.* Cambridge, Mass.: Harvard University Press.

Homans, George. 1961. *Social Behavior.* New York: Harcourt, Brace and World.

Hurrell, Andrew, and Benedict Kingsbury. 1992. *The International Politics of the Environment.* Oxford: Clarendon Press.

Iklé, Fred Charles. 1964. *How Nations Negotiate.* New York: Harper and Row.

Kimball, Lee. 1992. *Forging International Agreement: The Role of Institutions in Environment and Development.* Washington, D.C.: World Resources Institute.

Klir, G. J. 1985. "The Many Faces of Complexity." In *Science and Praxis of Complexity,* ed. S. Aida et al. Tokyo: United Nations University Press.

Krasner, Stephen, ed. 1983. *International Regimes.* Ithaca, N.Y.: Cornell University Press.

Kratochwil, Friedrich. 1989. *Rules, Norms, and Decisions.* Cambridge: Cambridge University Press.

Kremenyuk, Victor. 2002. "Systems of International Negotiations." In *International Negotiation,* ed. Victor Kremenyuk. San Francisco: Jossey-Bass.

Lang, Winfried. 1989. *Internationaler Umweltschutz.* Vienna: Orac.

Lax, David, and James Sebenius. 1991. "Thinking Coalitionally." In *Negotiation Analysis,* ed. H. Peyton Young. Ann Arbor: University of Michigan Press.

Levy, Marc, Oran Young, and Michael Zürn. 1994. "The Study of International Regimes." International Institute for Applied Systems Analysis, WP 94-113, Laxenburg, Austria.

Lipson, Charles. 1991. "Why Are Some International Agreements Informal?" *International Organization* 45 (4): 495–538.

Malgren, Harald B. 1973. *International Economic Peacekeeping in Phase II.* New York: Quadrangle.

Morgenthau, Hans J. 1960. *Politics among Nations.* New York: Knopf.

Munton, Don, and Geoffrey Castle. 1992. "Air, Water, and Political Fire: Building a North American Environmental Regime." In *Canadian Foreign Policy and International Economic Regimes,* ed. C. Cutler and M. Zacher. Vancouver: UBC Press.

Myers, Norman. 1995. "Environmental Unknowns." *Science* 69 (July 21): 358–360.

Neufeld, Mark. 1993. "Interpretation and the 'Science' of International Relations." *Review of International Studies* 19 (1): 39–61.

Olson, Mancur. 1965. *The Logic of Collective Action.* Cambridge, Mass.: Harvard University Press.

Patterson, Matthew, and Michael Grubb. 1992. "The International Politics of Climate Change." *International Affairs* 68 (April).

Porter, Gareth, and Janet Brown. 1995. *Global Environmental Politics.* Boulder, Colo.: Westview.

Powell, Robert. 1994. "Anarchy in International Relations Theory." *International Organization* 48 (3): 313–344.

Preeg, Ernest. 1970. *Traders and Diplomats.* Washington, D.C.: Brookings Institution.

Putnam, Robert. 1988. "Diplomacy and Domestic Politics: The Logic of Two-Level Games." *International Organization* 42 (3): 427–460.

Rawls, John. 1971. *A Theory of Justice.* Cambridge, Mass.: Harvard University Press.

Rittberger, Volker, and Peter Mayer, eds. 1993. *Regime Theory and International Relations.* Oxford: Clarendon Press.

Rittberger, Volker, and Michael Zürn. 1990. "Towards Regulated Anarchy in East-West Relations: Causes and Consequences of East-West Regimes." In *International Regimes in East-West Politics,* ed. Volker Rittberger. London: Pinter.

Rosenau, James, and Ernst-Otto Czempiel, eds. 1992. *Governance without Government.* New York: Cambridge University Press.

Ruggie, John G. 1983. "International Regimes, Transactions, and Change." In *International Regimes,* ed. Stephen Krasner. Ithaca, N.Y.: Cornell University Press.

Sand, Peter. 1990. *Lessons Learned in Global Environmental Governance.* Washington, D.C.: World Resources Institute.

Scapple, Karin. 1996. "The Helsinki and Sofia Protocols: Can They Be as Effective as the Montreal Protocol?" Paper presented to the International Studies Association, San Diego, Calif.

Scharpf, Fritz. 1989. "Decision Rules, Decision Styles, and Policy Choices." *Journal of Theoretical Politics* 1 (1): 149–176.

Sebenius, James. 1984. *Negotiating the Law of the Sea.* Cambridge, Mass.: Harvard University Press.

Sjöstedt, Gunnar, ed. 1993. *International Environmental Negotiations.* Newbury Park, Calif.: Sage.

Snidal, Duncan. 1985. "The Limits of Hegemonic Stability Theory." *International Organization* 39 (4): 579–614.

Spector, Bertram. 1994. "Decision Analysis." In *International Multilateral Negotiations,* ed. I. William Zartman. San Francisco: Jossey-Bass.

Spector, Bertram I., Gunnar Sjöstedt, and I. William Zartman, eds. 1994. *Negotiating an Environmental Regime: Lessons from UNCED.* London: Graham and Trottman.

Sprinz, Detlev, and Tapani Vaahtoranta. 1994. "The Interest-Based Explanation of International Environmental Policy." *International Organization* 38 (1): 77–106.

Stein, Janice, and Louis Pauly, eds. 1993. *Choosing to Cooperate: How States Avoid Loss.* Baltimore: Johns Hopkins University Press.

Susskind, Lawrence. 1995. *Environmental Diplomacy.* New York: Oxford University Press.

Victor, David, Kal Raustiala, and Eugene Skolnikoff, eds. 1998. *International Environmental Commitments.* Cambridge, Mass.: MIT Press.

Weber, Max. 1978. *Economy and Society.* Edited by Guenther Roth and Claus Wittich. Berkeley: University of California Press.

Winham, Gilbert. 1977a. "Complexity in International Negotiation." In *Negotiations,* ed. Daniel Druckman. Newbury Park, Calif.: Sage.

———. 1977b. "Negotiation as a Management Process." *World Politics* 30 (1): 87–114.

———. 1986. *International Trade: The Tokyo Round Negotiations.* Princeton, N.J.: Princeton University Press.

———. 1990. "The Prenegotiation Phase of the Uruguay Round." In *Getting to the Table,* ed. Janice Stein. Baltimore: Johns Hopkins University Press.

Wolf, Amanda. 1997. *Quotas in International Environmental Agreements.* London: Earthscan.

Young, H. Peyton. 1994. *Equity.* Princeton, N.J.: Princeton University Press.

Young, Oran. 1983. "Regime Dynamics." In *International Regimes,* ed. Stephen Krasner. Ithaca, N.Y.: Cornell University Press.

———. 1986. "International Regimes: Toward a New Theory of Institutions." *World Politics* 44 (1): 104–122.

———. 1989a. "Politics of Regime Formation." *International Organization* 37 (3): 349–376.

———. 1989b. *International Cooperation.* Ithaca, N.Y.: Cornell University Press.

———. 1991. "Political Leadership and Regime Formation." *International Organization* 45 (3): 281–308.

Young, Oran, George Demko, and Kiliparti Ramakrishna. 1996. *Global Environmental Change and International Governance.* Hanover, N.H.: Dartmouth College.

Young, Oran, and Gail Osherenko, eds. 1993. *Polar Politics: Creating International Environmental Regimes.* Ithaca, N.Y.: Cornell University Press.

Zartman, I. William. 1997. "The Structuralist Dilemma in Negotiation." In *Research on Negotiation in Organizations,* ed. Roy Lewicki. Greenwich, Conn.: JAI Press.

————, ed. 1987. *Positive Sum: Improving North-South Negotiations.* New Brunswick, N.J.: Transaction.

————, ed. 1994. *International Multilateral Negotiations.* San Francisco: Jossey-Bass.

Zartman, I. William, and Maureen Berman. 1982. *The Practical Negotiator.* New Haven, Conn.: Yale University Press.

Zartman, I. William, Daniel Druckman, Lloyd Jensen, Dean G. Pruitt, and H. Peyton Young. 1996. "Negotiation as a Search for Justice." *International Negotiation* 1 (1): 79–98.

Zartman, I. William, and Jeffrey Z. Rubin, eds. 2000. *Power and International Negotiation.* Ann Arbor: University of Michigan Press.

2

Deconstructing the Negotiations of Regime Dynamics

Bertram I. Spector

"GETTING IT DONE" is why regimes are negotiated. "It" includes all of the activities required to implement cooperative regimes, be those regimes designed to monitor world trade, promote European security, protect the ozone layer, protect human rights, or notify other states in the event of nuclear accidents. Our focus is not only on the institutional structures, substantive goals, and achievements of the regimes discussed in this book but also on how these regimes get their work done. We examine the processes by which these regimes are governed, operate, and evolve—and in many cases these are negotiation processes. Sometimes these processes work well, helping the regime attain its goals, and sometimes the processes are faulty, making the goals more difficult to achieve. As suggested in the preceding chapter, getting it done can be conceived largely as a multilevel, multilateral negotiation process, but one that is distinguishable from the neotiations that produced the regime in the first place. Regimes operate in a "postagreement" negotiation environment that certainly bears some resemblance to its antecedents but has many characteristics of its own. This chapter decomposes the organic postagreement negotiation process presented in the previous chapter into its domestic and international dimensions and compares the pre- and postagreement stages analytically. In doing so, the chapter examines the differences among various postagreement regime negotiation processes and then distinguishes between negotiation processes in global and regional regimes.

The untidy life cycle of regime dynamics takes the form of multiple recursive negotiations, each exposing conflicts and resolving issues. The more difficult questions of how these negotiations propel regimes toward outcomes and how differences in negotiation dynamics yield differences in regime effectiveness over time are addressed later in this chapter by reference to a comparative database focused on regime negotiations. By moving to this next level of detail—by inspecting and analyzing the anatomy of postagreement negotiation processes—we develop the investigatory tools to examine current and past regimes and begin to explain how these negotiations indeed make a difference in the evolution of regimes. Propositions derived from this investigation are examined in the case studies in part II of this book.

Regimes and Negotiation

When the euphoria of regime formation subsides, the difficult work of implementing the negotiated agreement begins. Implementation often entails many changes, both domestic and international, and concrete and cognitive. The process usually requires the regime's signatories to alter their practices in specified ways, but in many cases the details of how this ought to be done and the implications of alternative practices have not been fully evaluated. The diplomats who initiated the regime often leave this additional work for others to resolve, compounding uncertainty. Thus, implementation is seldom simply a rote process of putting into action what was decided at the negotiating table. It requires a creative and inventive negotiating process of its own, this time focused on ironing out the details of regime goals and the completion of partial agreements in a mutually acceptable way.

Certain changes must occur in order to implement regime provisions. At the national level, laws and regulations must be changed, prescribed actions performed, standards revised, targets modified, and enforcement and monitoring mechanisms put in place. At the international level, new regimes often entail new norms and procedures to follow, new institutional structures to build, and governance rules to abide by.

These changes can be characterized as a new postagreement negotiation process focused on firmly establishing and stabilizing the regime, one that involves new actors, new issues, new venues, and new conflicts. Successful regime formation negotiations thus generate continuous subsequent negotiations. The prevalence of negotiation activities extends from immediate regime implementation to governance, expansion, and evolution of the regime over time. In fact, once an international regime is formed, there are often few alternatives—other than dropping out of the regime entirely—to continuing the process of negotiation.

The heady issues that marked the initiating negotiations—developing overall principles and formulas that satisfy the concepts of justice and fairness to the parties—are usually supplanted in the postagreement negotiations with more practical concerns of how to settle specific disputes over particular provisions, set specific targets, draw certain boundaries, monitor and evaluate compliance, adjust standards as the need requires, and so on. This does not mean that postagreement negotiations are pedestrian. On the contrary, they address the very issues that citizens in the signatory countries can feel, see, and smell, impacting lives directly and evoking strong emotions. Moreover, postagreement negotiations are essential to understanding and explaining the viability of the initiating regime negotiations. The constructive formulas and the halfway solutions and sidelined problem areas all come to the surface in the postagreement period, either to help or to haunt.

By explaining the operations of regimes using a negotiation framework, we are recasting the regime concept in a behavioral light—in terms of joint decision making, problem solving, evolution, and collective choice. What this framework adds is an understanding of how regimes govern themselves and change in response to their environment; it can be described as a process of regime life cycles (Levy, Young, and Zürn 1995). This behavioral approach looks at how actors modify their utilities, enhance and retract cooperation, learn, redefine roles, and cause internal realignments. Behavioral regime dynamics thus trace a continual pattern of redefinition, adaptation, and restructuring brought about in large part through the process of negotiation. This chapter deconstructs the postagreement negotiation process into its components to seek an explanation of how and why regimes "get it done."

Regime Life Cycles: From Preagreement to Postagreement Negotiation

Postagreement negotiation is like other negotiation processes in many respects. It is characterized by a set of interested actors with mixed motives and the absence of a clear, mutually acceptable solution, but also by a desire on the part of all actors to create such a solution. By definition, these negotiations occur *after* the successful or at least partially successful negotiation of a regime agreement. In the realm of many scientific negotiations, environmental issues among them, only partial solutions appear to be possible in the short run due to incomplete understanding of these issues. The instability of partial and incomplete agreements necessitates continued negotiations and drives the process forward. Sometimes these negotiations are carried out in a formal setting, but sometimes an informal approach to negotiation is taken. Sustained negotiation often has no clear-cut conclusion; it continually self-reinforces the need for additional negotiation with the goal of completing or perfecting the regime's agreements.

Postagreement negotiation can thus be defined as *the dynamic and cooperative processes, systems, procedures, and structures that are institutionalized to sustain dialogue on issues that cannot, by their very nature, be resolved by a single agreement.*[1] The purpose of postagreement negotiation is to continue the dialogue to push forward the development of the agreement and its implementation in an evolutionary fashion. These sustained negotiations are the dynamic mechanism by which international cooperation can be enhanced by improving and adding to past agreements, completing or modernizing them, operationalizing their effects, and attempting to perfect solutions so that all participants feel satisfied with the outcome.

Several major aspects of the postagreement process distinguish it clearly from preagreement negotiation. First, postagreement negotiation focuses on "getting it done" as opposed to "getting to yes." The difficult tasks of identifying the necessary trade-offs, finding common ground, and achieving consensus among nations are the principal activities that occupy preagreement negotiators. They seek broad frameworks that all can agree to, but they often shift the burden of some difficult tasks to the postagreement period, including devising implementation processes, procedures, rules, and standards; building institutions and approaches to implement them; monitoring and enforcing the impact of these new approaches; and coordinating with other actors. Getting it done is typically more concerned with negotiating details than with negotiating over principles and norms. It defines where an agreement that is acceptable at the conceptual level is empirically tested to determine its feasibility in a practical sense—that is, whether it can be successfully implemented, governed, monitored, and enforced.

Getting it done is not always thought of as a set of negotiating activities. It is often viewed as a bureaucratic task to administer the implementation of negotiated solutions. But many of the decisions that must be made at both the national and international levels still must be negotiated—among parliamentarians, between national and local officials, between government agencies and domestic stakeholders, and between national agencies and international or regional-level agencies. These actors, each with its own, often conflicting, interests, must negotiate to find mutually acceptable solutions. Because of the influx of these new players, interests, and issues, getting it done can easily become more complicated than the initiating negotiations.

Second, postagreement negotiation deals very much with *continuities.* These talks begin where preagreement talks leave off. They take up the unfinished business of partial agreements to act upon their successes *and* failures. Sustained negotiation is needed not only to implement the agreements that were struck in earlier talks but to deal with the intractable issues that could not be settled amicably among the parties as well. Both types of challenges flow through as tasks for the postagreement period.

Important legal precedents, norms, and principles are also carried forth from the initiating negotiations. These represent the shared beliefs and values that were agreed to previously and now govern the continued negotiations. All of the negotiations and compromises that went into developing these precedents should, theoretically, facilitate progress in postagreement negotiations, serving as points of departure for tackling new and perhaps more difficult issues.

Beyond this common ground of accepted tenets, continued personal relationships play a large role in the course of postagreement talks. Many of the same people involved in the initial negotiations often continue to represent their parties in the aftermath. After all, as individuals they have amassed a valuable base of knowledge through the experience of the initial talks that would be difficult to replicate or pass on to others. The continuity of personnel involved in negotiation is important not only in the transmission of knowledge but also in facilitating opportunities to find innovative solutions. Informal personal relationships that develop over the course of the initial negotiations can be useful in promoting understanding across differing positions, finding ways to bridge the gaps between conflicting interests, and reducing the time sometimes needed to "break the ice" and separate the formalities from the real work at hand.

Continuities are ultimately manifested in the experiences of the parties from the initiating negotiation. They now have developed expectations of other parties, of the body of norms and principles produced, and of the likely effects of chosen solutions. This experience is in part built on feedback from negotiating partners and domestic stakeholders and on monitoring the effectiveness of negotiated actions and responses. Overall, these continuities represent learning by the involved parties, learning that can help stimulate a positive progression in resolving or managing the problem, either by undoing past mistakes or generating creative solutions.

As indicated in the previous chapter, the third major distinguishing factor between pre- and postagreement negotiation is the *multilevel or multitheater complexity* of the latter. The political willingness of domestic leaders in government, industry, and nongovernmental organizations to comply with negotiated agreements reached at the international level is a major driving force in the postagreement phase. These leaders can help to create or block a national consensus to implement international commitments. In addition, domestic institutions responsible for aspects of implementation are required to interface with their international counterparts to report on compliance and enforcement, receive new regulatory initiatives, and negotiate on verification and international governance issues. These linkages and interactions between the national and international levels are multiplied by the number of countries that are signatories to an agreement. The coordination of these interactions is left to the international level.

The conception of international negotiations as a two-level game (Putnam 1988; Evans, Jacobson, and Putnam 1993) goes to the heart of the complexity of postagreement negotiation. National defections (that is, refusal to accept, ratify, or abide by a negotiated agreement) can nullify the effect of international treaties, domestic issue linkages with international agreements can generate new coalitions that favor or undermine implementation, and uncertainty in domestic politics can be used tactically to feign incapacity at the international bargaining table.

The fourth distinguishing characteristic of postagreement negotiation is *evolution*. Postagreement negotiation marks several transitions:

◆ *From initiation of a regime agreement to its implementation.* Preagreement talks hammer out initial solutions and often frame breakthroughs in finding mutually acceptable approaches to solving problems or disputes. Those solutions come to fruition in the aftermath of those talks through the sustained mechanism of negotiation and bargaining among the implementers. Implementation, though, deals with a partly new set of issues, concerns, and interests involved more with the detailed rules and procedures needed to get it done than with the broader norms and principles of getting to yes. This natural evolution from initiation to implementation often travels through uncharted waters; initial agreements are usually vague about implementation requirements. This is sometimes necessary to be able to achieve the initial agreement altogether; the agreement's mandate may be acceptable to the signatories, but its implementation must be individually interpreted to be palatable domestically. This necessitates continued negotiations to decipher the initial agreement's intent and to translate that intent into feasible implementation approaches at a more local level. Most important, while the initial agreement may be conducted at an international level, much of the implementation must be negotiated at the domestic level, involving actors and interests that were previously unrepresented.

◆ *From uncertain expectations to established relationships.* When the initiating negotiations got under way, many things were yet to be defined—the issues and issue linkages, actor positions and interests, and actor relationships. Overcoming these uncertainties is time-consuming and often results in the negotiations taking only halting steps toward an outcome. The postagreement negotiation is free of many of these problems. By the end of the initial negotiations, most of these initial uncertainties have become established facts. Parties know the positions and interests of other signatories, the issues and approaches to solving the problem have been clarified and consensus may have been reached on their scope and meaning, and the parties usually have developed informal working relationships with one another—working in caucuses or coalitions toward mutually accepted goals. Certainly, as the complexities of domestic interests get intertwined with the implementation of the international agreement, new uncertainties may emerge: internal blocking coalitions, the intricacies of national treaty acceptance, the bureaucratic machinations of national agencies responsible for implementing new regulations, and so on. But a firm basis for common understanding at the international level is usually established as a result of the initiating experience.

◆ *From staunch national sovereignty positions to international interdependence.* With acceptance in principle of the initiating international commitment, the boundary between sovereignty and interdependence arguments often begins to blur. Demands to preserve national sovereignty have usually softened by the time postagreement negotiation occurs. Acceptance of the initiating agreement reflects national realization that international coordination and interdependent action are required to have a meaningful impact on the problem at hand. Thus, overcoming sovereignty objections, at least at the conceptual level, is often less of a problem in the postagreement period. On the other hand, sovereignty issues certainly do come to the fore concerning the *details* of implementation, when constraining regulations and reporting requirements are imposed to comply with international commitments. Powerful domestic stakeholders who may be asked to bear the costs of an agreement then often bring pressure on government officials to push sovereignty rights issues to protect domestic interests and thus weaken implementation.

◆ *From creation of new formulas to their transformation into details.* Preagreement negotiations deal primarily with inventing a package of principles and norms that is accepted as fair and just by the parties.

Postagreement negotiations deal with inventing ways to make those principles and norms a reality, through the building of detailed, though flexible, rules and procedures that can be implemented by all the parties in accordance with the differences of each national system (see Sjöstedt, this volume). But rule building is not the only task of the postagreement period. Over time, accepted principles and norms must be interpreted and changed; the consensus of a previous period may change as well because of new information, feedback from past implementation actions, and political rethinking. The evolutionary process embodied by postagreement negotiations often includes not only implementation but also expansion of the original goals of the agreement through a renegotiation of basic principles and norms.

◆ *From regime formation to regime operation.* Postagreement negotiations typically seek completion of partial outcomes. A major purpose of postagreement negotiation is to see that regimes evolve and are strengthened over time by spelling out the roles and obligations of the various parties, harmonizing efforts, evening out costs, verifying compliance, and pressuring noncompliant parties (Porter and Brown 1991). Barriers may get in the way of this strengthening objective— the regime may lack effectiveness because the parties lack the political will to make it succeed—but postagreement negotiation provides a forum for dismantling those barriers and seeking ways of truly solving the problems and resolving the disputes that led to the initial agreement.

There are two fundamental types of postagreement negotiations, though they are often intertwined. The first, *implementation negotiations,* follow the successful conclusion of a negotiated agreement in order to settle disputes, handle misunderstandings, deal with future adjustments to the agreement, and manage the day-to-day governance of the agreement among the signatories. The objective of these negotiations is to ensure that the negotiated outcome is well implemented.

The second, *expansion negotiations,* expand upon and extend the initiating agreement, deal with issues that were not addressed in sufficient detail, improve and flesh out the agreement, and make a partial accord more complete. As indicated earlier, partial incremental agreements tend to predominate on environmental issues due to scientific uncertainty concerning many of the problems and possible solutions, and the need for continued learning about effects and consequences. Partial agreements are also customary when there is political uncertainty on how to devise fair and equitable approaches. When a partial agreement is designed consciously, diplomats will usually negotiate simultaneously a sustained, institutionalized negotiation forum to continue the work they have begun. These negotiations often become a major component of an international regime.

Sustained negotiations present diplomats and policymakers with the challenge of progressively reframing the problems, adjusting strategies and perceptions, and refining solutions in postagreement negotiations. The UN Conference on Environment and Development (UNCED) in 1992, for example, has propagated such a system of postagreement negotiation under the umbrella of a regime on sustainable development dealing with climate change, biodiversity, deforestation, desertification, and other issues, which certainly will occupy the diplomatic, scientific, and interested nongovernmental communities well into this century (Spector, Sjöstedt, and Zartman 1994). The research community is in parallel confronted with new challenges of analyzing systems of partial linked agreements and an increasingly fuzzy demarcation between negotiation and implementation.

Ultimately, the principal research question surrounding regime dynamics and postagreement negotiation is that of *effectiveness*, the extent to which the problem is solved. Negotiation analysis, while focusing its attention on how process leads to outcomes, usually defines outcomes as agreements reached at the bargaining table (Kremenyuk 2002). Many diplomats and international civil servants, however, conceive of negotiation outcomes not as the agreements themselves but as the implementation and effectiveness of those agreements. For them, the questions are: Are agreements implemented at all and do they produce the intended effects on the problem that initiated negotiations in the first place? Postagreement negotiation often occurs over a long time frame and rarely in a logical or sequential order. While most countries intend to implement the changes they have agreed to, some may find it in their interest to consciously deceive their fellow signatories and have no intention of making the necessary modifications to law, regulation, or lifestyle. Yet other nations may have the best of intentions to implement their commitments but find that they lack the capacity or resources to follow through on them. The success of many negotiations can thus be determined only by evaluating the effectiveness of the postagreement negotiation process in transforming words into concrete realities through compliance with agreements. In large part, the postagreement negotiation process can therefore be viewed as the yardstick by which to judge the quality and effectiveness of the initiating negotiation process.

Deconstructing the Postagreement Negotiation Process

A conceptual framework of regime dynamics and the postagreement negotiation process is presented in figure 1. It depicts the multiple negotiation processes that operate concurrently and at several levels to make up regime governance. Domestically, *ratification negotiation* is usually required to achieve formal acceptance of regime agreements by each national government. Domestic ratification can be conceived of as a prototypical negotiation process in itself, bringing together the various domestic stakeholders who have an interest in some aspect of the agreement (Spector and Korula 1993). After ratification, *rule-making negotiation* is required at the national level, by which laws and regulations are enacted to conform to the stipulations of the regime. Such rule making almost always requires negotiation among domestic stakeholders in nongovernmental, as well as governmental (often parliamentary), organizations. Finally, *negotiation concerning monitoring, reporting, and enforcement* functions is necessary to provide feedback to national and international agencies on the success or failure of laws and regulations. Some of the most effective monitoring and reporting is performed by NGOs and scientific groups serving as watchdogs

Figure 1. Regime Dynamics in a Postagreement Negotiation Framework

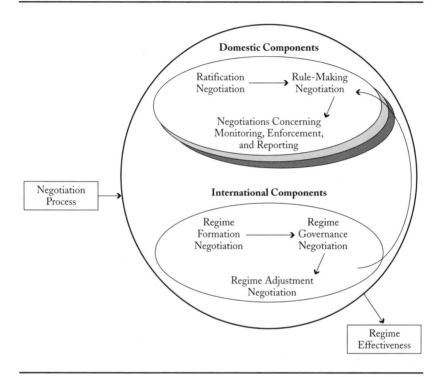

over national implementation procedures. Lively debates and ultimately bargaining between such NGOs and government agencies that are officially empowered with monitoring functions can result in improved and enforced national compliance with an international regime.

There are three negotiation subprocesses in the international component as well. First, *regime formation negotiation* involves the implementation and institutionalization of the agreed-upon rules and procedures. Many partial or imprecise sets of rules and procedures must be further elaborated through negotiation during the initial implementing period. In *regime governance negotiation*, information concerning participant actions is collected; compliance is monitored, verified, and enforced; and disputes are resolved. Negotiation is often the process through which problems with compliance, enforcement, and rule interpretation are worked out. The final subprocess is *regime adjustment negotiation*, in which the rules, procedures, and targets originally established in the negotiated regime might be modified in conjunction with new information collected on the effects of compliance and as science learns more about the problem—for instance, in the case of environmental issues. If significant changes to a regime are required, renegotiation may be called for. Otherwise, adjustments may be reflected in the need for additional domestic rule making.

Each of these six postagreement negotiation processes is distinguished by a different set of target issues and actors. They are not necessarily sequential phases; many overlap and can occur in parallel with others. The boundaries between phases easily blur; regime formation, for example, is a continuous process that precedes, but then usually operates simultaneously with, regime governance functions. Tables 1 and 2 summarize each phase's functions and participants.

The expectations for the negotiation process and the outcomes at each phase can be widely different. For example, ratification and acceptance may evoke the participation of a large variety of domestic stakeholders, each with its own pet interests to maximize. In comparison, rule making may be a more orderly process, but federal national systems such as the United States often require legislation and standard setting not only at the federal level but at a myriad of local levels as well. Regime governance, at the international level, requires negotiation among national parties and their responsible institutions to monitor, mediate, and enforce the implementation and operation of an agreement. All phases are usually multilateral processes; some include nonstate actors, some operate as informal negotiation processes, others as more formal processes, and some interact with others as they progress in parallel. The outcomes sought from each phase are also very different. For example, ratification yields national acceptance, rule making produces legislation and regulation, and enforcement results in accommodations between governmental regulating authorities and local governments, industry, or citizen groups that must comply with new decrees.

Table 1. Domestic Postagreement Negotiation Processes

Acceptance/Ratification Negotiations: Domestic negotiations concerning the formal acceptance of internationally negotiated agreements at the state level. These negotiations involve participation by various stakeholders, including government ministries and agencies, political parties, business, NGOs, and the public. They usually take the form of both formal negotiations in institutional settings, such as in national parliaments, and informal negotiations and debates among the bureaucracy and in the public media.

Rule-Making Negotiations: Domestic negotiations concerning the design and development of new or modified legislation, regulations, criteria, standards, and targets that are intended to bring the state into conformity with the provisions of an accepted international agreement. Formal participants are usually legislators and bureaucrats in government ministries and agencies who have the authority to make and change regulations. Other participants often get involved in influencing these negotiations, especially lobby groups representing business, political parties, NGOs, and the public.

Enforcement, Monitoring, and Reporting Negotiations: Domestic negotiations concerning the methods and approaches for implementation of new legislation and regulations. Many economic stakeholders often participate in these negotiations with national legislators and government officials, since these stakeholders are usually the parties that will have to change their behavior in line with new rules. The desired outcome of these negotiations is usually compliance with these new laws and regulations.

Table 2. International Postagreement Negotiation Processes

Regime Formation Negotiations: International negotiations concerning the operational implementation of a regime characterized by a set of principles, norms, rules, and procedures to govern a particular issue area in accordance with or referring to one or more internationally negotiated agreements. These negotiations concern how agreement provisions are operationally defined, formalized, and implemented to create a regime. Issues in such negotiations can include, for example, membership rules, voting rules, institutional development, and relationships among regime members and other external entities.

Regime Governance Negotiations: International negotiations concerning the ongoing operation and governance of an international regime, including such issues as coalition building and functioning, leadership, development of consensual understanding on issues, dispute resolution, monitoring and reporting, and the entry of new members and departure of old members.

Regime Adjustment Negotiations: International negotiations concerning renegotiation of current agreements to bring them into line with new information, new thinking, new issues, and feedback from current activities. These negotiations can result in regime enlargement and contraction.

Analysis

How do these diverse negotiation processes propel regimes? What makes them essential explanatory elements of regime dynamics? A systematic comparative analysis of twenty-six international and regional regimes was conducted to examine the internal workings of postagreement negotiation processes and their impact on those regimes. This analysis sought to evaluate the nature of the various postagreement negotiation processes, the extent to which they are, in fact, distinct and can explain regime dynamics, and the interlinkages and handoffs among these processes.

A virtual expert panel supported the data collection.[2] Officials from the international commissions and secretariats responsible for major environmental treaties, as well as experts who have followed the implementation of particular treaties, responded to a detailed questionnaire. Of the twenty-six responses, each related to a different international environmental regime.[3] Eleven of these regimes were global and fifteen were regional in scope. Respondents were asked to characterize thirty-two negotiation process attributes categorized into several baskets: issues, situation, structure, actors, process, strategy, and outcome. The respondents provided their judgment on each attribute across four postagreement negotiation processes: national ratification, regime formation, regime governance, and regime adjustment.[4] The respondents were also asked to use their expert judgment to classify the common behaviors they have observed over time and across countries and to rank these behaviors (high, medium, low, and none).

The resulting analysis focuses specifically on the common and distinguishing dynamics across these four major postagreement negotiation processes (see table 3). In general, the findings show that domestic-level ratification negotiations are often different in process from international regime negotiations. In contrast, there are fewer process differences among the three regime negotiation stages. There are many distinctions, on the other hand, between the process characteristics of regional and global regime postagreement negotiations (see table 4). The most prominent general trends are described below.

Table 3. Differences across Postagreement Negotiation Processes
(*N* = 26 regime experts; results are in percentages)

Postagreement Negotiation Factors	Domestic-Level Negotiations	International-Level Negotiations		
	National Ratification Negotiations	Regime Formation Negotiations	Regime Governance Negotiations	Regime Adjustment Negotiations
Issues: Large number of issues dealt with	45	54	45	38
Predominance of technical issues	5	22	26	19
Predominance of political issues	10	17	13	14
Much change or redefinition of issues	15	25	5	17
Situation: Major time deadlines	15	29	14	18
Strong publicity/media coverage	20	17	19	18
Strong third-party involvement	5	9	5	9
Large number of influencing external events	25	17	15	32
Participants had better ways of solving differences than to negotiate	17	9	10	18
Structure: Long time frame during which negotiations occurred	85	83	76	81
Talks are predominantly formal	60	48	48	55
Predominantly institutional setting	88	84	76	70
Actors: Government is major actor	82	96	95	90
NGOs are major actors	50	78	50	46
Extensive prior negotiating experience	71	58	62	52

Predominance of technical issue experts	9	42	38	14
Predominance of political officials	35	17	0	14
Large number of the same actors involved as in the originating negotiations	55	67	67	67
High level of cooperation among negotiators	33	35	29	38
Process: Predominantly characterized by problem solving	56	52	48	60
Predominantly characterized by win–lose	19	36	33	32
Frequent impasses	22	18	15	14
Basically characterized by reaching general principles and then bargaining over details	81	65	77	70
Strategy: High imbalance of power resources	29	35	38	48
Active use of pressure tactics	6	4	5	5
Outcomes Achieved: Partial outcomes	15	27	38	48
Basically perceived as fair	60	57	53	45
Ratified and accepted	67			
High speed in ratification	21			
Changes implemented in national laws, regulations, and targets to comply with agreements	38			
Regimes formed and states participate		77		
High conformity and compliance with treaty provisions			43	
Effective regime operation			30	
Political willingness to modify goals, targets, and means				50

Table 4. Differences across Negotiation Processes within Regime Types (*N* = 26 regime experts; results are in percentages)

Postagreement Negotiation Factors	National Ratification Negotiations		Regime Formation Negotiations	
	Global Regimes (*n* = 11)	Regional Regimes (*n* = 15)	Global Regimes (*n* = 11)	Regional Regimes (*n* = 15)
Issues: Large number of issues dealt with	40	50	50	57
Predominance of technical issues	0	10	20	23
Predominance of political issues	0	20	10	23
Much change or redefinition of issues	10	20	10	36
Situation: Major time deadlines	10	20	10	43
Strong publicity/media coverage	10	32	10	21
Strong third-party involvement	0	11	10	8
Large number of influencing external events	10	40	0	31
Participants had better ways of solving differences than to negotiate	0	33	0	15
Structure: Long time frame during which negotiations occurred	100	70	80	86
Talks are predominantly formal	50	70	60	38
Predominantly institutional setting	100	67	100	67
Actors: Government is major actor	90	75	100	93
NGOs are major actors	75	0	100	33
Extensive prior negotiating experience	80	64	80	43

Predominance of technical issue experts	0	15	30	50
Predominance of political officials	40	31	10	21
Large number of the same actors involved as in the originating negotiations	70	40	90	50
High level of cooperation among negotiators	44	22	40	31
Process: Predominantly characterized by problem solving	22	100	30	69
Predominantly characterized by win-lose	22	14	40	33
Frequent impasses	11	33	10	25
Basically characterized by reaching general principles and then bargaining over details	67	100	50	77
Strategy: High imbalance of power resources	0	63	30	38
Active use of pressure tactics	0	13	0	7
Outcomes Achieved: Partial outcomes	22	9	40	17
Basically perceived as fair	67	55	30	82
Ratified and accepted	30	93		
High speed of ratification	0	36		
Changes implemented in national laws, regulations, and targets to comply with agreements	40	36		
Regimes formed and states participate			78	77
High conformity and compliance with treaty provisions			22	57
Effective regime operation			11	43
Political willingness to modify goals, targets, and means			25	64

Postagreement Negotiation Processes (Table 3)

DOMESTIC RATIFICATION NEGOTIATIONS. More so than other regime negotiations, these domestic-level negotiations are characterized by formal and institutional settings (usually national parliaments), actors with extensive political experience (usually parliamentarians), problem-solving processes (to satisfy domestic stakeholders), incremental processes in which general principles are agreed upon first and details ironed out later, and final agreements that are perceived as fair and just for all the parties. In comparison with other regime negotiations, ratification negotiation processes involve significantly fewer technical issue experts (the issues dealt with domestically are often more political in nature), fewer veterans of the initiating negotiation (the venue is now at the domestic level), proceedings that are less like a win-lose situation (all domestic stakeholders have to learn to embrace the ratified regime), and fewer partial outcomes (ratification is the sole objective).

REGIME FORMATION NEGOTIATIONS. These negotiations have a distinct profile. In comparison with the other negotiations, formation talks involve a large number of issues, greater change in and redefinition of issues; more time deadlines; more institutionalized settings; and greater involvement on the part of NGOs, technical issue experts, and veterans from the initiating talks. Participants in formation negotiations are less likely to have better alternatives than negotiation to resolve their differences than are their counterparts in other regime negotiations.

REGIME GOVERNANCE NEGOTIATIONS. Governance negotiations, more so than other regime negotiations, are characterized by a predominance of technical issues. In comparison to the other postagreement negotiation processes, governance negotiations involve fewer changes in the issue portfolio and are subject to fewer external influences. In addition, governance negotiations tend to be less characterized by problem solving than the other regime negotiation processes. Many of the important issues in governance negotiations are settled in informal settings through a process of consensuation (Lodge and Pfetsch 1998).

REGIME ADJUSTMENT NEGOTIATIONS. These negotiation processes tend to be more influenced by external events than are the other regime negotiations; adjustment to the regime is motivated by changing issue agendas among the signatories over time. They also tend to be more characterized by problem-solving activity, greater imbalances of power among stakeholders, and achievement of only partial outcomes. At the same time, adjustment negotiations tend to be less likely than the other regime negotiations to involve NGOs, to be plagued by impasses, and to result in outcomes that are perceived as fair by all participants.

These results demonstrate a clear change in the manifest dynamics that occur within regimes throughout their life cycle. Not all the dynamics of all negotiations are the same. Ratification negotiations, by definition, focus on domestic politics and less on technical issues. The process is viewed very much as an incremental and cautious problem-solving situation, seeking basic agreement on general principles first and then proceeding to bargaining over the details to ensure an orderly and broadly accepted outcome that all stakeholders can agree to because they have bought into it along the way. Participants view it as a win-win process; it yields comprehensive outcomes that elaborate how the country will comply with and implement the regime.

In contrast, regime formation negotiations are multilateral and fluid. They involve a large number of issues that can change and be redefined as the negotiations proceed. Many old and new stakeholders participate. Whereas the ratification process is a formal and institutionalized process at the national level, regime formation talks are wide ranging and dynamic—their purpose is to create something new. Participants are committed to the process; they believe that negotiating regime formation is truly the best approach to achieving the objectives set out in the initiating regime agreement. At this early stage in the regime life cycle, the stakeholders are not easily diverted by external events; they usually stay the course to establish the regime as earlier negotiated.

Regime governance negotiations—the mainstay of everyday regime operations—are focused, as one might imagine, primarily on resolving differences over technical issues and addressing new technical issues that arise. Regime members negotiate within the regime's boundaries, rules, and procedures; they do not look for alternative venues to resolve issues. In fact, these governance negotiations can be characterized as businesslike and focused on achieving results, and they are therefore less likely to be diverted by external issues.

As regimes age, regime adjustment negotiations emerge with a very different profile from their predecessor processes. These negotiations —because they deal with regime re-formation—are more political in nature and expose the power differentials among stakeholders. Achieving what are perceived to be fair outcomes by all is *not* the objective here. Official actors are involved, less so NGOs. External political pressures can influence the proceedings, which are marked by a lot of give-and-take. The outcome is more likely to be a partial agreement.

Negotiation Processes across Global and Regional Regimes (Table 4)

GLOBAL REGIME RATIFICATION NEGOTIATIONS. These negotiations over global regime ratification, in comparison to those for regional regime ratification, take a long time to resolve in national legislatures. They tend to be conducted in more institutional settings, NGOs tend to more prominent in the talks, and the participants are more likely to be experienced negotiators.

REGIONAL REGIME RATIFICATION NEGOTIATIONS. The predominant issues in regional regime ratification talks are likely to be more political, more influenced by external events, and more subject to publicity and media coverage than those in global regime ratification negotiations. Impasses are likely to be more frequent, power imbalances among actors are likely to emerge, and actors are likely to have other ways to solve their problems. The approach to these negotiations is through problem solving and incremental bargaining over details, backed up by agreement on general principles. The outcome of these negotiations, ratification of the regional regime, is generally quicker than for global regimes.

GLOBAL REGIME FORMATION NEGOTIATIONS. These negotiations are more formal and institutionalized than their regional regime counterparts. More NGOs are involved at the global level, and negotiators are more experienced and likely to be veterans of the initiating negotiations. Talks concerning global regime formation are more likely to yield partial outcomes than are regional regime negotiations.

REGIONAL REGIME FORMATION NEGOTIATIONS. Regional regime formation negotiations, more than global regime formation talks, tend to be dominated by political issues that get redefined as the talks progress. Time deadlines often constrain the talks, and media coverage and external events tend to influence progress. Technocrats and political officials are more frequently involved in these negotiations, which are more characterized by problem-solving behaviors and by frequent impasses. Compared with global talks, regional talks are more likely to be perceived as fair, to yield outcomes that are complied with, and to build in future flexibility to achieve regime effectiveness.

There are clear differences in the negotiation processes across global and regional regimes. On the one side, the negotiations of global regimes are generally more structured (formal and in institutionalized settings), involve more NGO stakeholders and more experienced official negotiators, and result in more partial outcomes than regional regimes. On the other side, the negotiations that propel regional regimes are more dynamic than their global counterparts, involving more issue redefinition, external influences, power plays, impasses, media coverage, problem-solving behaviors, and technocrat involvement. The results of regional regime negotiations also appear to be more stable: They are more likely to be considered fair, to achieve significant compliance and effectiveness, and to be characterized by flexibility. In general, global regime negotiation processes are characterized by their structural and actor factors, while regional regime negotiations are predominantly distinguished by issue, situational, and process factors.

Discussion

Six general propositions can be drawn from this analysis. The regime data suggest a flow of activity from one set of negotiations to another throughout the life cycle of a regime. During ratification negotiations, the scene is domestic, the setting formal and institutional, the actors political, the process incremental, and the outcomes driven by the desire to achieve agreements considered fair by all stakeholders. During regime formation negotiations, the number of relevant issues grows, issues tend to change and get redefined, and new actors appear. In regime governance negotiations, technical issues predominate; the focus is on doing the very business that the regime was established to accomplish through continuous negotiations that resolve technical, operational problems. Finally, adjustment negotiations renew regimes to deal with new realities and are typified by power imbalances and external effects—the influences of change—and problem-solving approaches. Overall, postagreement negotiations to build and govern regimes tend to be rather similar; regime adjustment negotiations tend to be a different species, highlighting the disparities between establishing and changing a regime through negotiation processes.

Proposition 1. Regime negotiations at the domestic level tend to be predominantly political, but regime negotiations at the international level become more technical, involve new actors, and develop a zero-sum dynamic that can destabilize effective regime operations.

Proposition 2. When external events and power imbalances begin to exert significant pressure on a regime, negotiations are required to adjust the rules and norms by which the regime operates.

◆   ◆   ◆

Variation—and progress—through the life cycle of negotiation processes tends to revolve around changes in actors, situation and structure, and strategies and process. With regard to negotiation actors, political influence in the early acceptance stages dissipates and gives way to civil society and technocratic influence during the regime formation and governance stages, which finally gives way to reduced NGO involvement over time as state actors gear up to adjust the regime for changing circumstances. So, for example, ratification negotiations tend to include primarily politically oriented negotiators with prior experience. Formation negotiations introduce more NGO actors and technical experts into the talks. Governance negotiations tend to reduce the influence of political actors, and adjustment negotiations reduce the NGO presence. Auer (1998) demonstrated the transformation over time of particular groups of scientific experts from objective technocrats to partisan national advocates when they were placed in the position of negotiating implementation details in the postagreement talks on the Baltic Sea environmental regime.

Situational factors provide the context for negotiating and often have a significant impact on both the process and the outcome (Druckman 1993a). Regime negotiations are likely to be influenced by different types of external events—for example, parliamentary debates and public demonstrations—as NGOs become more involved; witness the disruptive impact of NGO demonstrations on the World Trade Organization negotiations in Seattle in December 1999. How do these situational factors influence the negotiation life cycle? As regimes form, the issues that negotiations must deal with, their changeability, and the number of deadlines all increase. Then, as regimes begin to deal with operational governance concerns, technical problems may increase but changeability in the set of issues under consideration stabilizes. As regimes adjust to changing circumstances over time, the influence of external events increases and the number of issues that are central to regime negotiations sharply decreases to a smaller core set.

Boyer (1999) examined the evolving nature of postagreement negotiation strategies in the several conventions that emanated from the 1992 United Nations Conference on Environment and Development.

His analysis suggests that the evolving strategies and actor relationships over the five years of postagreement negotiations recommend changes to national implementation mechanisms, reframing of key issues, greater facilitation and mediation in the regime governance process, and strengthening of NGO inputs. Problem solving and formula-detail processing during the ratification stage were transformed into power imbalances and stalemates by the regime adjustment stage.

There are indications in the data that the postagreement negotiation stages hold the potential for more conflict than the preagreement negotiations. Postagreement stages tend to be more characterized by win-lose processes and greater imbalances in power resources. Comparable data were referenced to characterize the degree of conflict-cooperation in preagreement negotiations that lead to regimes. In Druckman's data (1993b), initiating talks are primarily cooperative, problem solving in approach, and open, with infrequent use of persuasive tactics. Subsequent postagreement negotiations tend to be relatively less cooperative. For example, there were much lower ratings for cooperative relations, problem solving, and infrequent use of persuasive tactics in the postagreement talks than in preagreement talks. This suggests that the unfinished business of the originating negotiations sows the seeds for future discontent in the sustained regime-based talks that follow. The cooperative efforts to establish a regime often take place in a shadow of conflicting interests that were not effectively resolved in the initiating stages; this can yield deadlock and can significantly challenge the joint political will to find mutually acceptable solutions.

Proposition 3. Variation in fundamental negotiation factors such as actors, situation and structure, and strategies and process can signal progress or retreat in regime dynamics.

The nature of negotiation outcomes changes over the regime life cycle. In terms of comprehensiveness, ratification negotiations are more likely to yield comprehensive agreements, but partial outcomes become more likely as regimes mature. Likewise, outcomes tend to be perceived as fairer early in the regime, but over the life cycle of the regime they come to be seen as less so. Ratification negotiations have a generally high acceptance rate but are slower and are less likely to result in domestic implementation of reforms in response to the international agreement. Regime formation negotiations are effective in stimulating wide participation by the international participants. As the regime matures and negotiations turn toward regime governance, compliance with the treaty is only moderate and regime administration is viewed as relatively ineffective. Finally, when regimes reach the stage of necessary adjustment, negotiations yield only moderate willingness to modify goals, targets, and means.

Proposition 4. Comprehensive and fair agreements that enjoy wide participation and acceptance in the beginning tend to break down over the course of the regime's life and need to be renewed and renegotiated.

What is it about the negotiation process that propels regimes toward different types of outcomes? According to our data, regional regimes tend to result in more comprehensive agreements that are perceived as fairer than global regime outcomes. Regional regimes also have a higher level of compliance, more effective operations, and greater willingness to adjust their ground rules over time. These outcomes appear to be stimulated when political issues predominate and regime issues are in transition and in need of redefinition. These outcomes also result from greater deadline pressure and media publicity, more external influences, more alternative solutions and problem-solving approaches, more frequent impasses, and a progression from resolving principles to negotiating details.

Global regime negotiation outcomes are typified by more partial agreements that are perceived as being less fair and having lower levels of signatory compliance, less effective regime operations, and less willingness to change existing rules and agreements over time. What process factors propel these results? Greater formality and institutional settings for the negotiations, mixed with more NGO actor involvement, negotiators with more extensive prior negotiation experience, and more participation by veterans of the originating negotiations appear to produce these outcomes.

Proposition 5. In regional regime negotiations, issue, situational, and process factors are instrumental in influencing regime outcomes.

Proposition 6. In global regime negotiations, structural and actor factors tend to affect regime outcomes the most.

Conclusions

How can postagreement negotiation shape regime formation, governance, and evolution; produce outcomes and influence regime effectiveness; and feed back improvements to support future regime negotiations? Several implications of this framework and analysis will be addressed by the cases presented in this book.

The Impact of Precedence

Postagreement negotiation can occur, by definition, only if an earlier negotiation succeeded in establishing a full or partial agreement. Thus, continuing negotiations are always conducted within the shadows of earlier negotiations, both in terms of the way process and issues are handled and in terms of the norms that determine the types of outcomes that are viewed as fair and just. The emergence of a negotiated regime suggests agreement on a set of principles and a cooperative framework upon which continued discussions can be based. But does such a structure necessarily promote or facilitate subsequent agreements within the context of the regime? Does cooperative precedent provide an obvious path for reducing conflict, thereby making postagreement negotiation primarily a cooperative and not a mixed-motive process? These are negotiations among friends established by the prior agreement, in which a degree of understanding and consensual knowledge makes for a common framing of the problem and its solution. One might suspect that under such circumstances, further negotiation should thrive, modeling itself on the preceding positive environment.

However, it is easy to hypothesize just the opposite. Postagreement negotiations can become more conflict ridden and unstable because they involve new actors and because they proceed to tackle the more difficult details that were deferred in regime formation negotiations. In fact, one could postulate that the effectiveness of the regime itself will be judged ultimately on its ability to weather this storm. The need for continued negotiations in the first place suggests that only a partial agreement was struck initially. Perhaps it was possible to deal with only the relatively easy issues in these accords, leaving the difficult or intractable ones for later. If so, deadlock may ensue unless creative approaches are found to resolve disputes.

The Impact on Regime Governance and Regime Evolution

Postagreement negotiations are nested, layered negotiations in which broad frameworks often yield detailed protocols, and detailed protocols are renewed, expanded, or canceled over time in additional accords. This evolution of the initiating regime agreement is carried out primarily through the vehicle of postagreement negotiation in the service of governing and adjusting the established regime. What, in fact, needs to evolve? Issues often must be reconceptualized and redefined as new information emerges or as actions by signatories are taken into account. The modes of cooperation within the regime, including the process by which issues and disputes are resolved, often need revamping over time to deal with greater participation, new events, or new technologies for monitoring, or to achieve greater efficiencies. In addition, with changes in national political administrations and the development of new agreements elsewhere, the signatories may find new and more efficient ways of cooperating with one another, achieving a better balance between the need for interdependence and national sovereignty.

Table 5. Postagreement Negotiation Paths within Regimes

	Maintain Status Quo	**Seek Change**
Cooperative	Stable Implementation	Stable Expansion
Conflictual	Unstable Implementation	Unstable Expansion

As postagreement negotiations move from dealing with issues of principle to details, a totally new process may emerge that shapes the governance and the evolution of the regime. What could be considered a perfect laboratory for searching for solutions through problem solving might be transformed into a bargaining environment, one sustained more by making trade-offs on details. Moreover, a situation of shared understanding emerging from the initiating negotiations might change drastically as increasing familiarity with other parties' interests and sensitivities gives way to a more tactical, self-interested style of bargaining.

Negotiation Paths

Postagreement negotiation processes can evolve along different paths. Many factors influence the nature of the postagreement process—political will, interests, and capacity, among others. Two fundamental elements affecting postagreement negotiation paths are the type of relationship between the parties and the extent to which the parties seek change in the underlying norms and principles of the initiating agreement. Table 5 presents a simple typology that identifies four basic paths.

A *stable implementation path* is likely if the parties are relatively cooperative and jointly seek to implement an already negotiated agreement. This path implies that certain norms and principles are well established and there is a political commitment and willingness to implement them. Implementation is threatened, though, if the parties are not of like mind and are still in dispute over important interest areas. In this case, an *unstable implementation path* has been engaged that may be marked by uncertainty about the issue and the definition of the problem. The parties may not be totally committed to implementation and may still retreat back to their national sovereignty arguments. Intractable issues that could not be resolved in the initiating agreement may still be present, producing a high risk of stalemate. While general norms and principles may be spelled out in the initiating agreement, they may still be tentative and subject to change. Postagreement negotiation here involves revisiting these norms and principles before the rules, procedures, and details can be worked out. Because of the lack of consensus, these negotiations can devolve into prolonged conflict with little to show in terms of implementation.

A *stable expansion path* involves the evolution of norms, principles, and rules within a cooperative context to achieve a new breakthrough in an understanding of the problem and the solution. The *unstable expansion path* suggests negotiations where the parties have evolved from the initiating agreement in different directions, producing a new conflict of interests that has yet to be resolved. While all parties seek change, the negotiations must begin to address these diverging interests within a context that was once acceptable to all parties but may not be propitious for resolving them now.

Why study postagreement negotiation processes? The objective of this study is to initiate a broad analysis of the system of negotiation that continues *after* initial regime formation negotiations conclude. The goal is both analytical and practical. Postagreement negotiation is an important process bridging the gap between national policy and international relations that is little understood. Practically, if we can reliably diagnose the problems and explain the successes of regimes in postagreement negotiation processes, we can provide useful feedback to the initiating negotiation process—identifying novel approaches and structures that can avert or alleviate difficulties that might reduce the effectiveness of the regime during the implementation period.

Thus, the ultimate goal is to instate a learning cycle in which the outcomes of the negotiation process can yield meaningful recommendations for improving future negotiations. The anticipated benefit is a more efficient negotiation process that not only identifies satisfactory principles and achieves acceptable formulas but frames them in such a way that implementation of these principles and formulas produces the results intended.

The case studies presented in the second section of this book use the analytical structures, concepts, and propositions presented in these opening chapters to organize their analyses and reach conclusions about the process of postagreement negotiation within international regimes. The experience of these regimes supports the conceptual framework presented here and yields new insights into the workings of this important phase of international negotiation.

Notes

1. Postagreement negotiation is related to Raiffa's (1985) concept of postsettlement settlements. However, while Raiffa discusses the benefits of sometimes returning to the table after an agreement has been reached to seek an improved settlement, the goal of postagreement negotiation encompasses this function plus the additional tasks of reaching mutually acceptable solutions concerning implementation, feedback, and adjustment of agreed-upon formulas over the longer term.

2. This research was conducted while the author was resident at the International Institute for Applied Systems Analysis, Laxenburg, Austria, as director of the Processes of International Negotiation (PIN) Project.

3. The twenty-six regimes are the Single European Act, Paris Convention on Third Party Liability in the Field of Nuclear Energy (1960), Lisbon Agreement on Cooperation for Combating Pollution in the Northeast Atlantic (1990), South Pacific Forum Fisheries Agency Convention (1978), Protocol on Land-Based Sources of Pollution of the Barcelona Convention, Geneva Convention on Long-Range Transboundary Air Pollution and related protocols, Helsinki Convention on the Protection of the Marine Environment of the Baltic Sea Area, International Convention for the High Seas Fisheries of the North Pacific Ocean, IAEO Convention on Assistance in Case of Nuclear Power Accidents, Convention for the Mutual Recognition of Inspections in Respect of the Manufacture of Pharmaceutical Products, United Nations Outer Space Treaty (1967), Kuwait Regional Convention and its Protocols for the Protection of the Marine Environment, International

Undertaking on Plant Genetic Resources, Convention on Biological Diversity (1992), Amended London Guidelines for Exchange of Information on Chemicals in International Trade (1989), Montreal Guidelines for the Protection of the Marine Environment against Pollution from Land-Based Sources (1985), Convention on Future Multilateral Cooperation in the Northwest Atlantic Fisheries, Washington Convention on International Trade in Endangered Species, World Heritage Convention, Mediterranean Action Plan, Convention on the Conservation of Antarctic Marine Living Resources, Convention for the Protection of the Natural Resources and Environment of the South Pacific Region and Protocol for the Prevention of Pollution of the South Pacific Region by Dumping (1986), Montreal Protocol for the Protection of the Ozone Layer, North Atlantic Salmon Conservation Organization, Basel Convention on the Transboundary Movement of Hazardous Wastes, and Kingston Protocol on Specially Protected Areas and Wildlife (1990).

4. The domestic postagreement negotiation stages of "rule making" and "enforcement and monitoring" were not included in the questionnaire because the expert panel had limited knowledge of these stages across all signatories.

References

Auer, Matthew R. 1998. "Colleagues or Combatants? Experts as Environmental Diplomats." *International Negotiation* 3 (2): 267–287.

Benedick, Richard Elliot. 1991. *Ozone Diplomacy.* Cambridge, Mass.: Harvard University Press.

Birnie, Patricia W., and Alan E. Boyle. 1992. *International Law and the Environment.* Oxford: Clarendon Press.

Boyer, Brook. 1999. "Implementing Policies of Sustainable Development: Turning Constraints into Opportunities." *International Negotiation* 4 (2): 283–293.

Druckman, Daniel. 1993a. "Situational Levers of Negotiating Flexibility." *Journal of Conflict Resolution* 37: 236–276.

―――. 1993b. "A Comparative Methodology for Analyzing Negotiations." International Institute for Applied Systems Analysis, Working Paper WP-93-34, Laxenburg, Austria, July.

Evans, Peter, Harold Jacobson, and Robert Putnam. 1993. *Double-Edged Diplomacy.* Berkeley, Calif.: University of California Press.

Haas, Peter M. 1989. "Do Regimes Matter? Epistemic Communities and Mediterranean Pollution Control." *International Organization* 43 (3): 377–403.

Haggard, Stephan, and Beth A. Simmons. 1987. "Theories of International Regimes." *International Organization* 41 (3): 491–517.

International Institute for Applied Systems Analysis (IIASA). 1992. "Compliance Research Projects List." IIASA, Laxenburg, Austria, November.

Kremenyuk, Victor, ed. 2002. *International Negotiation: Analysis, Approaches, Issues.* 2nd ed. San Francisco: Jossey-Bass.

Levy, Marc. 1993. "European Acid Rain: The Power of Tote-Board Diplomacy." In *Institutions for the Earth*, ed. Peter M. Haas, Robert Keohane, and Marc Levy. Cambridge, Mass.: MIT Press.

Levy, Marc, Gail Osherenko, and Oran Young. 1991. "The Effectiveness of International Regimes: A Design for Large-Scale Collaborative Research —Research Design Version 1.1." Dartmouth College, December.

Levy, Marc, Oran Young, and Michael Zürn. 1995. "The Study of International Regimes." *European Journal of International Relations* 1: 267-330.

Lodge, Juliet, and Frank Pfetsch. 1998. Guest Editors, "Negotiating the European Union." *International Negotiation* 3 (3).

Parson, Edward A. 1993. "Protecting the Ozone Layer." In *Institutions for the Earth*, ed. Peter M. Haas, Robert Keohane, and Marc Levy. Cambridge, Mass.: MIT Press.

Porter, Gareth, and Janet Brown. 1991. *Global Environmental Politics.* Boulder, Colo.: Westview.

Putnam, Robert D. 1988. "Diplomacy and Domestic Politics: The Logic of Two-Level Games." *International Organization* 42 (3): 427–460.

Raiffa, Howard. 1985. "Post-Settlement Settlements." *Negotiation Journal* 1: 9–12.

Sand, Peter. 1991. "International Cooperation: The Environmental Experience." In *Preserving the Global Environment*, ed. J. Mathews. New York: W. W. Norton.

Shaw, Roderick W. 1993. "Acid Rain Negotiations in North America and Europe: A Study in Contrast." In *International Environmental Negotiation*, ed. Gunnar Sjöstedt. Newbury Park, Calif.: Sage.

Sjöstedt, Gunnar, Bertram I. Spector, and I. William Zartman. 1994. "The Dynamics of Regime Building Negotiations." In *Negotiating International Regimes: Lessons Learned from the United Nations Conference on Environment and Development*, ed. Gunnar Sjöstedt, Bertram I. Spector, and I. William Zartman. London: Graham and Trotman.

Spector, Bertram I., and Anna R. Korula. 1993. "Problems of Ratifying International Environmental Agreements: Overcoming Initial Obstacles in the Postagreement Negotiation Process." *Global Environmental Change* 17 (4): 369–381.

Spector, Bertram I., Gunnar Sjöstedt, and I. William Zartman, ed. 1994. *Negotiating International Regimes: Lessons Learned from the United Nations Conference on Environment and Development (UNCED)*. London: Graham and Trotman.

Susskind, Lawrence. 1994. *Environmental Diplomacy*. New York: Oxford University Press.

Széll, Patrick. 1993. "Negotiations on the Ozone Layer." In *International Environmental Negotiation*, ed. Gunnar Sjöstedt. Newbury Park, Calif.: Sage.

Thacher, Peter. 1991. "Background to Institutional Options for Management of the Global Environment and Commons." In *Global Security and Risk Management*. Geneva: World Federation of United Nations Associations.

Young, Oran. 1989. *International Cooperation: Building Regimes for Natural Resources and the Environment*. Ithaca, N.Y.: Cornell University Press.

3

Norms and Principles as Support to Postnegotiation and Rule Implementation

Gunnar Sjöstedt

THE COMMON UNDERSTANDING of international regimes may be summarized as follows: A group of governments institutes an international treaty containing formal rules prescribing how states are to perform in a given context. In the area of environmental politics the rules thus established typically require reduction of the emissions of specified pollutants, say CFCs or CO_2, before a certain target date. The effectiveness of a regime depends on the extent to which it solves the problem—for instance, reducing hazardous emissions according to the agreed-upon timetable. Research on international regimes has increasingly focused on state compliance with rules and assessments of effectiveness (Haas, Keohane, and Levy 1993). Regimes are primarily analyzed as a given structure of institutions. Rules and compliance with them continue to be emphasized, whereas other main elements of the conventional conceptualization of a regime—norms, principles, and procedures—receive little attention (Krasner 1983; Levy, Young, and Zürn 1995).

This perspective directs the attention of researchers away from the political processes by which international regimes are created and developed. Leading scholars in the field claim that we have sufficient basic knowledge of the history of international regimes. What we need to know more about is if, why, and how regimes actually give direction to state performance. They argue that the literature on regime formation has occupied center stage long enough (Levy, Young, and Zürn 1995).

However, regime operation cannot be separated from regime formation. Regimes cannot at any time safely be assumed to be "mature," having reached their final form. In some sectors this state of things is quite clear. For example, international regime building is a comparatively new phenomenon in the environmental area; most of the approximately 150 multilateral treaties on transboundary environmental issues were created after the Stockholm 1972 United Nations Conference on the Human Environment (UNCHE). Although these conventions have produced noteworthy results, we can expect continued regime building regarding most environmental topics, ranging from global problems such as climate change and depletion of the ozone layer to local ones such as management of hazardous wastes and the preservation of freshwater resources. The Uruguay Round of multilateral trade negotiations under the auspices of GATT/WTO (the General Agreement on Tariffs and Trade/World Trade Organization) attests to the fact that older and well-institutionalized international regimes may still undergo considerable change.

Recurrent revision of a regime thus represents something more complex and far-reaching than a marginal modification of an existing system of rules. For example, the periodic rounds of GATT/WTO multilateral trade talks have helped retain the effectiveness of existing trade rules (Winham 1986, 2002). This proposition has been named the bicycle theory, the essence of which is that stability presupposes dynamic movement. The cyclist cannot keep the bike standing unless he or she keeps it moving. The bicycle theory suggests that if the GATT/WTO treaty had not been recurrently renegotiated, its effectiveness as a regime would have been much less than it actually has been.

A complete assessment of regime effectiveness will have to take regime dynamics into account. The main aspect of regime dynamics highlighted in this project is postagreement negotiation. This concept covers all sorts of consultation and negotiation of a recursive and intersessional character. Recursive negotiations often take the form of regular conferences of parties (COPs) or other more sporadic course corrections. Intersessional activities on the domestic and interstate level have a direct impact on how the regime under negotiation will develop. However, the character of the evolving regime also affects intersessional activities as well as the regime-building process more generally. In order to identify and assess this regime-to-process impact, it is useful to distinguish between the four basic types of regime element: rules, norms, principles, and procedures.

Background

The increasing emphasis on rule compliance has led to the misconception of regimes as fairly stable systems of international rules. A consequence is that regimes are often treated as if they were the result of a unisequential process of international bargaining, in which a set of rules is established in a treaty (Haggard and Simmons 1987). Mainstream analysts do not explicitly assert that regimes are typically created by a single bargaining session. However, this is effectively their position since they do not take into account the fact that processes of regime formation have usually been pluri-sequential; the regime has been built in a series of negotiation rounds, each of which has often resulted in a separate agreement. This pattern of regime-building process has been particularly frequent with regard to complex environmental issues. International cooperative efforts to cope with the depletion of the ozone layer in the stratosphere or with the need for increased security cooperation in Europe are good illustrations, as discussed in the subsequent chapters by Pamela Chasek and Janie Leatherman.

The two cases depict a regime-building process characterized by development through a series of consecutive negotiations. However, although each such stage of the regime-building process can be portrayed as a distinct event, separate negotiations are positively interlinked. For example, the diplomatic interaction that generated the Montreal Protocol was strongly conditioned by the Vienna Convention as well as by the negotiations producing it, just as the conversion of the Conference(s) on Security and Cooperation in Europe into the Organization on Security and Cooperation in Europe was a sequence necessary for the continued life of the regime under new circumstances. In fact, the continuity within each pair of processes was so profound and so complex that their separateness may be contested.

Continuity between two consecutive negotiation sessions related to virtually the same agenda manifests itself in various ways. Intersessional activities represent one type of bridge between them. Two significant categories of intersessional activities are pre- and postnegotiation. Prenegotiation activities take the form of informal consultation among a group of parties, the purpose of which is to pave the way for a formal negotiation session. The function of prenegotiation, for instance, may be to attain a consensus between key governments that negotiations are to be conducted on a particular set of issues or to indicate objectives and an agenda for the expected future talks.

Postnegotiation activities involve continued talks between the parties concerned after an agreement has been achieved. As indicated by the ozone and security cases, in pluri-sequential processes of regime formation the post- and prenegotiations occurring between two rounds of multilateral talks may be intertwined. For instance, the failure of negotiating parties to agree on binding commitments to reduce the emission of CFCs in 1985 forced them to start postnegotiations after the Vienna Convention had been signed in order to avoid complete failure to cope with the ozone problem. At the same time these consultations functioned as prenegotiations in relation to the future conference forming the Montreal Protocol.

However, direct couplings between two rounds of negotiation on essentially the same issues are not the only manifestations of continuity. In the case of the ozone negotiations, the outcome of the Vienna process strongly conditioned and directly guided the talks on the ozone problem ending with the Montreal Protocol. This "conditioning effect" was very complex in the sense that the actors in the Montreal process were influenced by the Vienna Convention and the related negotiations in a variety of ways. For example, one form of continuity from Vienna to Montreal was the widely perceived need to transform the objectives of the Framework Agreement into operational commitments in the Montreal Protocol regarding CFC emissions. Another type of intersessional continuity consisted of the consolidation of an increasingly certain and widely shared underpinning of scientific knowledge about the problem of ozone depletion, its consequences, and its ramifications. The anatomy and mechanisms of international regimes need clarification if we are to understand the variety of ways in which the evolving regime can exert its influence on the regime-building process.

The Anatomy of International Regimes

According to the standard definition, a regime is the "implicit principles, norms, rules and decision-making procedures around which actors' expectations converge in a particular issue area" (Krasner 1983, 1). Rules are usually considered to represent the core element of a regime since they are specific prescriptions for action (Krasner 1983;

Rittberger 1993; Mitchell 1994; Susskind 1994). Rules thus represent the crucial link between regime guidance and actor performance. Procedures have to do with the day-to-day management of the regime— for example, the maintenance of an organization or a monitoring system. Procedures may also give direction to how negotiations and other forms of international cooperation are to be conducted from a practical point of view. Norms and principles represent background factors in which rules are rooted. Norms are values that are shared by the actors pertaining to the regime concerned (Ullman-Margalit 1977). Principles should be thought of as quasi-institutionalized consensual knowledge on the issues covered by the regime. They particularly pertain to causal relationships between key variables (Krasner 1983; Haas 1990; Haas, P. 1992).

An important quality of an international regime is the interrelationship among its four elements—rules, norms, principles, and procedures. This topic has not attracted much scholarly attention, since the most common approach has been to treat regimes as an entity, especially with regard to regime operation. When analysts have discussed regime effectiveness they have had one particular element of the regime in mind: rules (Young 1992; Underdal 1992; Mitchell 1994). In the standard analysis, regime operation has therefore been considered to be approximately the same thing as state compliance with international rules. A regime has been considered to operate well when compliance with its rules has been high, and its effectiveness has been considered low when governments have only moderately lived up to its formal prescriptions. The other elements of the regime—norms, principles, and procedures—are rarely mentioned.

A focus on rules is clearly appropriate to the analysis of how regimes operate. The rules stand out as the teeth of the regime, representing the formal commitments of the signatories to undertake clearly specified policy measures, such as reducing the emissions of hazardous pollutants to a certain degree according to a certain timetable. Governments have usually signed an environmental agreement because they have found this to be in their own best interest. Furthermore, a government will risk considerable political cost domestically as well as abroad if it breaks the rules of an international treaty. It may also be the subject of sanctions by other countries and international organizations in line with the stipulations of the treaty whose rules have not been honored (Chayes and Chayes 1993; Jacobson and Brown Weiss 1995). Governments signatory to a regime have many reasons for being particularly concerned with the element of an international regime that is represented by a set of rules.

There are several possible reasons why the other elements of regimes might be excluded from analysis. It might be argued that, in comparison to rules, norms, principles, and procedures are so insignificant that ignoring them sacrifices little explanatory power (Levy, Young, and Zürn 1995). Another view might be that as regimes develop over time there is a nearly perfect co-variation between different regime elements, which hence always retain the same relationship to one another regardless of the regime. Under these circumstances the analyst would gain very little by including all regime elements in the assessment.

However, although either of these hypotheses may possibly be valid in individual cases, they cannot be regarded as general characterizations of international regimes. Consider, for instance, the case of the GATT/WTO regime governing international trade, considered by many to be one of the strongest international regimes (Cox and Jacobson 1973). This regime is widely considered to have teeth, the most visible expression thereof being the set of detailed rules prescribing which trade policy measures are permitted and which are not. However, another pertinent quality of GATT/WTO is that the rules are strongly anchored in other elements of the regime. Hence the GATT/WTO regime includes carefully specified procedures for the guarding of the GATT treaty and the interpretation of rules, notably the celebrated panel system for dispute settlement (Jackson 1969). The GATT/WTO rules are based on a solid platform of norms and principles related to the conduct of "free trade," which have been summarized in the preamble of the treaty. The principles are based on mainstream academic thinking about international commercial policy and neoclassic free trade theory. They thus explain the rationale for adhering to the GATT/WTO rules: that such a policy promotes world economic growth, and, at least in the long term, maximizes welfare in the individual nations. The significance of the principles lies in the fact that they are part of a hegemonic doctrine, directly derived from neoclassic free trade theory, shared by professional trade policymakers around the globe. The preamble of the GATT/WTO treaty also includes guiding norms, prescribing the need for the development of global welfare within the context of economic and trade policies sustaining an open world economy (Dam 1970). Hence, in the case of GATT/ WTO the operation of the regime through state compliance with the rules cannot be fully understood unless the interplay of the rules with other regime elements—notably norms and principles—is fully taken into consideration.

Neither can it be safely assumed that a changing regime is characterized by simultaneous changes in rules, norms, principles, and procedures. It is not difficult to find examples of regimes where regime elements have developed unevenly—for instance, in such a way that the growth of the rules has been more protracted than that of other regime elements. The case of the depletion of the ozone layer offers one illustration. The Vienna Convention of 1985 contained practically no formal rules related to the emission of CFCs and other hazardous pollutants (Lang 1986). Still, there certainly existed an embryonic ozone regime before formal rules for CFC emissions were first established in the Montreal Protocol. In its earliest stage, therefore, the ozone regime consisted of regime elements other than rules. One important component was an emerging consensual knowledge shared by the actors taking part in the regime-building process concerning the causal relationships between the emissions of certain identified pollutants and the depletion of the ozone layer in the stratosphere. Evolving regime principles often involve the formation of issue-related consensual knowledge within the context of a regime-building process. Simultaneously, general guidelines were developed for continued negotiations on the ozone problem. These activities should be described as norm building rather than rule making. Therefore, another reason for recurring post-agreement negotiations is to work out changes from norms to principles to procedures to rules—and to backtrack when necessary.

Hence, one tentative conclusion is that in the ozone case the development of norms and principles in the initial stage of the process was a prerequisite for adoption of rules with teeth in consecutive process stages unfolding in Helsinki, Montreal, London, and Copenhagen. Accordingly, the transition from the first to the second main phase of the regime-building process was significantly conditioned by norm building and the formation of consensual knowledge paving the way for the ensuing establishment of formal rules.

There is ample evidence that the various elements of an international regime do not necessarily unfold hand in hand at the same pace. Other examples suggest that a given process stage, such as a certain conference or negotiation round, may be dominated by the development of one particular regime element, say norms or principles. In this regard a comparison is useful between the global negotiations on global warming in the Inter-governmental Panel on Climate Change (IPCC) and the preparations for the United Nations Conference on Environment and Development (UNCED) in Rio de Janeiro in 1992.

The negotiations on climate change dealt with an extremely complex and difficult agenda. The underlying hypothesis is that emissions from human activities—production, heating, transport, and consumption— in turn generate greenhouse gases that will increase the average surface temperature of the globe. The result will supposedly be large-scale societal costs or even ecological catastrophes. A main problem of the negotiations on climate change was from the beginning—and remains —the lack of reliable scientific knowledge about the multitude of processes and relationships contributing to the warming of the atmosphere or the effects of such a development. Study groups including leading scientists from around the world have been organized to make an inventory of the state of knowledge regarding the various specific problem areas pertaining to the issue of climate change. The establishment of such consensual knowledge has been a protracted, complex, and cumbersome process that has dominated the negotiations so far. Accordingly, in the regime-building effort related to climate change, the development of principles preceded the formation of other elements, rules included (Zaelke and Cameron 1990). For at least a decade negotiations focused essentially on the establishment of a viable consensual body of knowledge.

In the end the UNCED process generated a fruitful outcome, including two framework agreements on climate change and biodiversity and Agenda 21, a vast strategic plan for future environmental cooperation in the UN system. Nevertheless, UNCED produced few binding rules. For this reason critics have argued that UNCED was essentially a failure (Susskind 1994). However, a fair assessment of UNCED would have to take into account regime elements other than rules. Within the context of the UNCED process extensive stocktaking took place, aggregating great amounts of information on the activities of the various UN agencies related to sustainable development. This work can be described as the formation of guiding principles, based on an emerging consensual knowledge, for future regime building in the UN system for the purpose of promoting sustainable development. In UNCED knowledge formation was closely associated with norm building, not least in relation to the concept of sustainable development itself (Spector, Sjöstedt, and Zartman 1994).

Mechanisms of Regime Operation

Following the conventional analysis that regime operation is equal to state compliance with international rules, the proposition that rules represent the only significant interface between a regime and the performance of states is represented by track 1 in figure 1. However, the analytical model represented in figure 1 also indicates three other possible causal relationships between the elements of a regime and state behavior. Thus, figure 1 maintains that norms as well as regime principles may sometimes have an essentially autonomous, intentional effect on actor behavior. Track 3 represents an impact caused by the norm component of the regime. Track 4 represents the option that institutionalized consensual knowledge and regime principles condition and steer state behavior independently of the impact of other regime elements. Together, tracks 1, 3, and 4 indicate the complexity of regime dynamics—how the effectiveness of the regime may evolve over time,

Figure 1. Regime Dynamics: Some Basic Hypotheses

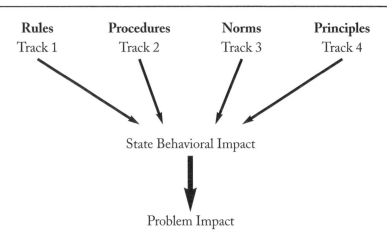

Including developments that are not necessarily consistent with one another. Tracks 1, 3, and 4 suggest that such changes may be of at least three different kinds, relating to rules, norms, and principles. Track 2, finally, represents a scenario in which variation in state behavior within a regime can be explained primarily as part of the process of regime adjustment itself.

Comprehensive assessments of the way regimes operate and of their effectiveness must take all four tracks indicated in figure 1 into full consideration—something that has been rarely done in the academic debate on how international regimes influence state behavior. The analysis below includes a number of suggestions in this regard.

Track 1: The Impact of Rules on Signatory States

The impact of track 1 on state behavior corresponds essentially to the conventional understanding of regime operation. According to this perspective, a regime begins to operate when states start to actively respect its rules (Underdal 1992; Young 1992). Rules themselves have usually been regarded as a fairly static structure of formal prescriptions for state performance on the issue covered by the regime. A principal proposition put forward in the present study is that regime rules are seldom, if ever, perfectly clear and uncontested by all parties concerned. This is particularly true for rules that have not yet become "mature" but are likely to be developed further in future rounds of regime-building negotiations. In such cases, state compliance with international rules is likely to be associated with differing kinds of postsessional activities for the purpose of interpreting them. Here belong various types of state interaction, ranging from formal postagreement negotiations to clarify rules to situations in which rule interpretation is handled by overt confrontation between leading powers. The trade wars between the United States and the European Union are one well-known example of the latter type, which in a complex way have been related to the GATT rounds (Coneybeare 1987; Sjöstedt 2000). For example, in the Tokyo Round of the GATT 1973–79, the specter of trade war and unilateralism on the part of the United States helped persuade the governments of key countries that new multilateral trade negotiations were necessary.

Track 2: The Support of Norms, Principles, and Procedures to Rule Implementation/Postagreement Negotiations

Realist and neorealist authors claim that regimes essentially express the current interests of a winning coalition of states (Strange 1983). The real impact of the regime depends on the political power of its supporting coalition rather than on the strength of supporting norms and principles. The effectiveness of a regime is dependent on the ability and willingness of the supporting coalition to serve as a guardian of the regime and sanction free riders and governments breaking the rules. There are clear indications that norm creation and the construction of principles through the establishment of consensual knowledge may have a strong impact on how the regime operates in the short as well as the long run.

In the short-term perspective, norms and principles may, separately or jointly, have a significant supportive impact on the postsessional activities related to rule interpretation or modification. Norms included in a regime, referring, for instance, to justice and fairness, may underpin and legitimize its rules and hence significantly facilitate their implementation. A well-known example is the GATT/WTO regime. The rules have their roots in norms and principles embedded in the doctrine of free trade, which is internalized in key decision makers in most countries. If rules are consistent with widely shared norms, the political costs of noncompliance will be much higher than if the rules of a regime partly contradict an underlying normative structure.

In contrast, norms contradicting the rules of a regime may be employed to support a position of nonacceptance or noncompliance. This is by no means a theoretical case. Particularly in the UN system it has not been unusual that evolving regimes have been crippled by an inconsistent and contradictory normative structure (Rothstein 1979). For instance, governments in many developing countries have had reservations about certain environmental treaties because they share the normative conception that industrialized countries have the greatest responsibility for global environmental problems such as ozone depletion or climate warming and should therefore pay the major part of the necessary abatement costs. The logic of this view is that the alarming accumulations of pollutants in the atmosphere and the stratosphere have been primarily caused by rapid industrialization in Europe and North America during the last two hundred years. Environmental degradation has been the price industrialized countries have paid to reach the high level of economic development that distinguishes them from developing countries. Thus, in line with the widely acknowledged norm that "the polluter pays," industrialized countries should bear the larger part of the costs required to master problems such as ozone depletion and climate warming (Agarwal and Narain 1991). In contrast, developing countries have the right to continue to give economic considerations priority over ecological ones. The strength of this argument has been further reinforced by being combined with norms representing an established interpretation of fairness or justice in purely economic terms—the right of developing countries to receive special and preferential treatment on issues of economic development.[1] This view has been aired in many multilateral negotiations on environmental issues, not least at the 1992 United Nations Conference on the Environment and Development (Spector, Sjöstedt, and Zartman 1994; Susskind 1994). Thus, normative support may push an implementation process forward, but contradictions between the norms and rules included in the same regime may produce counterforces hindering rule implementation.

Normative support of rules may also strengthen actor expectations that other actors will honor the rules of the regime. Convergence of expectations can be expected to improve, or sustain, an atmosphere of cooperation in a "process community" engaged in a regime-building enterprise. For example, the fundamental norms and principles of trade underpinning the international trade regime have seemingly helped to sustain the confidence of individual governments that most of the time other states will resist the temptation to gain short-term domestic political benefits by means of free-riding. This evaluation of the situation makes it easier for a government to disarm the argument for protecting certain industries or regions put forward by sectoral interest groups against the risk that other countries will cheat or bend the rules.

Norms and principles also play an important part in supporting or facilitating pre- and postnegotiations or other types of intersessional activities. A basic scenario can be useful to clarify these functions of the regime. In this scenario, negotiations on an environmental agreement have just been concluded. The outcome is generally regarded as disappointing; binding commitments to reduce the hazardous pollutant covered by the regime-building process do not go very far. Many delegations share the view that continued discussions are necessary in the near future in order to find a formula to cut targeted emissions more decisively. This scenario corresponds fairly well to the situation in the negotiations on, for example, ozone depletion or acid rain in the earlier stages of the regime-building process related to these problems. The current state of the negotiations on climate change is rather similar. It may be argued that the scenario reflects a recurrent—indeed, typical—stage of the regime-building process concerning complex environmental questions.

A critical feature of this scenario is that many of the parties involved have a common interest in developing a regime to achieve a viable collective solution (for example, reduced emissions of hazardous substances) to the environmental problem confronting them (for example, ozone depletion). But at the same time there are differences of interest between leading nations or coalitions of states with regard to how abatement costs are to be distributed. In this situation, key bargaining issues have been how much, and how fast, individual states will have to reduce the critical emissions and how the substitution of new, "green" technology for old, polluting production facilities is to be financed. In many countries, governments are constrained by sectoral interests claiming that demands for cleaner technology will jeopardize the competitiveness of key industries—for example, the opposition of industries dependent on cheap energy to the introduction of a CO_2 tax. The existence of an embryonic regime may be of critical importance in enabling the negotiating parties to break such a deadlock. Established procedures such as scheduled recurrent meetings to review the results of the recent round of negotiation offer an important forum for postnegotiations and continuing regime-building activities. With such meetings scheduled, there is no need to take new diplomatic initiatives or to develop a novel formula for continued negotiation. This means that the demand for visible political leadership can be kept very low if this is required. Otherwise the initiation of negotiations typically presupposes an initiative by a great power or a grand coalition of states. The existence of procedures and calendars for routine consultations may also serve as a face-saving device for countries with a strong domestic opposition to upgraded commitments in the regime concerned. The governments of such countries need not take a position on whether the regime should be extended but instead can simply signal their intention to participate in routine consultations.

Principles also have a particularly important role to play. Our initial overview of actual cases of environmental regime building indicates the importance of knowledge and knowledge formation in such processes. It is also clear that the functions and roles of knowledge are of different kinds. For example, in the case of acid rain in Europe, the successful regime-building process was triggered by sudden extensive media exposure of the latest scientific evidence that long-range transboundary air pollution produces acid rain (Hordijk, Shaw, and Alcamo 1990). Publication of this information alarmed politicians and the public, pushing the hitherto neglected issue of acid rain onto the political agenda. The cases of ozone depletion and acid rain are good examples of regime-building processes in which the collective systematic gathering of knowledge and information clearly represented extensive and ostensibly important phases.

Such consensual knowledge is an aggregate of cognitions that reflect what relevant actors know about the problem(s) at issue, rather than their attitudes toward them. Knowledge is considered to be consensual when it reflects what the quasi-totality of the actors involved in negotiations acknowledge as valid. (Sjöstedt 1994, 66). Basically, consensual knowledge represents a frame of reference offering concepts and interrelationships between concepts, facilitating effective interparty communication. In some cases, consensual knowledge does not represent much more than a professional jargon.

However, in processes with complex issues that are comparatively unfamiliar to the parties involved, or at least most of them, it has often been necessary to establish a fairly elaborate language of negotiation. Consensual knowledge may also serve as a code of interpretation of critical causal relationships pertaining to the substance of the issues, a kind of analytical model. As indicated by the RAINS computer model used in the negotiations on acid rain, some elements of consensual knowledge may become quite elaborate and formalized. Consensual knowledge may also be framed in such a way that it implies, or even explicitly recommends, a certain line of action. Hence, a body of consensual knowledge identifying a problem of climate warming resulting from the emission of CO_2 and other greenhouse gases clearly indicates that the solution to this problem lies in the elimination of these hazardous discharges (Grubb 1989).

These functions of consensual knowledge may substantially facilitate intersessional negotiations linking two rounds of environmental regime building. When the pool of issue-related knowledge concerning, say, the depletion of the ozone layer was built up, this development meant something different from merely "participant education" in a general sense. The effective development of consensual knowledge—for example, in numerous multilateral environmental negotiations—has often been an important step toward agreement on the operational element of the regime—the rules—in spite of the fact that parties have not yet started bargaining over commitments.

However, an emerging comprehensive consensual knowledge of leading environmental issues such as ozone depletion, biodiversity, or acid rain has not only given general direction to the negotiations by specifying the kind of policy measures necessary to cope with the problem at hand—for example, reduced industrial emissions of certain substances. In several cases of environmental regime building, the refining of consensual knowledge has also included estimates of the magnitude of the policy measures required—for example, how much the emission of various specified pollutants must be limited.

Preliminary talks in intersessional discussions about what in a scientific sense has to be done to cope with a certain environmental problem have often been combined with discussions of what should be done in a more normative sense. The multiparty discussions within the UN system have, for example, generated a number of basic norms, which seemingly provide guidance for state behavior in environmental regime-building processes. One is the notion of sustainable development, while another is "the polluter pays" principle, formally sanctioned at UNCED in Rio de Janeiro in June 1992.

Tracks 3 and 4: Regime Operation Bypassing the Rules

The most certain indication of the existence of an international regime is the existence of a set of formal rules that have an observable impact on state performance. The main function of norms and principles incorporated in international regimes is undoubtedly to underpin the rules and give them legitimacy and clarity. Norms and principles may, however, also have a direct impact on how national governments, businesses, and other actors behave. There are at least three different ways in which norms and principles may guide actor performance directly, at least to some extent: opinion building, education, and doctrine internalization.

The existence of a regime does not affect public opinion automatically. However, the existence of norms and principles embedded in an international regime may be referred to in domestic political campaigns. The institutionalization of the regime's norms or principles may lead to what may be called an awareness effect. UNCED and the World Conference on Sustainable Development (WCSD) ten years later are examples. Both were events of global dimensions. A hundred heads of state or government took part in the Rio de Janeiro and Johannesburg conferences in June 1992 and August 2002. Hundreds of nongovernmental organizations (NGOs) had in some way taken part in the preparatory work. Three thousand accredited representatives of NGOs were present in Rio when UNCED concluded; eight thousand NGO representatives were accredited to the WCSD. The awareness effect seemingly encouraged NGOs in various countries to promote the ideas of sustainable development. In this work, NGOs and political parties could refer to norms and principles that had been developed in the UNCED process.

Furthermore, UNCED and WCSD were extensively covered by the mass media; it has been estimated that nine thousand members of the press were present in Rio de Janeiro and four thousand at Johannesburg. These circumstances have led some analysts to conclude that one of the main achievements of UNCED was to increase the awareness of the general public throughout the world of the significance of global environmental problems, and particularly the complex connections between environment and development.

Education refers to the behavior of whole populations or broad societal groups—for example, when a group of people such as farmers or owners of cars changes its behavior in line with the objectives of an international regime in ways that cannot be explained as simply compliance with rules. The actors involved learn that some of their behavior leads to hazardous consequences, say, for the environment. One example would be marginal changes in lifestyle in order to reduce the emission of greenhouse gases by reducing the use of motor vehicles or making windows and doors draft-proof. Another example is farmers learning from regime norms how best to maintain forests and wetlands to preserve biological diversity. This proposition means not that all the information that the individual farmer needs to protect biodiversity comes from an international regime but that consensual knowledge from an evolving regime is directly linked to a larger body of scientific knowledge concerning a particular issue. The regime principles help identify this body of knowledge and highlight its significance.

Doctrine internalization is similar to education but connects the regime with key decision makers, not with the public. The neoclassical theory of free trade embedded in the GATT/WTO regime represents an illuminating case of doctrine internalization. The regime principles that guide the conduct of trade policy are a summary description of an authoritative academic theory, which may easily be formulated as a doctrine guiding economic policy. This doctrine is shared and internalized by key decision makers in governments and other institutions that formulate trade policies. In this sense, the network of trade policymakers resembles what Peter Haas (1992) and others have referred to as epistemic communities. There are indications that doctrine internalization in this sense is now occurring in relation to currently evolving regimes pertaining to complex environmental issues.

Conclusion

An article written by leading regime analysts argues that one of the flaws of the standard conception of an international regime is that its components are indistinguishable. The authors also accept the assumption of conventional analysis that rules represent the critical element. Their basic definition of international regimes retains the difference between rules and other regime elements, which they describe as "principles, norms . . . procedures and programs that govern the interactions of actors in specific issue areas" (Levy, Young, and Zürn 1995). The main motive for keeping these categories seems to be their utility for classifying international regimes into analytical categories. This analysis recalls the difficulties of distinguishing unambiguously between regime elements. For example, rules are supposed to differ from norms in that they are more formal, but the threshold for sufficient formalization remains to be determined. Consensual knowledge about certain critical causal relationships—for example, emissions and ozone depletion—seems to attain a normative dimension: a prescription to cope with a particular environmental problem and also how.

However, the present analysis strongly suggests that the distinction between principal regime elements should be preserved. There are indications that the interplay between norms and principles—partly institutionalized consensual knowledge—may be of crucial importance for understanding how regime-building processes function in their earlier stages, particularly with regard to intersessional consultations and negotiations. Another area that needs further analysis is the process by which norms and principles underpin or strengthen rules when a regime has become operational in the sense that states have started to follow its prescriptions. Finally, norms and principles may have a considerable autonomous impact on actor behavior in the issue area covered by the particular regime.

Note

1. Recall that the norm of special and preferential treatment for developing countries has been formally acknowledged in the organizations of the United Nations and related organizations such as GATT/WTO.

References

Agarwal, A., and S. Narain. 1991. *Global Warming in an Unequal World: A Case of Environmental Colonialism*. New Delhi: Centre for Science and Environment.

Benedick, R. 1990. "Lessons from the Ozone Hole." *EPA Journal* 16 (2).

———. 1991. *Ozone Diplomacy: New Directions in Safeguarding the Planet*. Cambridge, Mass.: Harvard University Press.

Buxton, V. 1988. "The Montreal Protocol." *European Environment Review* 2 (July).

Coneybeare, John A. C. 1987. *Trade Wars: The Theory and Practice of International Commercial Rivalry*. New York: Columbia University Press.

Chayes, A., and A. Chayes. 1993. "On Compliance." *International Organization* 47.

Cox, R., and H. Jacobson, eds. 1973. *The Anatomy of Influence: Decision-Making in International Organization.* New Haven, Conn.: Yale University Press.

Dam, K. 1970. *The GATT: Law and International Economic Organization.* Chicago: University of Chicago Press.

Finnemore, M., and K. Sikkink. 1998. "International Norms Dynamics and Political Change." *International Organization* 52 (4): 887–917.

Grubb, M. 1989. *The Greenhouse Effect: Negotiating Targets.* London: Royal Institute of International Affairs.

Haas, E. 1990. *When Knowledge Is Power: Three Models of Change in International Organizations.* Berkeley, Calif.: University of California Press.

Haas, P., ed. 1992. "Knowledge, Power, and International Policy Coordination." Special issue of *International Organization* 46 (1).

Haas, P., R. Keohane, and M. Levy, eds. 1993. *Institutions for the Earth: Sources of Effective Environmental Protection.* Cambridge, Mass.: MIT Press.

Haggard, S., and B. Simmons. 1987. "Theories of International Regimes." *International Organization* 41 (3).

Hasenclever, A., P. Mayer, and V. Rittberger. 1997. *Theories of International Regimes.* Cambridge: Cambridge University Press.

Hordijk, L., R. Shaw, and J. Alcamo, eds. 1990. *The RAINS Model of Acidification: Science and Strategies in Europe.* Dordrecht: Kluwer.

Jackson, J. 1969. *World Trade and the Law of GATT.* Indianapolis, Ind.: Bobbs-Merrill.

Jacobson, H., and E. Brown Weiss. 1995. "Strengthening Compliance with International Environmental Accords: Preliminary Observations from a Collaborative Project." *Global Governance* 1 (2).

Katzenstein, P., ed. 1996. *The Culture of National Security: Norms and Identity in World Politics.* Ithaca, N.Y.: Cornell University Press.

Krasner, S. 1983. *International Regimes.* Ithaca, N.Y.: Cornell University Press.

Lang, W. 1986. "Luft und Ozon Schutsobjekte des Volkerrechts." *Zeitschrift für Ausländishes Öffentliches Recht und Völkerrecht* 46 (2).

Levy, M., O. Young, and M. Zürn. 1995. "The Study of International Regimes." *European Journal of International Relations* 1 (3).

Mitchell, R. 1994. *Intentional Oil Pollution at Sea: Environmental Policy and Treaty Compliance.* Cambridge, Mass.: MIT Press.

Moravcsik, A. 2000. "The Origins of Human Rights Regimes." *International Organization* 54 (2): 217–252.

Rittberger, V., ed. 1993. *Regime Theory and International Relations.* Oxford: Clarendon Press.

Rothstein, R. 1979. *Global Bargaining: UNCTAD and the Quest for a New International Economic Order.* Princeton, N.J.: Princeton University Press.

Rummel-Bulska, I. 1986. "Recent Developments Relating to the Vienna Convention for the Protection of the Ozone Layer." *Yearbook of the Association of Attenders and Alumni of the Hague Academy of International Law,* vols. 54–56.

Sand, P. 1985. "Protecting the Ozone Layer: The Vienna Convention Is Adopted." *Environment* 27 (5).

Sjöstedt, G. 2000. "Asymmetry in Multilateral Negotiation between North and South at UNCED." In *Power and Negotiation,* ed. I. William Zartman and Jeffrey Z. Rubin. Ann Arbor: University of Michigan Press.

Sjöstedt, G., ed. 1994. *International Environmental Negotiation.* Newbury Park, Calif.: Sage.

Spector, B., G. Sjöstedt, and I. W. Zartman, eds. 1994. *Negotiating International Regimes: Lessons Learned from the United Nations Conference on Environment and Development (UNCED).* Boston: Martinus Nijhoff.

Strange, S. 1983. "Cave! Hic Dragones: A Critique of Regime Analysis." In *International Regimes,* ed. D. Krasner. Ithaca, N.Y.: Cornell University Press.

Susskind, L. 1994. *Environmental Diplomacy: Negotiating More Effective Global Agreements.* New York: Oxford University Press.

Szell, P. 1985. "The Vienna Convention for the Protection of the Ozone Layer." *International Digest of Health Legislation* 36 (3).

———. 1993. "Negotiations on the Ozone Layer." In *International Environmental Negotiation,* ed. G. Sjöstedt. Beverly Hills, Calif.: Sage.

Ullman-Margalit, E. 1977. *The Emergence of Norms.* Oxford: Oxford University Press.

Underdal, A. 1992. "The Concept of 'Regime Effectiveness.'" *Cooperation and Conflict* 27 (3).

Winham, G. 1986. *International Trade and the Tokyo Round Negotiation.* Princeton, N.J.: Princeton University Press.

Young, O. 1989. *International Cooperation: Building Regimes for Natural Resources and the Environment.* Ithaca, N.Y.: Cornell University Press.

————. 1992. "The Effectiveness of International Institutions. Hard Cases and Critical Variables." In *Governance without Government: Order and Change in the World of Politics,* ed. J. Rosenau and E.-O. Czempiel. New York: Cambridge University Press.

Zaelke, D., and J. Cameron. 1990. "Global Warming and Climate Change: An Overview of the International Legal Process." *American University Journal of International Law and Policy* 5 (2).

Zartman, I. W. 1978. *The Negotiation Process: Theories and Applications.* Beverly Hills, Calif.: Sage.

Part II
Case Studies

4

The Mediterranean Action Plan

Lynn Wagner

THE MEDITERRANEAN ACTION PLAN (MAP) began in 1975 as an action plan with loose goals to be followed by agreements that would tighten members' obligations to reduce marine pollution. Over the past quarter century, the MAP contracting parties have negotiated changes in the regime's focus, added regulations and issues covered under the regime, and reached domestic implementation agreements. Repeated negotiations at biennial meetings, through specially convened expert groups, and within domestic bureaucracies have provided the vehicle through which the contracting parties have arrived at these decisions. This study highlights these processes and the factors that have affected MAP postagreement negotiations, focusing particularly on those elements that Bertram I. Spector's analysis found to be influential (see chapter 2)

The MAP process provides an example of the roles that consensual knowledge, norms, and principles play in regime-building negotiations.[1] Scientists, mostly under the coordination of the United Nations Environment Programme (UNEP), played an important role in developing the Mediterranean Action Plan in 1975. Government representatives formally negotiated the agreement only after scientists had made their recommendations and UNEP had drafted proposals describing its vision for MAP. Scientists have also affected postagreement negotiations. This chapter traces the processes through which this influence has affected the talks. It then focuses on relationships Spector identified regarding domestic and international postagreement negotiations. Spector's study of twenty-six environmental regimes found that domestic postagreement negotiations are more formal than international negotiations and that regime adjustment negotiations are more likely to be affected by external events than are regime-building negotiations. This chapter examines these relationships in light of the experience of MAP.

Regime-Building and Adjustment Negotiations under the MAP Regime

The MAP regime has incorporated flexibility and change into its modus operandi. This flexibility has facilitated its change in focus from preservation of fisheries to integrated planning to sustainable development. The original agreement in 1975 envisioned such change, inasmuch as it represented a decision to cooperate rather than a blueprint of how cooperation would take place. The contracting parties have negotiated the form of that cooperation through protocols, decisions to change the MAP's institutional structure, and smaller adjustments along the way. They have filled originally recognized gaps and responded to changing international and national approaches to environmental issues. This introduction highlights some of these changes and the mechanisms through which they have taken place.

The Regime's Evolving Approach

The regime was established to solve a problem, and problem definition dominated the early stages of MAP. Perceptions of environmental degradation in the Mediterranean region began in the 1950s, with ship-generated marine pollution as the major concern. The focus turned to the protection of living resources, especially fisheries, in the 1960s. In 1969, sixteen Mediterranean states attending a convention organized by the Food and Agriculture Organization (FAO) requested FAO to examine the requirements for a convention on Mediterranean marine pollution (Boxer 1982, 326–327), although many governments recognized that an even broader pollution problem existed—for example, beaches were closed to tourists and local problems with sewage-plant disposal were highly publicized. Jacques Cousteau drew attention to the problem in the 1970s by publicizing the disappearing Mediterranean shore-life (Haas 1990, 83). UNEP provided $19 million along with administrative support (Kaul 1993) to help channel these ongoing efforts, fund scientific studies of the problem, and lead the Mediterranean states to extend the regime's focus beyond the preservation of fisheries. UNEP initially directed its funds to scientists in the region, anticipating that their research would convince politicians to take action. The fact that sixteen Mediterranean countries had begun looking into a regionwide agreement on marine pollution facilitated acceptance of the subsequently negotiated agreements, but UNEP's strategy to cultivate these scientists as regime supporters remains a critical factor in the speed with which the politicians ratified the agreements and began addressing the problem as defined by the MAP regime. (See Zartman's Proposition 2, which points out the value of a regime "imposing" an agenda [chapter 1 of this volume.)

Peter Thacher (1993, 10), who was deputy executive director of UNEP during MAP's early days, reports that the emphasis of MAP gradually shifted from assessing to reducing pollution flows. Through the 1975 Mediterranean Action Plan, the Mediterranean countries identified the problem and agreed to UNEP's conceptualization of the regime. Through the 1976 Convention for the Protection of the Mediterranean Sea against Pollution, they agreed to a legal framework and identified issue areas (e.g., "pollution from ships" and "pollution from land-based sources") for which they could develop follow-up protocols. Along with the convention, the Mediterranean states simultaneously negotiated the first two protocols, on dumping and emergencies, which identified concrete actions the contracting parties should take to address these issues.

Throughout MAP's almost thirty-year existence, the contracting parties have continued to identify pollutants to be regulated, to decide how they should be regulated, and to make other necessary regime adjustments. After the initial flurry of agreements, the contracting parties returned to the negotiating table to focus on nonpoint sources, such as runoff from the land, through the 1980 Land-Based Sources Protocol. This agreement's adoption signified that countries were willing to go beyond the initial, broad agreements to specify levels of pollutants they would abate, but agreement did not come without negotiations over how they would accomplish this objective. The biggest disagreement during these talks was over how pollutants should be controlled: by emission controls, as preferred by the Europeans, or through ambient standards, as advocated by the South. The text called for certain substances to be eliminated (the "black list") and others to be strictly limited (the "grey list"). The developing countries were concerned about the detrimental economic effects that could arise if the emission of certain substances was banned. They also argued that their coasts had experienced less pollution and would be better able to assimilate emissions. The industrialized nations had greater coastal pollution and called for emission standards. The negotiators compromised by applying emission standards for the grey list, based on suggestions by the UNEP secretariat (Haas 1990, 113–115). This protocol required more changed activities at a greater cost than had previous agreements, and its three-year wait for ratification, compared with the initial protocols' two, signaled the start of longer periods before adopted texts entered into force. As the changes required at the national level have increased, so has the time necessary for governments to prepare and gather support for ratification.

As with the Land-Based Source Protocol, some regime adjustments have added to or revised the regime's legal framework. The Mediterranean states negotiated protocols regarding hazardous wastes and pollution resulting from offshore exploration during the early 1990s. Following the United Nations Conference on the Environment and Development (UNCED) in 1992, the contracting parties reviewed their initial agreements in light of the emerging international emphasis on sustainable development and amended the convention and protocols. Table 1 lists the legal agreements adopted by the Mediterranean countries. These components create the framework for cooperation on environmental problems in the Mediterranean Sea. Other decisions have taken different forms but share the objectives of strengthening the regime and expanding it in directions that were not specifically foreseen in the original plan. At their biennial meeting in Genoa in 1985, for example, the contracting parties set ten priorities, some with time-constrained goals.[2] By 1989, the contracting parties had adopted eight common measures to regulate pollution covered under the Land-Based Sources Protocol (UNEP 1990, 6). Exogenous influences inspired many of the changes to the legal structure, while cybernetic learning loops, decisions to adjust the regime's basic formula, and system maintenance through biennial meetings have also compelled the Mediterranean states to return to the negotiating table (see Zartman, this volume).

Just as the convention put off specified details for discussion at a later time, the protocols also put off decisions on key issues, which led to renewed negotiations once parties had recognized the need and

Table 1. MAP Legal Components

Year Adopted	Convention or Protocol
1975	The Mediterranean Action Plan
1976; amended 1995	Convention for the Protection of the Mediterranean Sea against Pollution (1995 amendments changed the name to Convention for the Protection of the Marine Environment and the Coastal Region of the Mediterranean) (Convention)
1976; amended 1995	Protocol for the Prevention of Pollution of the Mediterranean Sea by Dumping from Ships and Aircraft (1995 amendments add: "or Incineration at Sea") (Dumping Protocol)
1976; formally distinct amended version, 2002	Protocol Concerning Cooperation in Combating Pollution of the Mediterranean Sea by Oil and Other Harmful Substances in Cases of Emergency (Emergency Protocol)
1980; amended 1996	Protocol for the Protection of the Mediterranean Sea against Pollution from Land-Based Sources (Land-Based Sources Protocol)
1982; formally distinct amended version, 1995	Protocol Concerning Specially Protected Areas and Biological Diversity in the Mediterranean (Specially Protected Areas Protocol)
1996	Three annexes to the Protocol on Specially Protected Areas and Biological Diversity in the Mediterranean
1994	Protocol on the Protection against Pollution Resulting from Exploration and Exploitation of the Continental Shelf, the Sea Bed and Its Sub-soil (Offshore Protocol)
1996	Protocol on the Prevention of Pollution of the Mediterranean Sea by Transboundary Movements of Hazardous Waste and Its Disposal (Hazardous Waste Protocol)

Source: Medwaves, various issues.

developed the will for further agreement. In some cases, past agreements specified the timing for further negotiations. The Land-Based Sources Protocol identified when decisions on control systems should be discussed: after the protocol entered into force (Boxer 1982, 345). New developments and agreements have depended on push-and-pull factors from the multilateral regime as well as international stimuli and domestic considerations. The adoption of eight common measures to regulate pollution covered under the Land-Based Sources Protocol, for example, was necessitated by an absence of domestic regulation in some countries. This selective absence is one type of disparity among parties that Zartman's Proposition 4 (this volume) suggests performs "the motor role in moving regime negotiations through their recursive iterations." In this case, we also see Zartman's Proposition 3—"parties continually seek to adjust regime rules . . . to fit their approach to the problem rather than simply complying"—at play. Those countries with domestic regulation tried to negotiate an exclusion from the MAP requirements. The related text on lubricating oils notes that the European Community (EC) members were bound to EC regulations and therefore had adopted legislation to control the substance (UNEP 1989, annex V, p. 6).

The lack of domestic legislation that necessitated these common measures, as well as the decision to adopt time-bound goals, follows in part from MAP's lack of enforcement procedures. Bliss-Guest, while a program officer for UNEP's Regional Seas Programme Activity Centre, wrote that "an independent enforcement agency or mechanism would certainly not be feasible at present in any region because of political realities" (1981, 278). Enforcement relies on peer pressure at the governmental level, rather than policy and interest-driven decisions or groundswells of grassroots opinion. Accordingly, members have negotiated reporting requirements to increase awareness of both compliance and noncompliance. At the third biennial meeting, in 1983, the parties unanimously endorsed a proposal for yearly national reports on measures adopted concerning implementation (UNEP 1983, 13). The parties strengthened the reporting requirement in 1989 by specifying that each party must file an annual report on its fulfillment of MAP obligations. Annual reports are filed late, but this process has resulted in more attention being paid to the actions or inactions of each state (Chircop 1992, 20). Inconsistencies and delinquencies in reporting data regarding production, consumption, and disposal of regulated substances remain, however, and decrease this tool's effectiveness.[3] The contracting parties' tardiness or selective noncompliance with reporting requirements and legislative changes has meant that compliance levels are unknown and certainly not complete. The conclusion returns to the issue of implementation.

Regime Structures and Participants

MAP regime-building, governance, and adjustment negotiations take place in a variety of standard forums. The contracting parties negotiate every two years in the Ordinary Meetings of the Contracting Parties to the Barcelona Convention and informally through other institutionalized and ad hoc meetings and structures. The contracting parties have convened expert groups to negotiate each proposed protocol and the amendments to the convention. Bureau representatives, who serve two-year terms, work with the UNEP-MAP Coordinating Unit in Athens to oversee short-run operations. The bureau expanded from four to six representatives following the accession of three ex-Yugoslavian states[4] to the Convention. The Coordinating Unit oversees MEDPOL, MAP's research and monitoring component. The bureau coordinates the activities of regional activity centers (RACs) in Malta (REMPEC, which deals with oil and chemical pollution), France (Blue Plan—integrated planning), Croatia (Priority Action Programmes), Tunisia (Specially Protected Areas), Italy (Environment Remote Sensing), and Spain (Cleaner Production).[5] MEDPOL and the RACs each have networks of national focal points with whom they communicate (Chircop 1992, 20). Following UNCED, Tunisia proposed and delegates ultimately agreed to establish a Mediterranean Commission on Sustainable Development. This body reflects the newest approach to environmental problems and seeks to formulate methods, policies, and strategies for sustainable development (*Medwaves* 1996–97, 33:6).

The dispersed locations of the MAP institutions underpin a deliberate and widely heralded aspect of this regime: the cultivation of scientists' support and the encouragement of active governments in the regime. The scientific community was separate from the process community in the early stages, and UNEP cultivated it as a strategy to produce its desired outcome. The scientific-monitoring component of MAP began following the 1975 agreement, and the developing countries were satisfied that participation in MAP would result in technology transfer, in part through the RACs and monitoring equipment set up on their own soil. Institutions of the MAP regime were located in the most active states, which encouraged these states to become and remain active in the regime.

Civil society—a critical component for implementation—did not participate as a major player from the start, however, and is a crucial missing piece in the original regime design. While UNEP, scientists, and government officials were establishing the MAP structures and focus, nongovernmental organizations (NGOs) were just beginning to develop their capacity to address Mediterranean pollution. Some had started awareness-raising activities, including Jacques Cousteau's efforts to publicize Mediterranean pollution problems and a meeting of metropolitan authorities to draft an international antipollution code for Mediterranean cities (Boxer 1982, 331). Compared with the role NGOs have played in more recent environmental regimes, however, they did not play a strong role during the initial MAP negotiations. The World Wide Fund for Nature (WWF), for example, established its Mediterranean Office in Rome in 1991, at which point its involvement in MAP "became effective" (Guarrera 1993). Since establishing its Mediterranean Office, WWF has attempted to influence the regime, but the regime originally influenced it to open the office. This chapter returns to the questions of regime design and implementation after pursuing its primary objective: tracing the processes and factors driving the MAP regime changes.

Driving Factors, Domestic and International Negotiations, and Change

This discussion of postagreement negotiations in the MAP regime sketches important influences related to "norm-building" (Sjöstedt, this volume) and rule-making processes. It moves from the overarching influence of efforts to develop consensual knowledge to more specific issues regarding the regime's interface with other international activities and the role of domestic actors and institutional structures in ratification and implementation. The section illustrates the generally stagelike, stable process through which postagreement negotiations have progressed. During MAP's initial stages, organizers encouraged a learning process and established the machinery through which learning has continued. The first part of this section explores these efforts and the development of consensual knowledge. The other two parts highlight factors that affected the transfer of this knowledge into postagreement domestic and international negotiations. They also consider Spector's hypotheses regarding differences between initial and postagreement negotiations at domestic and international levels, highlighting factors and processes that have affected the MAP regime's evolution and implementation.

Consensual Knowledge, Norms, and Principles

The early MAP experience involved efforts to establish norms and principles.[6] UNEP facilitated their development and dissemination through its efforts to build a scientific consensus, which was then expected to generate a political consensus. This strategy, and additional UNEP inducements that convinced the developing countries that the regime would involve technology transfer, influenced governments' decisions to adopt the initial and subsequent international agreements to reduce Mediterranean pollution. It also established the machinery —for example, the regional activity centers—for continued development of scientific information. Long time periods have been required to build up a scientific consensus on some issues, however, and complete political commitment has often been even slower to develop. The following discussion identifies some of the actors and actions associated with this heavily analyzed aspect of the MAP regime.

MAP's three phases (as identified by Jeftic 1994, 5) illustrate the efforts to change attitudes toward Mediterranean pollution and necessary individual and collective responses. The changes in focus recognize the need to build consensus through a learning process. Phase I, from 1975 to 1981, focused on strengthening national capacities so that all countries would participate and methodologies for implementation could be developed. Phase II, from 1981 to 1995, focused on assessment and monitoring of pollution, research on pollution, and development of common measures for pollution control. Phase III began in 1995 and is scheduled to extend to 2005. It emphasizes the development of pollution control measures and checks country compliance using measures the country itself has adopted (Jeftic 1994, 5). Throughout these phases, national representatives negotiated their participation and set the standards to which they would adhere, agreeing to hold themselves to progressively higher expectations. Their policy changes are attributed to the development of a consensual knowledge of pollution problems and the necessary responses.

UNEP's efforts to build national scientific capacity and expertise regarding the Mediterranean pollution problem are credited with the fact that initiating negotiations were a "problem-solving exercise" rather than a concessional bargaining session (Thacher 1993, 132). When it launched the MAP talks, UNEP took into account the uneven nature of the Mediterranean nations' scientific capacities and initiated a process to build up the scientific community. UNEP and the participating scientists used this strategy to push for action on the part of governments (Zartman 1992, 119). Although doing so slowed the negotiation process, UNEP believed that the agreement would be stronger if each nation's decision was based on domestically produced assessments of marine pollution (Haas 1990, 80). This "epistemic community"—a knowledge-based community that uses its expertise to influence state objectives (Haas 1990, 52)—included UNEP scientific officials and national scientists. They were generally responsible for building the consensual knowledge in favor of reducing marine pollution. To turn knowledge into state action, however, political decision makers had to share in the consensus about Mediterranean pollution and the responses that were required. The communication process between these two groups has been critical for advancing the regime. This strategy continued after the 1975 agreement and is credited with speeding and changing the course of states' participation (Haas 1990).

The strategy's importance also stems from its modification, to some degree, of the regime's top-down nature. One analyst notes that MAP was built to address decision makers in the region and that they are generally the only participants (Chircop 1992, 26). As noted previously, the public in general and NGOs in particular were just becoming aware of Mediterranean pollution problems. The Mediterranean governments were also only beginning to address these problems and they looked to FAO and then UNEP to take the initiative. UNEP's strategy of involving scientists broadened the domestic base of regime supporters and participants. Individual citizens—the ultimate target for norm internalization and behavioral changes in environmental regimes —were not involved during this stage, limiting the cybernetic effect of domestic acceptance on the course of negotiations and prompting suggestions that the regime lacked popular constituencies (Chircop 1992, 26). The conclusion considers the impact that this lack of broad-based support may have had on postagreement negotiations.

UNEP's strategy began in September 1974, when forty marine scientists from ten Mediterranean states attended a meeting cosponsored by UNEP. The participants agreed on a list of sources and channels of pollution in the Mediterranean Sea. They also proposed seven monitoring and research projects, which UNEP then funded (Haas 1990, 91–92; Thacher 1993, 125). UNEP thus secured an international consensus on the need for a comprehensive action program, which gave the plan clout when placed before the Mediterranean nations' foreign ministries. UNEP sponsorship of scientific research allowed the scientists to study the problem and resulted in support among the scientists for UNEP (Thacher 1977, 311). Such rewards for scientists also caught the attention of developing countries desirous of technology transfer and thus affected the negotiations.

The Mediterranean Pollution Monitoring and Research Programme (MEDPOL) was established following the 1975 agreement and increased the amount of scientific information available during negotiations on the convention. Equipment distribution and personnel training dominated the program's first two years (Boxer 1982, 342), a focus that convinced the foreign ministries of developing countries that MAP would lead to technology transfer. These actors were thus encouraged to continue their participation. The decision to locate MAP institutions in the most active nations also encouraged the Mediterranean countries to become and remain active in the regime (Haas 1990, 79–80).

An examination of the change in Tunisia's negotiating position during the Land-Based Sources Protocol illustrates the process by which consensual knowledge and learning have affected MAP negotiations (Chasek, Wagner, and Zartman 1996). During talks on the Land-Based Sources Protocol, Tunisia originally opposed placing fluorides and phosphorus on a list of strictly limited substances (the grey list). Tunisia believed this limitation would affect phosphate mining along its coast. Following evaluation of information from UNEP, however, Tunisian scientists realized the environmental need to control these substances. They then convinced their foreign ministry officials to include them in the protocol (Haas 1990, 114). In this case, Tunisia held up international agreement until its domestic scientific and then political communities were convinced of the need to act.

The contracting parties' 1989 decision to refocus MAP on integrated planning provides another example of the role that learning has played in adjustment negotiations for the regime. It also illustrates the long time period required for the scientific community to develop expertise and influence the political decision makers. Originally, France's scientists were the only ones with experience in integrated planning. The original international agreement on this subject, the Blue Plan, was adopted in 1977 without a base of consensual knowledge. France and UNEP nursed this component along during its early years (Haas 1990, 119–120). Ten years later, scientists in other nations had participated in Blue Plan projects and gained experience with integrated planning methods. They had also reported back home to their political decision makers. At the 1987 Ordinary Meeting, the UNEP executive director submitted a report regarding the change in MAP focus to integrated planning. The contracting parties negotiated and approved a final amended report at the following Ordinary Meeting in 1989. MAP coordinator Aldo Manos called the decision to refocus on integrated planning a "crucial evolution" in the regime (*Medwaves* 1991, 22:5). The scientists and politicians had learned that a simple concentration on marine pollution from point sources was no longer adequate; integrated planning was necessary.

The consensual knowledge of the regime has not always been accurate or based on complete information, however, highlighting the strategic role that this factor can play in negotiations. For example, politicians initially acted in part through the mistaken belief that the Mediterranean currents were so strong that pollutants from one country would wash up on the shores of others. The marine scientists knew that the currents were not this strong but recognized that this belief increased the politicians' incentive to reach an agreement and did not disabuse them of this misconception (Haas 1990, 70). In another example, France blocked MEDPOL projects that could produce results disputing its position on pathways and pollutants to be regulated by the Land-Based Sources Protocol (Haas 1990, 101). France did not want to introduce information that would alter its problem definition and others' positions. These examples again demonstrate the influence that scientific information has had on negotiating positions and thus decisions regarding the regime's direction. They also indicate that the consensual knowledge of the day may not be the norms and principles on which the regime hangs its hat in the long run.

Efforts to develop consensual knowledge and build regime norms have influenced the direction and speed of postagreement negotiations, but other factors have also influenced this process. The French example illustrates that conflicting priorities influence a participating country's motivation to act on regime norms and principles. In the Tunisian case we also saw the need to convince scientists and political decision makers that environmental concerns outweighed their economic concerns before the international negotiations could conclude. The following discussion focuses on political decision makers' roles and the domestic and international political processes through which the contracting parties get the regime's work done.

Domestic Negotiations and Change

Several themes emerge from an examination of the cybernetic loop in the MAP-related domestic postagreement negotiations. The first is the role of individuals returning to their domestic bureaucracies after learning about Mediterranean pollution issues at international meetings. Much of this influence stems from their exposure to scientific assessments and receipt of assistance for domestic assessments, as discussed above. In addition, the creation of domestic environmental institutional structures gives these individuals a formal voice and provides the machinery that states can use to implement the MAP agreements —machinery that was lacking in the earlier stages. Further, analysts suggest that the authority of these agencies vis-à-vis other government agencies corresponds to the level of implementing legislation each nation has passed (Raftopoulos 1992, 94; Antoine and Baouendi 1992, 83). These agencies' role in ratification and development of implementing legislation explains the increased formality of domestic versus international talks that Spector found in his study of twenty-six environmental regimes.

The experiences of Algeria and Egypt demonstrate the authority of domestic environmental agencies in bringing about domestic postagreement negotiations. Neither country had an environmental authority in 1975, so enforcement of the MAP agreements first required establishing new structures. Many developed countries already had such bodies and therefore focused on consolidating and enforcing legislation to control marine pollution (Saliba 1990, 11). In Algeria and Egypt, actors in the MAP initiating discussions returned to their countries, gained a foothold in their bureaucracies, and influenced their politicians' decisions to create environmental agencies and comply with the international agreement. But the scientific consensual knowledge developed at the international level has not always neatly transferred to domestic environmental agencies and then translated into action. As in Tunisia and France, competing issues and agencies slowed this transition.

Efforts in Algeria to establish an environmental authority and pass legislation were limited until its scientists were given a significant role in the political decision-making community. Algerians do not enjoy broad freedom of association; as a result, decision-making processes are especially dependent on elites (Antoine and Baouendi 1992, 95). The Algerian government established a coordinative environmental organization in 1974. However, Algerian officials believed that industrial development was a higher priority than environmental protection, and the environmental body did not initially affect policy. After 1975, marine scientists used the organization to gain a foothold in the Algerian administration, and environmental issues slowly gained priority. In 1975 government officials were alerted to the danger that marine pollution posed to Algeria's fishery yields and they requested a coastal pollution assessment. The assessment, conducted with UNEP-donated equipment and training, confirmed the warning and prompted concern within the government and elites. Finally, in 1983 a National Agency for Environmental Protection was created and legislation was passed to control marine pollution (Haas 1990, 137, 157). The critical ingredients appeared to be individuals with knowledge about the issues, a communication link with the government, and a governmental legislating agency. These factors did not exist after the initial MAP agreement in 1975. As a result, the necessary domestic policy negotiations did not occur immediately following the relevant international decisions.

The Egyptian experience presents a second study of domestic post-agreement negotiation processes. In 1981, a National Environmental Committee was created to determine whether Egypt should ratify the Land-Based Sources and the Specially Protected Areas Protocols. Until this point, scientists had been isolated from government decisions. The National Environment Committee included scientists who had worked with UNEP on MAP-related projects. Not surprisingly, the committee recommended immediate compliance with MAP. In addition to this group's recommendation, Mostafa Tolba, the Egyptian microbiologist who was UNEP executive director, lent his influential voice to urge the Egyptian government to support MAP (Haas 1990, 138). However, full compliance with MAP was still a long way off. A presidential decree in 1981 established the Egyptian Environmental Affairs Agency, which was to prepare national plans, study legislation, provide information, propose standards, and coordinate environmental policy. Environmental control depends on the agendas of the sectoral institutions, however, and most relevant action has been taken by presidential decree (Raftopoulos 1992). As a result, the Environmental Affairs Agency has exercised only limited influence.

The Egyptian experience shows the importance of individuals with knowledge of the issues and a communication link with the government. The creation of an environmental agency does not in this case seem to have speeded the passage of relevant legislation. The agency can bring environmental issues to the table, but competing issues and stronger agencies can limit implementation. The increasingly contentious nature of the issues addressed by MAP protocols may add to the number of such challenges and slow the pace of implementation.

International Postagreement Negotiations

Numerous overlaps and influences from the initial negotiations, domestic negotiations, and other international agreements have affected MAP's international postagreement negotiations. The initial negotiations resulted in a loose agreement to cooperate on Mediterranean pollution problems, the details of which would follow later. Negotiators in 1975 anticipated that the first round of postagreement negotiations would include talks over the Dumping and Emergency Protocols. They believed that a protocol on land-based sources of pollution would be more difficult to negotiate and intentionally delayed work on it. Still other issues, such as the dangers of hazardous waste, came to the contracting parties' attention for reasons external to the regime and were handled as they arose. This minichronology raises two issues for further examination: driving factors for the decision to undertake regime adjustment negotiations, and reasons why later negotiations have been more contentious.

Spector (see chapter 2) found that regime adjustment negotiations are more likely to be influenced by external events. In the case of MAP, these external events came in the form of overlaps with other regimes. Developments and decisions made in other international or subregional forums affected MAP negotiators' preferences on how to regulate members' activities and whether to address certain issues during later adjustment negotiations. This experience also supports Spector's finding that postagreement negotiations tend to be less cooperative than the initiating negotiations. The MAP organizers intentionally put off negotiations on the Land-Based Sources Protocol and took up the Dumping and Emergency Protocols because they were advised that the former would be harder to negotiate. The contracting parties then gradually added new pollutants to the list and expanded the degree to which polluting activities would be regulated. As time passed, MAP negotiators reached issues for which certain contracting parties had already adopted regulations—such as the EC emissions standards —or that affected domestic industries—such as Tunisian phosphates. The increased obligations and costs involved with these later topics added greater friction to the talks compared with the problem-solving exercise during the initial decision to cooperate.

A number of the subjects for regime adjustment negotiations were foreseen at the time of the initial agreement. Negotiators knew that the regime would require the identification of specific pollutants and regulations to address them. They decided that no state could become a contracting party to the convention unless it also adopted a protocol and thus agreed to take specific action. The contracting parties adopted the convention and first two protocols one year after the initial agreement to cooperate. Government representatives advised UNEP in 1974 that a protocol covering land-based sources would be harder to complete than the Dumping and Emergency Protocols. It therefore was not scheduled to be among these first follow-up agreements (Haas 1990, 96–97). The contracting parties subsequently completed the Land-Based Sources Protocol in 1980.

Other recent regime adjustment negotiations have focused on issues that had not been foreseen during the initial negotiations. Exogenous factors in the form of overlapping or impinging regimes have driven the MAP contracting parties back to the negotiating table, with the parties incorporating into the MAP regime issues that they have learned about through other international forums. The parties' decisions to negotiate the Hazardous Waste Protocol and to amend the initial MAP agreements provide examples of such externally driven learning. The Hazardous Waste Protocol was inspired by the Basel Convention, a decision of 115 countries to control transboundary movement and disposal of hazardous waste. Leaders from several Mediterranean countries recognized the exposed position of the Mediterranean in this regard and proposed drawing up a document more closely adapted to needs of the region. This protocol served in some respects as post-agreement negotiations for the Mediterranean signatories of the Basel Convention, who sought to strengthen and clarify its commitments in their specific, regional context (*Medwaves* 1994–95, 31:2).

The UNCED meeting in 1992 inspired several changes in the MAP framework, including the creation of the Mediterranean Commission on Sustainable Development and the decision to revise and amend the MAP framework. Certain concepts, such as sustainable development, the precautionary approach, biodiversity, and the polluter-pays principle, were not familiar during the 1970s when the convention was adopted. The Mediterranean countries agreed in 1993 to "enter a broad-ranging discussion to examine—and possibly redefine—the legal and institutional basis of their cooperation" (*Medwaves* 1994, 30:9). At their 1994 meeting, experts pored over draft amendments from the contracting parties and secretariat. Participants negotiated to extend the scope of the convention to inland waters and estuaries and to include the precautionary and polluter-pays principles, the environmental impact assessment, and the integrated management of coastal zones. They also added a new preamble that referenced major declarations and decisions made during their Ordinary Meetings and considered and adopted changes to some protocols.

In addition to affecting the decision to negotiate, regime overlaps have affected negotiators' positions regarding regulations. During negotiations on the Land-Based Sources Protocol, for example, France and Italy desired to replicate, not complicate, the EC directives they were already committed to follow, identifying the emissions that should be treated and the substances whose emissions were banned

(Haas 1990, 73). Greece followed their lead, because it would soon join the European Community (Haas 1990, 111–112). This regime overlap influenced the negotiations again at a 1984 meeting. Those talks fell through because UNEP's proposed standards were inconsistent with EC standards and France's representative objected to accepting conflicting standards (Reed 1984, 31). For the EC countries these MAP negotiations in effect replayed EC-wide negotiations. Although such negotiation replays occur mostly in the domestic arena after international negotiations, France and Italy found themselves in two regimes that were regulating similar activities and they stressed to the Mediterranean community the obligations to which they were already committed.

The regime overlaps discussed above moved MAP negotiations forward in some cases and held them up in others. The Mediterranean states' growing awareness of environmental problems paralleled similar processes within the international community and smaller regional groupings. The growing and changing norms and principles through which the Mediterranean states approached the issue borrowed from and informed those adopted in other forums. The other forums were also busy negotiating related pacts and regulations. The above examples indicate that these other forums pushed and pulled MAP. New learning through these forums pushed the Mediterranean states to regulate new pollutants in their own regional context. Certain contracting parties slowed down progress, however, when MAP negotiations did not closely parallel regulatory requirements they had adopted elsewhere. As the MAP regime expanded, so did the possible overlaps with other regimes, and conflict resulted when the overlaps were not complementary.

The initial negotiations were termed a "problem-solving exercise" (Thacher 1993, 132), but as negotiations on later protocols moved to the heart of the problem, they tended to be "heavy-going" (*Medwaves* 1994–95, 31:2). Indeed, the original regime design anticipated that later negotiations would be more difficult than those initially undertaken. The post-1975 talks addressed progressively more difficult issues, obligations on states were stronger, and overlaps with existing agreements were more common. The regime allows states to accept protocols when their "political and social climates allow" (Bliss-Guest 1981, 279). Given the increasingly difficult issues and stronger obligations, it is not surprising that time between adoption and entry into force for each subsequent protocol was longer, even though national participants and government structures were established and familiar with the regime.[7] The first two protocols (the Dumping and Emergency Protocols) were ratified by the requisite six countries and entered into force in two years. The third protocol (Land-Based Sources) required three years and the fourth protocol (Specially Protected Areas) required four years. The completely revised Protocol on Protected Areas and Biodiversity also required four years to reach the requisite six ratifications. The amendments to the convention and protocols drafted in the mid-1990s require fifteen ratifications to come into force. This higher standard still had not been met six years after adoption (*Medwaves* 2001, 44:1; *Medwaves* 2000, 40-41:5; *Medwaves* 1997, 34:14).

Conflicts during the postagreement phase also stem from negotiators' interpretations of their initial compromises. These interpretations provide one of the driving forces for the negotiations that Zartman highlights in Proposition 3 (see chapter 1), which suggests that parties seek to adjust regime rules to fit their approach to the problem rather than simply complying with the regime. The original agreement signaled the start of the Mediterranean states' cooperation through the MAP machinery, but it did not necessarily imply that negotiators had secured complete agreement or assured agreement in the future. MAP's funding requirements, for example, were subject to an initial compromise and continue to be the object of "lively" meetings (Chircop 1992, 20). This subject remains a perennial stumbling block to implementation; the 1994 MAP budget deficit of $2.5 million, out of a total annual budget of $6.3 million, resulted in the cancellation or postponement of many activities (*Medwaves* 1994, 30:2). During the initial MAP negotiations, the northern Mediterranean states did not want a new bureaucracy for the regime, commitments to regulate their industrial practices, or requirements for financial support. The southern Mediterranean states, in contrast, wanted to enhance their marine science capabilities and adopt comprehensive regional arrangements (Haas 1990, 98–99). In some cases they wanted to be excused from certain obligations—a strategy to "leave," or to negotiate individual exceptions. The Mediterranean states initially struck a compromise: stronger monitoring and assessment proposals than the northern states desired but unspecified administrative arrangements. When UNEP turned MAP funding over to the states in 1979, the financial considerations under discussion became real. The compromise agreements may have resulted in neither group feeling truly responsible for its part of the de facto formula. The Mediterranean states "maintain their contributions to a minimum" (Chircop 1992, 20) and the southern states have not been comprehensive in their adoption of pollution regulations (Raftopoulos 1992, 94).

Conclusion

This study highlights the processes and factors that have affected MAP postagreement negotiations. It suggests a number of lessons, based on the experience of the Mediterranean Action Plan, for contracting parties seeking to accomplish their goals. Many of these findings seem intuitive; Spector even suggests some of them to explain his statistical findings. The nuances bear repeating, however, and in combination with the other case studies bring new understanding to the how and why of certain postagreement negotiation processes and relationships.

At the domestic level, participants in the international negotiations had to return and build consensus within their governmental structures to implement the MAP agreements, activating the cybernetic process. A bureaucratic base from which to address the regime's issues and communication between those who understood the consensual knowledge of the issue and the domestic bureaucratic structure were complementary precursors to ratification and legislative negotiations. Furthermore, the national environmental agency's authority vis-à-vis other agencies influenced whether environmental concerns prevailed over others during these negotiations.

At the international level, overlaps with other regimes pushed the regime forward in some cases and held it back in others. Negotiators capitalized on the consensual knowledge developed through other forums to add new issues and obligations to the MAP regime's legal framework, requiring new negotiations. However, some regime overlaps resulted in conflicts between the contracting parties' obligations to different regimes; negotiators in such cases need to coordinate or adopt regulations that allow adherence to different directives with similar impacts. Initial compromises have held up regime governance negotiations, such as the MAP budget, where negotiators have held on to their previous positions on the agreements—a case where system maintenance inertia overcame attempts to move the regime forward in new directions. Understanding the history of the agreements can provide a necessary context for understanding present negotiation conflicts.

Finally, UNEP's strategy of obtaining scientific support in addition and as an impetus to securing political support is hypothesized to have speeded the adoption of norms and principles within these two communities, with parallel impacts on the domestic and the international negotiations. The MAP regime's norm-building process among and within the MAP contracting parties has been quasi-institutionalized and deliberate from the start. The strategy initially included bribes of financing for scientific projects to hook the scientists and technology transfer to hook the politicians. The strategy established the precedent of relying on information and scientific exchange to reach agreements. This approach continues today, in part through the machinery—the regional activity centers—that was established early on.

Stepping back to view the whole MAP history, one can see evidence that decisions taken during early negotiations continue to play a role in the regime's evolution. Initial attempts to build consensual knowledge have been institutionalized through a phased approach to learning and implementation, suggesting a legacy that facilitates postagreement agreement. However, negotiators initially compromised on some issues and put off others that they expected would be more difficult to resolve. As a result, subsequent negotiations appear to have been more conflictual. The cooperative, "problem-solving" initiation has not precluded "heavy-going" negotiations later on, but it may have encouraged the negotiators to return to the negotiating table as often as they did and helped show the way to resolve the problems the regime was designed to handle.

The MAP postagreement process has followed fairly stable implementation and expansion paths, based on the learning process to establish norms and principles as elements of the regime. Political commitment and willingness have not always gone hand in hand with this learning process, however. A declaration that emerged from the contracting parties' Ordinary Meeting in 1985 recognized the lack of and need for political commitment to the agreements. At the same meeting, Mostafa Tolba noted, "The contracting parties have created an apparatus which has not yet been put to full use. . . . This elaborate organizational structure is in danger of being dismissed as a façade" (*Medwaves* 1985, 3:2).

This lack of commitment stems from perhaps the greatest legacy of the initiating talks: their top-down approach. UNEP's efforts to involve scientists served as a strategy to counteract this influence, but the fact remains that NGOs were not actively pushing negotiators in 1975 and governments looked to FAO and then UNEP to take the lead. These actors have since evolved, but the initiative on these issues still does not come from the bottom, and therefore the cybernetic component of the regime negotiation process has remained weaker than it otherwise would be. NGOs might benefit from the development of communication links with domestic bureaucracies, just as scientists did. The contracting parties hoped to address this situation through their decision in 1999 to create a full-time information officer within the Coordinating Unit to focus primarily on improving relations with the media (*Medwaves* 1999, 39:3). Further studies of the processes through which regime norms and principles translate to individuals' choices, and vice versa, would provide a better understanding of this element's role and potential in influencing regime evolution.

To use the watercourse metaphor, the norms and principles have begun to take hold at the water's surface, although much still remains to be done there. Even more needs to be done to stir the forces below before they can catch up and drive the top. The regime rules and regulations have been established, expanded, and amended, gaining recognition and affecting action. The MAP Coordinating Unit's news bulletin notes that without the Mediterranean Action Plan "environmental degradation would, most certainly, have continued, probably faster than now. Governments would have been less well informed" (*Medwaves* 1996, 32:1). Despite the evidence of the reluctance, or inability, of nations to comply with certain aspects of MAP, progress has been made in terms of pollution reduction and in attitudes toward the need for reduction. Ljubomir Jeftic, the senior marine scientist at MAP's Athens headquarters, said in 1991:

> When we started, probably 80 percent to 85 percent of Mediterranean beaches and their coastal waters were dirty and unsafe for swimming. Today, I think we have pretty well reversed the percentages. Around 80 percent of Mediterranean bathing waters are much cleaner and much safer . . . that is to say, safe[r] from microbiological contamination. (*BNA International Environment Daily*, November 18, 1991)

MAP coordinator Aldo Manos commented in 1988 that "[u]p until a few years ago, asking countries for data on the quality of the sea was like trying to get at military secrets. Today countries like Greece, France, and Italy volunteer information on safe and unsafe beaches, something unthinkable in the past" (*Financial Times* 1988, 20).

The circulation within the watercourse is constructive: information makes improvements possible and improvements make getting information easier. But work remains to be done. When asked in 1995 if he considered MAP a success, newly appointed MAP coordinator Lucien Chabason said that "success" was too strong a word. He noted that success will require regional coordination, well-organized MAP facilities, communication with the public, strengthening of and coordination between national ministries, and better involvement of local authorities and socioeconomic actors (*Medwaves* 1996, 32:6–7). For all its efforts over more than two decades, MAP is still not well known and the participation of nongovernmental actors is still lacking. National and intergovernmental authorities also fail at times to work in concert with

MAP's objectives. To paraphrase Mostafa Tolba, until the bottom of
the watercourse is stirred to action, movement at the top may be dismissed as a façade.

Notes

1. Sjöstedt (chapter 3 of this volume) defines these terms and discusses
their differences and interconnections. This chapter focuses on their impact
on actor behavior as a whole and does not distinguish between them.

2. In Genoa the contracting parties set ten priorities for the period
1985–95. Mostafa Tolba reports that three of the priorities represented the
first time that a group of nations had adopted time-constrained goals. The
priorities addressed the establishment of sewage-treatment plants, identification and protection of sites of common interest, and new marine and coastal
sites and reserves, among others (Tolba 1998, 41).

3. The lack of data has also meant that MAP policies may not be optimal
for their objective. For example, the lubricating oils common measure was
based on estimates that were extrapolated from those data that were reported
(UNEP 1989, annex V, p. 6).

4. Bosnia-Herzegovina, Croatia, and Slovenia.

5. The latter two, created in 1993 and 1995, respectively, are national
centers made available to MAP, with no MAP budgetary contribution
(*Medwaves* 1997, 34:7).

6. Sjöstedt (this volume; see also Spector, Sjöstedt, and Zartman 1994,
66) defines consensual knowledge as knowledge that "reflects what the quasi-
totality of the actors involved in a negotiation acknowledge as valid cognitions." He defines norms as the values that actors share regarding the regime
(see also Ullman-Margalit 1977) and principles as the "quasi-institutionalized
consensual knowledge about the issues covered by the regime." This chapter
focuses on their impact on actor behavior as a whole.

7. An additional reason for the longer time periods relates to the practical implication of an expanding regime: as more countries join the regime,
the minimum number of ratifications required for entry into force grows,
leaving more room for individual government's processes and debates to hold
up the agreement's entry into force. It is interesting to note that the most
recently revised protocol, the Emergency Protocol, was designated a "new" as
opposed to an "amended" protocol in part because the latter requires fifteen
ratifications while the former needs only six (*Medwaves* 2001, 44:1).

References

Antoine, Serge, and Abdelkader Baouendi. 1992. "Sauver la mer, la terre, le ciel!" In *La Méditerranée réinventée: Réalités et espoirs de la cooperation*, ed. Paul Balta. Paris: Éditions La Découverte.

Bliss-Guest, Patricia A. 1981. "The Protocol against Pollution from Land-Based Sources: A Turning Point in the Rising Tide of Pollution." *Stanford Journal of International Law* 17 (summer).

BNA International Environment Daily. 1991. "Nations Agree on Measure to Stem Pollutants Entering Mediterranean Sea." November 18.

Boxer, Baruch. 1982. "Mediterranean Pollution: Problem and Response." *Ocean Development and International Law Journal* 10 (3–4): 315–354.

Chasek, Pamela, Lynn Wagner, and I. William Zartman. 1996. "The Internationalization of North African Environmental Concerns." In *The North African Environment at Risk*, ed. Will D. Swearingen and Abdellatif Bencherifa. Boulder, Colo.: Westview.

Chircop, Aldo E. 1992. "The Mediterranean Sea and the Quest for Sustainable Development." *Ocean Development and International Law* 23: 17–30.

Financial Times. 1988. "Murky Threat to Homer's Sea." July 22, 20.

Guarrera, Luigi. 1993. Personal communication with Mediterranean programme coordinator, WWF International, December 7.

Haas, Peter M. 1990. *Saving the Mediterranean: The Politics of International Environmental Cooperation*. New York: Columbia University Press.

Jeftic, L. 1994. "MED POL Phase III Will Emphasise the Development of Pollution Control Measures and Checks on Compliance." *Medwaves* 30 (autumn): 5.

Kaul, Rajiv. 1993. "Power in Numbers." *Harvard International Review* 16 (1): 40–42.

Medwaves. (various issues). Athens: MAP Coordinating Unit.

Raftopoulos, Evangelos. 1992. *Compilation of Environmental Legislation Relative to the Barcelona Convention: Comparative Analysis*. UNEP/BUR/40/Inf.3. Athens: UNEP.

Reed, Carol. 1984. "Europeans Disagree on Pollution Control." *Chemical Engineering* 14: 31.

Saliba, L. J. 1990. "Making the Mediterranean Safer." *World Health Forum* 11 (3): 274–281.

Spector, B., G. Sjöstedt, and I. William Zartman. 1994. *Negotiating International Regimes: Lessons Learned from the United Nations Conference on Envi-*

ronment and Development (UNCED). London: Graham and Trotman/ Martinus Nijhoff.

Thacher, Peter S. 1977. "The Mediterranean Action Plan." *Ambio* 6: 308–312.

———. 1993. "The Mediterranean: A New Approach to Marine Pollution." In *International Environmental Negotiation,* ed. G. Sjöstedt. Newbury Park, Calif.: Sage.

Tolba, Mostafa Kamal. 1998. *Global Environmental Diplomacy.* Cambridge, Mass.: MIT Press.

Ullman-Margalit, E. 1977. *The Emergence of Norms.* Oxford: Oxford University Press.

United Nations Environmental Programme. 1983. *Report of the Third Meeting of the Contracting Parties to the Convention for the Protection of the Mediterranean Sea against Pollution and Its Related Protocols.* UNEP/IG.43/6. Athens: UNEP.

———. 1989. *Report of the Sixth Ordinary Meeting of the Contracting Parties to the Convention for the Protection of the Mediterranean Sea against Pollution and Its Related Protocols.* UNEP(OCA)/MED IG.1/5. Athens: UNEP.

———. 1990. *Common Measures Adopted by the Contracting Parties to the Convention for the Protection of the Mediterranean Sea against Pollution.* MAP Technical Reports Series no. 38. Athens: UNEP.

———. 1992. *Mediterranean Action Plan and Convention for the Protection of the Mediterranean Sea against Pollution and Its Related Protocols.* Athens: UNEP.

Zartman, I. William. 1992. "International Environmental Negotiation: Challenges for Analysis and Practice." *Negotiation Journal* (April): 113–123.

5

The Challenges of Regime Adjustment and Governance in the OSCE

From Cold War Confrontation to Democratization and Preventive Diplomacy

Janie Weatherman

SINCE ITS INCEPTION in the early 1970s, the Conference on and then Organization for Security and Cooperation in Europe (C/OSCE) has focused on soft security,[1] promoting the idea of the indivisibility of security across a divided Europe and the close relationship between individual security and security between states. But the end of the Cold War substantially altered the nature of the security threats facing Europe. This forced the OSCE to negotiate a shift from forging shared norms and principles to managing failed transitions to democracy and intrastate crises in real operational terms (CSCE 1997). Thus, the shift from Cold War conflict regulation and transformation to the post–Cold War management of internal conflicts, shoring up regional instability, and rebuilding societies in the aftermath of civil wars marked a fundamental change in regime governance in the OSCE.

The chapter begins with the origins of the idea for a European Security Conference and the negotiating dynamics that led to the 1975 Helsinki Final Act. This framework agreement created the Conference on Security and Cooperation in Europe, but its continuity, as well as its institutional competencies, was only minimally specified. Nevertheless, the postagreement period was full of surprises that propelled the infant multilateral process forward—not least the emergence of Helsinki human rights monitors in Eastern Europe. In the second part of the chapter, the focus turns to the impact of exogenous factors on regime change in the OSCE. On its way to becoming an international organization, the OSCE met with some successes but many failures as it took up the banner of preventive diplomacy—with the Balkans providing the real test of its mettle. Increasingly, the OSCE has given attention to the consolidation of democracy as a means of both preventing conflict and postconflict rehabilitation. In defining and pursuing its goals as it evolves, the OSCE regime continues to negotiate its norms, principles, and operations in a crowded field, with NATO, the European Union, and the Council of Europe all competing with the OSCE to establish new institutional missions.

The Spirit of Helsinki: Confronting the Problem of East-West Conflict

The formation of international regimes is one way states can respond to conflicts they face in their relations. In creating regimes, policy agents are motivated by power, interests, and values to find some order or means of regulating their interactions. The impetus for regime building comes from the recognition that cooperation needs to be organized, but some triggering problems often underscore the necessity to do so. The initiators then start a process that takes on a life of its own. Thus, regime building presents both new opportunities and unexpected challenges. While some states are actively trying to set up a new regime, others may be trying to block it or limit its scope, its coverage of issues, the stringency of its rules, and so on.

Such were the dynamics that stirred the creation of the OSCE. The idea can be traced back to the 1954 Soviet proposal to convene an all-European Security Conference to engage in a problem-solving exercise to work out the key issues of a divided Europe, beginning with the divided Germanys and their contested legal status. More broadly, it was intended to encompass efforts to work out disputes over the spoils of World War II and to manage the confrontation between two competing political systems in Europe, rendered all the more dangerous by an accelerating arms race between the United States and the Soviet Union. Matters of power, interest, and ideology as well as international stature and legitimacy were all at stake. However, by emphasizing "all-European" in its original proposal, the Soviet Union sought to exclude North American participation. As a result, the Soviets failed to garner support for the conference from Western European countries (especially West Germany) and neutral and nonaligned European states. Ultimately, the truncated meeting led to the founding of the Warsaw Pact in 1955, while West Germany became a member of NATO (Jakobson 1983).

Renewed efforts by the Soviet bloc in the 1960s, notably the 1966 Bucharest Appeal to launch a European Security Conference (ESC), were perceived by the West as continued attempts to manipulate divisions within NATO and disengage the United States from the defense of Western Europe. The West countered with a series of NATO proposals calling for mutual balanced force reduction talks (MBFR) in Europe to address conventional force buildups across the bloc divide. But negotiations leading to the mutual recognition of the two Germanys as sovereign, independent states and negotiations resolving issues related to the divided city of Berlin also served as preparatory and partial steps leading to the convening of the security conference. For small European states in general, and for the neutral and nonaligned states in Europe in particular, an inclusive security conference was critical, since they could use such a regional forum to advance their own security concerns, including nuclear disarmament. For them the nuclear arms race between the superpowers was a key triggering concern. Many of these states advocated a conference on European security through UN resolutions and initiatives in the Interparliamentary Union during the 1960s. While these efforts bore little fruit, they helped to lay the groundwork for a major diplomatic initiative that Finland undertook in May 1969, prompted in no small measure by Finland's concern with its own security in the wake of the 1968 Soviet invasion of Czechoslovakia and the increasing integration of Western Europe. A multilateral forum would give Finland some much needed cover: an opportunity, on the one hand, to emphasize its Western orientation as a democracy and market economy, and on the other, to enhance the credibility and acceptability of its active neutrality policy. In a memorandum inviting all European states plus the United States and Canada, Finland offered to host multilateral consultations on the proposed European Security Conference.[2] Finland early on assumed the role of "conductor," a third party committed to organizing and facilitating the prenegotiation process to bring all the essential parties into agreement to participate and to shape an acceptable agenda on which to initiate the consultations. Ultimately, this led to the participation of the United States and Canada, and the neutral and nonaligned states, along with European NATO and Warsaw Pact members, in multilateral preparatory talks that convened in Dipoli (outside Helsinki) in November 1972.[3]

A regime-building process had been initiated that would culminate in the 1975 Helsinki Final Act. What the participating states did not expect was the way the Final Act would resonate throughout the Eastern bloc at the grassroots level, galvanizing opposition forces there while creating new interests in the CSCE process among human rights activists in the West.

The Helsinki Final Act: A Framework Agreement

The CSCE came to life as a framework agreement that was politically but not legally binding. The agreement was signed at the level of heads of state. The main formula behind the agreement consisted of balancing security and stability against human rights—what has often been described in the CSCE as negotiating apples for oranges. Zartman's reference in chapter 1 to Homans' maxim applies here: it was really a matter of finding agreement on goods more valued by one party than they cost the other (Homans 1961, 62). To make sense out of a multilateral negotiation process that encompassed a panoply of issues ranging from principles of interstate relations to confidence- and security-building measures to economic cooperation and humanitarian concerns, there had to be a variety of ways of simplifying the negotiating tasks as well as giving them structure and direction. "Baskets" served as the key organizing device. The term was first proposed by a member of the Netherlands delegation at Dipoli and thereafter stuck. The baskets were, moreover, given numbers to avoid debate on the headings. Thus, the CSCE's organizational structure follows the trend in other regime-building efforts, whereby definitions are avoided in favor of developing lists of activities grouped around functional areas of cooperation, only later to be joined under a definitional umbrella. The basket approach was also a clever device since it helped bridge an impasse in the negotiations over the Soviet preference for negotiating deductively and the tendency of the West overall (though not necessarily France) to work inductively. The East thus sought a declaratory kind of peace agreement, while the West pushed for concrete, practical, cooperative measures to promote human rights and freedoms infused with Western concepts of political liberalism.

Basket I of the Final Act effectively enumerates a Decalogue of principles guiding relations between participating states and provisions to enhance security;[4] Basket II deals with cooperation on economic, scientific, and environmental issues; Basket III covers not only human rights issues relating to traditional civil and political rights but also economic, social, and cultural rights and humanitarian issues (Bloed 1993a); and Basket IV concerns the follow-up to the CSCE. Thus the approach to regime building set out in the Final Act is based on a framework agreement of general principles followed by specific protocols for applying them to narrower areas of cooperation. The Final Act vaguely calls for their elaboration in subsequent bilateral and multilateral encounters, including the convening of a follow-up meeting to review what had been achieved and consider new commitments. In this sense, the Final Act entertained very minimal provisions for the regulatory functioning of the regime, and no specific monitoring mechanisms were envisioned (Ghebali 1989, 60).

The multidimensionality of the CSCE concept of security lent itself to a broad application: It empowered people to demand of their own state the fulfillment of its international obligations; it also empowered people to pressure their government to hold other states accountable for violations. The communist bloc maintained that only the doctrine of socialist internationalism applied to relations between socialist states, but the West wanted an agreement based on universal applicability covering both interstate relations and the treatment of citizens by their own state. The West was determined not to negotiate a peace treaty, much less a special European legal order. For its part, the Soviet Union wanted to give the Decalogue legal force, but not the text of Basket III on human rights.

As a result, the Final Act is a compromise between the socialist camp's insistence on the primacy of nonintervention in internal affairs (Principle VI) and the West's emphasis on human rights and international cooperation (Principle VII). For the West the solution was to balance Principle VI with Principle X, fulfillment in good faith of obligations under international law.[5] The West also relied on the human rights provisions included in Basket III and Principle VII, on Respect for Human Rights and Fundamental Freedoms, to challenge Soviet efforts to reduce the Final Act's scope to Principle VI. These were the key elements of the formula around which the rest of the Final Act itself was negotiated.

These kinds of results could hardly have been foreseen during the initial CSCE negotiations, where the participating states carefully weighed their stakes as well as the costs and potential benefits of a final agreement. Ultimately, disparities in power played a key role in determining what would not be included in the 1975 agreement, with powerful states clearly demarcating areas where consensus would not be attainable. The CSCE's continuity after Helsinki became, in fact, one of the most hotly contested issues in the final phase of negotiations. The Soviet Union's initial enthusiasm for promoting the CSCE's institutionalization as a means of exercising influence over Western European security matters gave way to restraint as the political nature of the human rights bargain behind the Final Act became clear. Already concerned with the concessions they had made in Basket III, the Soviets pushed instead for a speedy close to the negotiations and a final agreement based on vague recommendations for further cooperation. And to minimize the significance of Basket III, the Soviets pursued a number of tactics. For example, during the Geneva negotiations the Soviets attempted first to block the reassembly of the Basket III committee before Basket I and especially the principles on nonintervention were negotiated. Later, they tried to introduce a preamble to Basket III that would have emptied the contents of that basket of any practical significance, and finally they tried to stonewall the negotiations using the consensus decision rule. Even though in the negotiations on Basket I Romania had cosponsored proposals with nonaligned European countries, and in Basket II Hungary had taken a more liberal position than either the GDR or the USSR, in Basket III the East negotiated on the basis of bloc solidarity (Kirk Laux 1984, 258–259).

The real significance of the Final Act lies in the new ground it broke, especially in launching multilateral approaches to confidence-

and security-building measures in Europe—however modest these initially were—and human rights. Notably, the latter had a penetrating character that extended beyond traditional human rights instruments. CSCE commitments entered into matters traditionally left to the discretion of the states. By the 1990s these came to include the structure of government, rule of law, and democratic pluralism. As Bloed (1993a, 50) notes, "[T]he myth that the political system of a state is irrelevant for adequate protection of human rights has been definitively discarded."

Decision-Making Process

The decision-making process was managed through a mix of both coalition-forming and consensus-building strategies. According to the rules of procedure, all states were to participate in the CSCE as sovereign equals guided by the rule of consensus, which covered both procedure and substance. Defined as the absence of any objections to the making of the decision in question, the consensus rule meant that final agreements either would be reduced to the least common denominator or would depend on some element of integration as well as trade-offs and package deals.

Three coalitions formed from the outset and wielded varying degrees of influence over the negotiation process. The EC states and NATO allies, including both the United States and Canada, made up the Western bloc. They did not always act with one voice, with EC states sometimes presenting their own proposals and often adopting an independent position as a way to promote European political cooperation (Ghebali 1989; Schoutheete 1980).[6] However, to coordinate the Western position in CSCE negotiations, EC states caucused first, then NATO. The emergence of these practices must be viewed within the context of the early, low-key U.S. role at Helsinki. The Nixon administration saw the CSCE as a regional enterprise that could jeopardize bilateral U.S.-Soviet accommodation on strategic nuclear issues, Vietnam, and other regional issues affecting international peace. As Maresca (1985) argues, in contrast to the European Community's emphasis on human rights, U.S. demands were limited to obtaining agreement based on mutual respect for different systems of government and nonintervention in internal affairs.

A second major coalition consisted of the Warsaw Pact states, the Eastern bloc. They were led by Soviet efforts to protect the socialist states' policy of resisting the application of international law and agreements in any area except between the competing ideological systems. The East challenged the West's conception of the universality of international law and sought special regional principles of interstate relations. Thus, the aim of the East was to achieve a final document based on broad declaratory principles that would legitimize Soviet foreign policy aims.

By default more than design, the third principal "grouping" (in CSCE parlance) consisted of the neutral and nonaligned countries in Europe (N+N): Finland, Austria, Sweden, Switzerland, and Yugoslavia, along with such microstates as Cyprus, the Holy See, Lichtenstein, Malta, Monaco, and San Marino. Their expectations for a cross-bloc rather than bloc-based approach to détente were also short-lived. Finland's early role as "conductor" in orchestrating the Dipoli Consultations contributed to expectations among the East and West that the N+N would perform intermediary services to overcome the polarized atmosphere that had already emerged during the preparatory talks. Sometimes this came at the expense of pursuing national proposals and N+N proposals, but often they were able to include key aspects of their own interests in the draft texts. Their third-party role was also necessitated by the rule of consensus as much as by the complex nature of multilateral negotiations among thirty-five participating states dealing with a multi-issue agenda. Thus, the N+N played an indispensable role in negotiating commitments between East and West on compromise language they carefully vetted across the bloc lines, including as much of all the participating states' positions as possible without incurring objections from others. In so doing, they often kept the CSCE negotiations alive, unlike U.S.-Soviet arms limitations talks, which were put on ice during the height of the renewed Cold War in the early 1980s. There were also some limited groupings that formed around specific issues, most notably the Mediterranean, for which Yugoslavia, Spain, and Italy in particular often took leading roles. Malta's singular interest in this issue ensured it a notorious bargaining role as a "defender," prepared as it was on more than one occasion (Geneva, Belgrade, Madrid) to hold up consensus among the other thirty-four participating states on a final document until its regional interests were satisfactorily taken into account.

Breathing Life into the CSCE: Postagreement Regime Evolution

As the CSCE turned from a one-time multilateral conference culminating in the 1975 Final Act into a follow-up process, it became the battleground on which the participating states tried to impose their own agendas on its further development and to circumscribe other states' behavior. This battleground encompassed three principal challenges: (1) how to extend CSCE commitments, especially in the face of Soviet reluctance to engage in further discussions on human rights issues; (2) how to institutionalize the process to provide durability and viability from one conference to the next; and (3) how to imbue it with governing capabilities to ensure that such tasks as monitoring, information gathering, implementation, and sanctioning of violations were undertaken. These negotiations unfolded over three follow-up meetings during the Cold War years: Belgrade (1977–78), Madrid (1980–83), and Vienna (1986–89), as well as numerous intersessional expert meetings. The process culminated in the November 1990 summit meeting of CSCE heads of state and the signing of the Charter of Paris. This manifesto marked a watershed in East-West relations and the metamorphosis of the CSCE. Since then, there have been follow-up meetings in Helsinki (1992), Budapest (1994), Lisbon (1996), and Istanbul (1999), and many meetings on the human dimension as well as security and economic cooperation. At stake was the making of a multilateral negotiation into a collective approach to the management of East-West security problems and, to the extent possible, their peaceful transformation.

Thus the Final Act was less the capstone than the foundation for a repeated set of regime-building negotiations. It limited the continuation of the CSCE to a skeletal follow-up meeting to be held in Belgrade in 1977, leaving the responsibility for procedures and modalities for monitoring and implementation to the postagreement phase. Specific measures such as regularized meetings, legally binding obligations, and any permanent organizational or administrative features were eschewed. Instead, the Final Act's minimalist approach directed the participating states to just three broad endeavors: (1) to pay due regard to and implement the provisions of the Final Act unilaterally, bilaterally through negotiations, and multilaterally through meetings of experts; (2) to proceed to a thorough exchange of views on the implementation of the provisions of the Final Act and, in this context, to deepen their mutual relations; and (3) to continue the multilateral CSCE process and cooperation within international organizations. Thus, from the outset, the CSCE had practically no capacities for monitoring compliance, taking enforcement action, or setting new standards and promoting regime governance.

The Helsinki Final Act was a novel approach with its own contradictions. It was both an agreement legitimizing the status quo arrangements of a divided Europe and a tool for challenging the political and security norms and principles on which the divisions were sustained. From its initiation, the CSCE has been defined by its comprehensiveness. This aspect of the 1975 Final Act set it apart from other international agreements, as did its broad conception of security and treatment of human rights in the context of other basic international principles guiding relations between states. Nevertheless, the Final Act's core principles contained significant ambiguities and escape clauses limiting its obligatory character. Therefore, the West insisted that new commitments be negotiated as a function of the review of implementation. So the CSCE developed incrementally as follow-up negotiations expanded on the original scope and depth of commitments in the Final Act. Some subsequent provisions embody recommendations within the domain of the Final Act that the Final Act had not dealt with in concrete terms or had dealt with only in limited fashion (for example, disarmament and minority rights), and others modify the substance of the previous recommendations (for example, confidence- and security-building measures and human rights).

For example, the presentation of proposals at the 1977–78 Belgrade follow-up drew attention to key issues on CSCE modalities and opened an important debate on expanding the military-security dimension of the Helsinki Final Act. At the 1980–83 Madrid review meeting, the participating states returned to the military-security issues and agreed on the parameters for an improved regime on confidence-building measures—renamed confidence- and security-building measures (CSBMs). The CSBMs were then negotiated successfully at the 1984–86 Stockholm Conference on Disarmament in Europe (CDE), thus giving substance to Principle II of the Final Act, refraining from the threat or use of force. To this end, the Stockholm Conference achieved agreements for the prior notification of certain military activities, constraining provisions, and compliance and verification procedures, including on-site inspection of military exercises. These provisions marked a breakthrough in East-West security negotiations in the post–World War II era and prepared the way for including on-site inspections in the U.S.-Soviet Intermediate Nuclear Forces agreement of 1987.

The on-site inspection provisions also set a precedent for negotiating more intrusive mechanisms for human rights—the first nonvoluntary CSCE human rights mechanism—agreed to at the Vienna follow-up meeting (Bloed 1993b, 42–43; Lehne 1991a, 170, 188). The Vienna Mechanism allows for a system of supervision to obtain information from another state (on possible violations) relating to the human dimension of the CSCE, including a binding commitment to hold bilateral consultations and provide information to all CSCE states. The Vienna Mechanism, which was used extensively during the transition period to the post–Cold War era and at least seventy times during 1989, was supplemented by the Moscow Mechanism, created in September 1991. To the previously limited intergovernmental procedures, the Moscow Mechanism added a system of missions of independent experts, or rapporteurs, which could be sent to a state against its will, as long as the initiating state had the support of at least five other CSCE states. The Vienna meeting was a turning point in the development of consensual understanding on human rights and on the formal observance and domestication of the CSCE principles in legislative practices, as well as foreign policy. By the conclusion of the meeting, "the idea of human rights as one of the elements uniting Europe was taking shape" (Lehne 1991b, 152).

To balance this, the Vienna Concluding Document enhanced the instrumentality of CSCE human rights principles and commitments by creating a linkage between these commitments and national legislation and by securing the right of individuals and groups to monitor the implementation of human rights. This led to provisions for "the right to know one's rights" and the dissemination of information on human rights, and to the elaboration of two principles of the Final Act: Principle VII, Respect for Human Rights and Fundamental Freedoms; and Principle IX, Cooperation among States (Lehne 1991a, 155). This included the participating states' recognition of their duty to "respect the right of their citizens to contribute actively, individually or in association with others, to the promotion and protection of human rights and fundamental freedoms" (§13.5). They committed themselves to "facilitate direct contacts and communication among these persons, organizations and institutions within and between participating States *and remove, where they exist, legal and administrative impediments inconsistent with the CSCE provisions*" (§26, emphasis added). The language is specific and incontrovertible. The strengthening of these commitments illustrates the diachronic aspects of rule making and the incremental development of CSCE regime governance and institutional competence.

The CSCE expert meetings leading up to the Vienna follow-up as well as the Vienna meeting itself and the expert meetings held shortly thereafter all provided the West with important opportunities to judge the social transformation under way in the Eastern bloc and the Soviet Union, which Gorbachev had initiated under his policies of perestroika and glasnost.[7] These policies brought a new Soviet approach to the law of peaceful coexistence, dropping the earlier distinction regarding international law between socialist and capitalist states, the former governed by socialist internationalism and the latter by international law. "In fact, it removed the legitimacy of socialist international law as a separate, regional, category of international law" (Hoedt and Lefeber 1991, 2).

Institutionalizing the CSCE

Institutionalization was the second challenge the CSCE states faced in the regime's postagreement evolution. The member-states had to determine modalities for a review of implementation and enforcement and decide whether the circumstances called for new normative commitments that might extend the Final Act or the adoption of revisions to delimit its scope. They also had to settle on procedures for the continuation of the CSCE, not just as concerned the Belgrade meeting in 1977–78, but beyond. Would the first follow-up be the end of the Helsinki process, or would it launch something more durable? While it is generally true that follow-up negotiations are less about finding formulas that satisfy the parties' conceptions of fairness and justice and more about finding practical methods of settling disputes over particular provisions or about adjusting goals, monitoring progress, and so forth, negotiations over these procedural matters themselves in the CSCE were tightly wrapped in notions of fairness and justice. Whereas the West saw the CSCE as an opportunity to criticize the Soviet bloc for its human rights violations, the East saw the first order of business in the follow-up process to be a matter of adjusting the regime rules to minimize these political costs and to defuse further pressure from domestic nongovernmental organizations (NGOs), both the underground organizations in the East and those monitoring compliance for the West. As Zartman notes in chapter 1, recursive regime negotiations are fundamentally about the question of costs under conditions of uncertainty. The aftermath of the signing of the Helsinki Final Act posed that question most acutely for the Soviet bloc: Will we cost ourselves unnecessarily now and forevermore (on the human rights commitments) in order to thwart the uncertain threat of future costs, especially the uncertain costs of the nuclear arms race and East-West security?

Among the most contentious issues at the first follow-up meeting in Belgrade was whether the Final Act implied a contingent relationship between the review of implementation and the possibilities for the parties (given the results of the review) to proceed to "the deepening of their mutual relations, the improvement of security and the development of co-operation in Europe, and the development of the process of détente in the future."[8] Expanding the CSCE's standard-setting, monitoring, and supervisory capabilities would not have been possible without the gradual institutionalization of the CSCE process itself. Other questions also emerged: Should review of implementation be completed before consideration of new substantive commitments, as implied by the order of the tasks enumerated in the Final Act? How long should a review go on? If there are serious shortcomings on the implementation of already existing CSCE commitments, should there be any discussion of new substantive commitments? Given these considerations, how long should the first follow-up conference last?

Negotiations at Belgrade became a test of what had been achieved in Helsinki, with the West treading old ground to achieve what had not been accomplished in the Final Act (especially on human rights and confidence-building measures) and the Soviet bloc attempting to maintain a posture of inertia on human rights issues while pushing for largely declaratory agreements on military-security questions. The growing U.S. interest in human rights, which the Carter administration made the centerpiece of its foreign policy, also introduced new dynamics into East-West relations that threatened to be the undoing of détente. The new administration's approach to the Soviet Union stood in stark contrast with Nixon and Kissinger's, which had given little importance to the CSCE initially and which applauded the substance of the Final Act (Maresca 1985) only belatedly. As the Basic Principle Agreement (BPA) of 1972 illustrates, the United States and the Soviet Union had defined détente in the early 1970s in terms of *limits* on superpower confrontation. The referent point was the status quo, not increases in cooperation as intended in the multilateral context of the CSCE concept of détente. The newfound U.S. interest in the CSCE led to a new set of tensions among NATO states, too, especially during periods when the European Community did not want to include the United States in working out a common position. For its part, NATO essentially reacted to EC positions. Within the European Community, the French maintained their own views, with French president Giscard d'Estaing seeking a special relationship between France and the Soviet Union. For its part, the European Community was satisfied that the N+N positions were closer to the EC positions than those of any other participant.

The lack of cohesion among the Western alliance members made it difficult for their views to prevail over those of the Soviet Union. The N+N nations concluded that this made it more important for them to take an active part; and so, with the CSCE facing an early demise, the N+N stepped in as both instrumental and facilitative third parties at Belgrade. They assumed key organizational responsibilities, including forging consensus on procedural solutions to the institutional structure and modalities of the CSCE follow-up process, and on the purpose of the review of implementation and the justification for new commitments. Thus, the first key N+N compromise came early at Belgrade, during the prenegotiations on the agenda and negotiating modalities. The compromise set aside a fixed period of time for review of implementation. This favored the West's position and thus succeeded in establishing a CSCE follow-up system predicated on the monitoring of compliance with the Final Act. The right of participating states to examine the record of implementation and to raise issues to this effect with the other signatory states as their prerogative and not as an infringement of state sovereignty was reconfirmed. This hard-won result was a product of considerable bargaining over the agenda for the Belgrade meeting (the "Yellow Book"), which was then put to the test throughout the very difficult Belgrade negotiations.

Belgrade also established that among the tasks of the follow-up were the drafting of a final, concluding document and attainment of consensus on it, which would specify the place and date of the next follow-up. This was also a product of the efforts of the N+N, which had insisted from the beginning that negotiations should continue until there was a consensus on a final document and agreement on the date and place for the next follow-up. The Belgrade follow-up also institutionalized the use of expert meetings as a means of sustaining East-West contact between sessions and of providing an exchange of views and the development of substantive documents on more specialized issues. It also provided an opportunity for increasing NGO participation, and thus improving the domestic dimension of the regime. Perhaps most important, Belgrade established accountability as a key element of the CSCE process, demonstrating through an open debate among thirty-five states that noncompliance could bring political costs. Even though the substantive agreement at Belgrade was meager,[9] this first follow-up was important and in many ways successful. It set up standards and precedents for making the CSCE process operative. The mere fact that the thirty-five participating states met and found ways of proceeding largely within the same framework established at Dipoli and Geneva suggested that the CSCE might be more robust and durable than it first appeared. Thus, the Belgrade Conference was a key step in the process of regime building and governance.

Compliance was not forgotten in the process of negotiating the evolution of the norms, principles, and rules. Belgrade marked the first time in the history of diplomacy that compliance with a multilateral instrument would be scrutinized, giving way to open criticism of other governments' failure to implement the agreement (Skilling 1984, 286). These mechanisms produced stronger machinery for dealing with violations than available to the UN human rights covenants. That this criticism was open and public is underscored by the practice followed by the U.S. delegation in the 1980–83 Madrid follow-up meeting and by other Western delegations of granting interviews with the press regarding specific individual human rights abuses that had been (or were to be) raised in the negotiations. "This political cost . . . was often insufficient to induce countries to fulfill their obligations, but it kept CSCE commitments relevant, more so maybe than other legally binding human rights instruments" (Lehne 1991a, 17). At Madrid the West even forced the Soviets to return to a review of implementation in light of the declaration of martial law in Poland, even though the period for review had been completed according to the timetable of the agenda. Thus, the West gained the right to raise questions on implementation at all times and thereby strengthened the role of the CSCE as a supervisory body.

The CSCE's institutionalization might not have succeeded had it not been for the role of the N+N. In the aftermath of the Geneva negotiations, the role of the N+N states as coordinators in the CSCE became customary. During the Belgrade and Madrid meetings, their facilitative efforts in promoting both the procedural and substantive aspects of the negotiating process were especially critical. In addition to their normal functions of facilitating the organization of the working committees, drafting texts, identifying the potential zone of agreement, and devising compromises, the N+N worked to stabilize the negotiating process at Belgrade and Madrid. Supplying a mechanism of continuity when none existed institutionally, the N+N defended the integrity of the CSCE rules of procedure, the credibility of commitments, and the CSCE's viability as a multilateral political process. They also worked to keep the superpowers' threatening tactics from bringing the CSCE to an end, assumed responsibility for negotiating failures, and contributed face-saving interventions at numerous crisis junctures that made it politically possible for both East and West to accept the other's demands. By accepting the importance of upholding the CSCE human rights commitments and the necessity of a thorough review of any violations, the N+N (led by Switzerland, Sweden, and Austria) helped ensure that the East could not diminish this aspect of the follow-up conference.

Learning in the CSCE

Several factors help explain why it was possible to negotiate an expansion and strengthening of CSCE standard-setting and governance capabilities. First, because the CSCE was a political, not a legal, agreement, the participating states could adjust their negotiating positions more rapidly to the social and political transformations sweeping across Eastern Europe. The CSCE began with the Decalogue's Principle VII, on human rights, and each succeeding CSCE agreement added to the commitments by making them increasingly specific and spelling out the meaning of earlier commitments by creating more rules and clarifying the scope of their application. "This type of interpretive rule-making takes the place of judicial interpretation. While not adjudicatory in character, it serves to anticipate and resolve disputes about the specific meaning of CSCE commitments . . . by eliminating or weakening legal arguments that have been or might be advanced to excuse nonperformance" (Buergenthal 1993, 6). The West used this approach to close loopholes and straighten wordings used by the Eastern bloc countries to evade CSCE commitments. Buergenthal (1993, 7, and 1991) argues that "these achievements would, on the whole, have been impossible had the participating states been drafting and voting on treaty provisions." Because they are of a political rather than legal nature, the CSCE commitments could also be adopted and modified more expeditiously than juridical obligations (Pentikäinen and Scheinin 1993, 110).[10] The West, with the support of the N+N, ensured that the CSCE remained relevant and responsive, for example, by negotiating new human contact provisions at the Madrid CSCE negotiations to counter the imposition of martial law in Poland and later scoring pioneering breakthroughs on human dimension commitments (for example, the national minority rights agreed upon in Copenhagen in 1990) even as the Cold War was ending.

Second, the CSCE had a reach that included learning loops tying domestic governance to international governance. This "legislative approach" was flexible because it was not subject to domestic institutional constraints, but the informal attitude toward monitoring infused the CSCE with a sense of purpose and direct relevance that most participating states had never anticipated. Since the Helsinki Final Act was not a treaty with legally binding commitments, the domestic post-agreement processes did not present the typical ratification requirements, with attendant domestic bargaining among governmental agencies, political leaders, parties, and lobbyist or other interest groups with a stake in bringing (or not bringing) it into force. Yet explicit provisions regarding monitoring and enforcement of CSCE provisions were absent, although the Final Act called for a review of implementation based on "a thorough exchange of views" at a follow-up conference.[11] Thus formal ratification bargaining was replaced by the rise of dissidents, refuseniks, peace movements, and NGOs as stakeholders and by the creation of various agencies as monitors of the Final Act. CSCE "expert meetings" also became an enduring feature of the CSCE process as a result of the Belgrade meeting, and this, too, enhanced the interaction of the delegations of CSCE participating states and NGOs.[12]

Third, the Final Act was widely disseminated in the Eastern bloc. The Soviets reproduced it in such organs as *Pravda* and *Izvestia,* loudly proclaiming it a foreign policy victory. While the official statements stressed the inviolability of frontiers as the most important of the ten principles of interstate relations,[13] citizens in the Eastern bloc learned about their right to know and act upon their rights and duties, including human rights, rights of emigration and religious association, and fundamental freedoms. These aspects of the CSCE, coupled with the Soviets' deliberate attempts to give it wide publicity throughout the Eastern bloc, helped create an awareness of a new East-West regime in formation. At first skeptical, individuals nevertheless began to make appeals to Moscow based on the Final Act. In May 1976, Yuri Orlov and ten others founded the first Helsinki monitoring group, the Public Group to Promote Observance of the Helsinki Agreement in the USSR.[14] This was followed by the emergence of groups in Ukraine, then Lithuania, Armenia, and Georgia, and in Czechoslovakia and Poland, of which Charter 77 received widespread recognition (Kirk Laux 1984, 262).

Gorbachev used CSCE norms and principles as a means of legitimizing institutional changes in the Soviet Union, so that doctrine internalization came to connect the CSCE process with key decision makers and their reform programs even in the Eastern bloc on issues they had long resisted. The first sign of major political change came to light in early 1986 when Gorbachev instructed the Soviet delegation at the CSCE negotiations in Stockholm on confidence- and security-building measures to accept on-site inspection, a major reversal of a long-standing Soviet position. At the Vienna review meeting, more surprises unfolded as Soviet foreign minister Eduard Shevardnadze announced that the Soviet Union gave great importance to Principle VII and, pointing to major legislative and administrative measures being adopted in his country to facilitate the resolution of humanitarian problems related to such matters as family reunification and mixed marriages, proposed to convene a conference of the CSCE in Moscow to consider the whole range of human dimension problems.[15] Gorbachev used such occasions to communicate that his political reforms were real and that the Soviet leadership was making good-faith efforts to bring Soviet policies into line with CSCE commitments.

By 1989, dissidents and opposition groups were using the Vienna meeting and its strengthened principles, as well as the convening of CSCE expert meetings in the Eastern bloc countries, to put greater pressure on their governments, the ecological conference in Sofia being a notable example (Leatherman 1993; see also Lehne 1991a). When the Sofia meeting was used by the activists as a "protective cover for unprecedented public protest activity against the Communist regime,"[16] Zhivkov's response of police brutality brought great criticism of the regime and led shortly thereafter to his ouster (Lehne 1991a). Honecker's attempt to live up to the CSCE commitments as a "passport to greater international respectability" (Brown 1991, 144) did little to stem the tide of East German vacationers in Hungary seeking to exit the Communist bloc. Pointing to its CSCE obligations and UN principles of freedom of movement, and emphasizing these multilateral commitments over bilateral ones, Hungary made the remarkable decision to allow the exodus of East Germans, a decision that helped unleash a series of events leading to the fall of the Berlin Wall in November 1989 and the "velvet revolutions" throughout the Eastern bloc.

The fourth factor that helps explain the expansion of the CSCE's capabilities is that, in addition to these domestic-level CSCE linkages, several governmental and intergovernmental monitoring activities were launched. Although the Council of Europe was stymied in its search for a role in the CSCE process (Ghebali 1989, 66), two other intergovernmental bodies played a role in CSCE monitoring: the North Atlantic Assembly (NAA) and the Interparliamentary Union. The

NAA was charged with analyzing the implementation of Basket III and compiling East-West agreements on these issues. The Interparliamentary Union served as a parliamentary process parallel to the CSCE, organizing regional conferences simultaneously with Helsinki and each CSCE follow-up meeting.

The U.S. Commission on Security and Cooperation in Europe was created "to monitor the act of the signatories which reflect compliance with or violation of the articles of the Final Act, with particular regard to the provision relating to Human Rights and Cooperation in Humanitarian Fields," and to report to members of Congress on its findings. The bill creating the commission was reluctantly signed into law by President Ford on June 3, 1976. Since then the commission has been one of the most significant organizations in documenting East-West compliance with the CSCE and human rights provisions, has played a vital role in the preparation of U.S. positions, and has provided commission members for U.S. delegations to CSCE meetings.

Although no formal organizational structure connected monitoring and advocacy groups in the East and West, CSCE review conferences offered a key opportunity for them to report on human rights abuses and to lobby national delegations for improvements in CSCE normative commitments. These efforts led to the founding of the International Helsinki Association (later Federation), under the honorary presidency of Andrei Sakharov. Its objective was to monitor the CSCE agreements from its headquarters in Vienna and to receive complaints of violations, as well as to mobilize assistance for those persecuted and seek amnesty for them (Skilling 1984, 318–319; Leary 1980).[17]

Exogenous Factors and Regime Change

The course of international regimes is shaped not only by their internal dynamics but by exogenous factors as well. During the Cold War, the rise of dissident groups in the East, the renewed interest in human rights monitoring in the West, and eventually Gorbachev's use of CSCE commitments to support reform at home were all important external forces shaping the CSCE's development. But the greatest external shocks came with the end of the Cold War. This momentous event posed two interrelated challenges for the CSCE. First, it had to redefine its core mission along with the tools for carrying it out. Second, it had to defend its mission within the context of other institutions in Europe with overlapping geographic and functional areas undergoing similar systemic challenges. NATO, the Council of Europe, and the European Union were pushed by events into competition with one another and with the CSCE to carve out new identities in the transformed landscape. While these organizations faced new demands to expand their membership to include former communist states, the CSCE was faced with losing one of its most distinctive attributes: comprehensive membership. These questions were debated repeatedly during the 1990s as the CSCE underwent three key stages of institutional redesign that took it from a multilateral process into a new sphere of responsibilities as an international organization. The first set of negotiations was rather limited in nature and resulted in the 1990 Charter of Paris. The second phase produced more important innovations in institutional operations and functions and included negotiations spanning the 1992 Helsinki follow-up and the 1994 Budapest Summit. The third phase shifted the primary focus from making the OSCE operational on its own to working out its relationship to other European institutions, as well as the United Nations, and culminated in the 1999 Istanbul Charter.

Power differentials among the CSCE participating states became more salient factors in the renegotiation of these CSCE purposes than they had been during the previous regime-building processes. This factor accounts in considerable measure for the "new CSCE" that emerged during the first few years following the end of the Cold War, but it does not explain the transformation of the CSCE in its entirety. To be sure, as the Cold War ended the powerful states were able to limit the efforts of the new power contenders (especially Germany) and the smaller aligned, neutral, and nonaligned states that sought to make the CSCE into a regional security organization with teeth. Of particular significance was the failure of CSCE participating states to reach agreement during the Charter of Paris negotiations for creating a strong Conflict Prevention Center (CPC) as part of the new CSCE institutional structure. Initial German proposals and those of smaller countries such as Czechoslovakia had called for the CPC to be the origin of a European collective security system to replace the two alliances. Despite support from the Soviet Union and the Eastern bloc, as well as the appearance of a Canadian proposal similar in intent, the project for developing a strong CPC was met with resistance by the United States, France, and Britain, each of which presented alternative proposals. The French-British proposal limited the CPC to the implementation of CSBMs and a procedure for the conciliation of disputes. The United States continued to push for the primacy of NATO in European security affairs. Before the failed coup attempt in Moscow, Soviet objections largely prevented the CSCE from developing procedures to take actions without a consensus and from intervening in Yugoslavia, arguing that the CSCE should prevent only conflicts between countries and not interfere in disputes within states (Weitz 1993, 353). Central and Eastern European states, which had lobbied for the strengthening of the CSCE in order to justify the dissolution of the Warsaw Treaty Organization, were left without what they perceived to be adequate security guarantees. These concerns, coupled with U.S. reservations, the lack of Soviet influence, and unified Germany's continued membership in NATO, helped to shape a post–Cold War CSCE based on a minimal organizational structure. It contains a mixture of old practices regarding follow-up and expert meetings, and new practices related to the emerging OSCE institutions centered on the promotion of democracy and peaceful political change, including economic liberty, social justice, and environmental responsibility based on market economies.

The 1990 Charter of Paris encapsulates these objectives in lofty language, declaring that the "era of confrontation and division of Europe has ended," and that "Europe is liberating itself from the legacy of the past." Whereas previously the only mention of democracy in CSCE documents was limited to the name of the German Democratic Republic, in the Charter of Paris the principles of democratic government are clearly invoked, with human rights and fundamental freedoms defined as central to democratic government. The charter was negotiated in a spirit of Western triumphalism, without nuance and reservations. It failed to acknowledge that the realization of human liberties could be undermined by the lack of national democratic traditions in the East and the great social and economic upheavals that the march toward market economies would bring in its wake. Thus the charter's shortcomings: a document based on nearsighted political euphoria that in effect failed to establish a new institution, whether in teleological, programmatic, structural, or real operational terms (Ghebali 1996, 23 and 24).

It was left to the 1992 Helsinki follow-up meeting to make something workable out of the charter's skeletal arrangement of the new CSCE. The need for more far-reaching institutional innovation was driven by the sobering reality that unlike at the Charter of Paris negotiations, diplomats could no longer ignore social upheavals, economic crises, and eruption of intrastate conflict (many of these violent) throughout the former communist bloc. In a short time span, the CSCE had to be transformed from a process largely devoted to the codification of the balance of power between East and West to its new responsibilities for "guid[ing] international change, including the disintegration of authoritarian empires, and oversee[ing] disputes among antagonistic nationalities" (Weitz 1993, 346). With collective security ruled out, the prevention, management, and resolution of conflicts became central objectives of the CSCE.

By 1995, the CSCE had been renamed the Organization for Security and Cooperation in Europe, and the key institutional changes inaugurated in the Helsinki follow-up were in place and running. Between summits, the central responsibilities for regime governance came to rest with the ministerial council. Meanwhile, daily consultations and decision making take place in the Permanent Council at the Vienna headquarters of the OSCE. Decisions are still adopted according to the consensus principle, although at the January 1992 Prague meeting of the CSCE Council it was decided that in "cases of clear, gross and uncorrected violation" of CSCE commitments, action could be taken without the consent of the state concerned. This option was exercised regarding the conflict in the former Yugoslavia (Serbia and

Montenegro) in May 1992, leading to its suspension (the only such suspension to date), which ended in November 2000 (Milinkovic 2001). There is also a provision for "consensus-minus-two," by which the OSCE can call on two participating states in dispute to seek conciliation, but this procedure has not been invoked. Decision making is coordinated by the chairman-in-office (CiO), the chief executive office of the OSCE, which rotates annually among OSCE states.

The Office on Free Elections (in Warsaw), set up to monitor elections, later became the Office on Democratic Institutions and Human Rights (ODIHR). Having principal responsibility for promoting the human dimension, it advocates the rule of law through projects that provide technical assistance and improve the administration of justice. It has also aimed at strengthening civil society, for example, by building dialogue between NGOs and governments on human rights issues, promoting public awareness through educational and TV programming and ODIHR publications, and hosting seminars open to NGO participation on issues such as national minorities and free media. It also contributes to early warning by monitoring the implementation of OSCE commitments. It establishes guidelines and procedures for creating democratic electoral systems and provides practical support for consolidating democratic transitions. For example, the ODIHR promotes democratic elections by making expert missions available before, during, and after elections to observe the entire process. Deployed on a long-term basis, often for six to eight weeks in the host country, these teams evaluate the legal and regulatory framework, the election administration and the role of the media, and other circumstances influencing the election campaign. They work together with short-term observer missions that monitor the actual election, often in collaboration with other international organizations, including the Council of Europe. The ODIHR issues a preliminary statement on the election soon after election day and then makes a final report with recommendations within thirty days, for which the ODIHR may also provide support to help implement (Rotfeld 1997, 146).

The OSCE also set up a Security Forum, which engages in arms control negotiations and disarmament and confidence- and security-building measures, regularly consults on security matters, and oversees implementation of agreed-upon measures. At the 1994 Budapest Summit, the OSCE adopted the Code of Conduct, a landmark development in the area of security cooperation that broke new ground with new norms regulating military-civilian relations in democratic societies. The Economic Forum (strongly advocated by the United States as a means of averting the rise of pan-European economic cooperation through the European Union) was mandated to contribute to stability and cooperation by monitoring economic and environmental developments, with an eye to alerting OSCE states of any threat of conflict, as well as facilitating economic and environmental policies of participating states with transitional economies. It is intended to enhance the OSCE's interaction with other international organizations as well as with NGOs and the private sector.

The OSCE institutional response to the challenges of national minorities questions in the post–Cold War era has its most innovative tool in the form of the Office of the High Commissioner on National Minorities (HCNM), which was set up at the 1992 Helsinki follow-up. According to this mandate, the high commissioner can gather information, carry out visits, and promote dialogue over situations that could develop into conflicts. The HCNM is designed for preventive action through early third-party intervention. The goal of the high commissioner is to improve the parties' relations and facilitate their recourse to nonviolent methods to solve their problems and, in so doing, promote the application of OSCE principles. Thus, the high commissioner aims at setting up procedures or processes that deescalate tensions and may make specific recommendations to these ends. If unsatisfied with the results, the high commissioner may issue an "early warning," whereby further action on his/her part is contingent on consideration by the Permanent Council and the consensus of the participating states. Former Dutch foreign minister Max van der Stoel, who served as the first high commissioner, has generally received high marks for his efforts involving minorities questions in numerous OSCE states, including Albania, Croatia, Estonia, the Former Yugoslav Republic of Macedonia, Hungary, Kazakhstan, Kyrgyzstan, Latvia, Romania, Slovakia, and Ukraine.

The 1999 Istanbul Charter for European Security, signed by the fifty-four OSCE participating states on November 19 after five years of protracted negotiations, further increases the OSCE's ability to deploy peacekeeping forces, enabling development of rapid expert assistance and cooperation teams (REACT) (van Santen 2000, 8–9). It also embraces "an emerging mild security guarantee" (Ghebali 2001, 79). Building on an idea vaguely formulated in the 1994 Code of Conduct on Politico-Military Aspects of Security, the charter commits OSCE members "to consult promptly . . . with a participating State seeking assistance in realising its right to individual or collective self-defence in the event that its sovereignty, territorial integrity and political independence are threatened" in order to "consider jointly the nature of the threat and actions that may be required" in defense of the OSCE's common values. The result was shaped by the nature of the negotiations between contrasting EU and U.S. positions on the one side and what proved to be more far-reaching proposals from the Russian side (Lundin 2000, 20).

At the heart of the debate are differing conceptions of the security risks and challenges confronting Europe. For the Russians, NATO expansion had been a central concern, whereas for other states the focus was on the stationing of foreign military forces without the consent of the host nation and using energy resources to apply political pressure (Ghebali 2001, 78). While Russia's opposition prevented any explicit reference to the stationing of foreign troops without the consent of the host state, the charter does not provide any means of restricting NATO expansion either. Instead, it reaffirms the rights of states to freely choose their security arrangements and declares that "no State, group of States, or organization can have any pre-eminent responsibility for maintaining peace and stability in the OSCE area or can consider any part of the OSCE area as its sphere of influence" (as quoted in Ghebali 2001, 78).

Three other key Russian demands also failed to find their way into the Istanbul Charter. First, Russia pushed for the rationalization of OSCE structures to enhance the overall importance of the OSCE (especially vis-à-vis NATO); second, it sought to make OSCE decisions binding (as a first step toward developing a legal foundation for the OSCE); and third, it argued for the institutionalization of the Security Model Committee—which was responsible for negotiating the Istanbul Charter—to adapt the OSCE to the changing security realities. The OSCE states resisted any major institutional redesign and instead the OSCE continues with the dichotomy, as Ghebali (2001, 80) describes it, "between the general political functions of the Permanent Council and the exclusively politico-military competencies of the Forum for Security Co-operation."

The real success of the Istanbul negotiations can be found in the provision for enhancing the OSCE's operational capabilities, especially in the areas of peacekeeping operations, long-term missions, and joint cooperative actions among international organizations. Here one can point especially to the European Union's initiative in pushing for the adoption of the Platform for Cooperative Security. But the fact that the charter limits the OSCE role in peacekeeping to case-by-case consideration, while other charter provisions call for an OSCE role in policing and reliance on the REACT concept, reflects the success of the U.S. negotiating position of limiting the OSCE peacekeeping role to civil tasks (Ghebali 2001, 81–82).

From Preventive Diplomacy to Consolidating Democracy

As this discussion of the OSCE's institutional redesign indicates, the organization has continued to develop politically flexible mechanisms for conflict prevention and management rather than legal approaches. Although the OSCE approach to early warning and conflict prevention did not start out as a coherent set of norms and principles, it has evolved into a comprehensive and broad view of preventive action, so that preventive measures can be introduced before the onset of violence and also in other phases of the conflict. Crisis management initiatives may also seek to limit the spread of conflict, while postconflict rehabilitation initiatives can work to prevent the renewed outbreak of violence (Abadjian 2000, 23; see also Leatherman et al. 1999).

Along with the HCNM, missions of long duration have proven to be among the most important tools used by the resource-limited OSCE in dealing with the security challenges of the post–Cold War period. Missions of long duration are basically of four types: (1) conflict prevention; (2) crisis management; (3) postconflict rehabilitation; and (4) liaison offices. Preventive missions are charged with engaging the parties in dialogue and monitoring and reporting on local conditions to higher OSCE authorities (the CiO, Troika, and Permanent Council) while collaborating with other OSCE institutions and officials, such as the ODIHR and the HCNM. Examples of conflict prevention missions include missions of long duration in Kosovo, Sandjak, and Vojvodina and missions to Skopje, Estonia, Latvia, and Ukraine (Abadjian 2000, 24; see also Leatherman et al. 1999; Ackermann 2000; William 2000; Mychajlyszyn 1998; Lähelma 1999; Anderson 1999).

Crisis management missions are sent with the objective of preventing an ongoing conflict from worsening while facilitating a search for solutions through monitoring and reporting as well as mediation and negotiation. Examples of these deployments include missions to Georgia, Tajikistan, Moldova, and Albania (Bloed 1998, 40). Postconflict missions operate to keep conflicts from re-igniting and to assist in rehabilitation, as seen in missions to Bosnia and Herzegovina, Croatia, and Kosovo and in activities related to the second stage of the OSCE Presence in Albania (Borchgrevink 1998; Ward 2000). Liaison offices in Central Asia and the Caucasus serve as a tool of preventive diplomacy "by timely identification of threats to security and implementing in practice of the Organization's fundamental principles of comprehensiveness and indivisibility of security" (Abadjian 2000, 25).

The OSCE began to use missions in the early 1990s when it deployed small teams of experts to countries for early warning and prevention, such as the OSCE missions in Latvia and Estonia. In recent years, reliance on missions has increased and the size and complexity of mission tasks have expanded to allow the OSCE to assist in postconflict rehabilitation, as in Bosnia, or to monitor crisis situations, as in Kosovo (Adler 1998). Proposed by Richard Holbrooke in negotiations with Serbian president Slobodan Milosevic without his having first consulted with the OSCE, the Kosovo Verification Mission in fall 1998 (Leurdijk 1999) numbered fourteen hundred (Walker 2001, 128). Although the monitors had to be withdrawn as negotiations broke down and war ensued in spring 1999, the OSCE presence was reinstated later in the year under the UN Mission to Kosovo (UNMIK).

It was the OSCE's early, failed policies toward the Yugoslav crisis in the early 1990s that led to its emphasis on conflict early warning and prevention and, more recently, democratic consolidation (Flynn and Farrell 1999). In early 1992 at the Prague Council Meeting, the OSCE adopted the "consensus-minus-one" provision and used it to suspend Yugoslavia until November 2000. This case, the only instance of a suspension within the OSCE, raised difficult questions about whether an international organization can exercise more influence by continuing the process of dialogue or through a policy of marginalization. Evidence suggests that Belgrade's behavior was not significantly affected by the OSCE action. And by suspending Yugoslavia the OSCE denied itself the possibility of taking other actions, including a role in conflict prevention and interventions by the HCNM (Milinkovic 2001, 21–23). Moreover, in light of the suspension, the Yugoslav authorities refused to renew the visas of OSCE missions to Kosovo, Vojvodina, and Sandjak, thus also diminishing the OSCE's role in the region (Perry 1998, 47). These decisions thus not only hampered the OSCE's ability to intervene early in the Yugoslav crisis but continued to undermine its effectiveness throughout the 1990s as the Kosovo crisis became increasingly acute.

The Yugoslav case stands as the exception, not the rule: Rather than marginalize states threatening peace and security by suspending their participation or shaming them publicly, as was the Cold War approach, the OSCE in other cases has tended toward engagement. This policy has been pursued through the deployment of OSCE missions of long duration, interventions by the HCNM, fact finding, rapporteurs, personal representatives of the chair-in-office, and assistance from the ODIHR. In addition, the OSCE summits, ministerial councils, and at times the documents and decisions of the Permanent Council embody a set of preventive measures (Abadjian 2000, 23; Leatherman

2003). The 1999 Istanbul Charter strengthened this approach both by focusing its long-term missions on democracy and mediation and by its introduction of joint cooperative actions. However, Russian determination to avoid any increases in the authority of the OSCE to intervene in the internal affairs of the participating states (given its concerns about NATO's unilateral intervention in Kosovo) has limited the innovativeness of joint cooperative actions. Thus, the charter conditions joint actions on the consent of the host state and therefore does not foresee the possibility of introducing sanctions, lest the state refuse OSCE assistance. But at least the OSCE has negotiated a move in the direction of an additional mechanism for providing assistance to states facing structural challenges in implementing OSCE commitments, as Albania, for example, did in 1997 when public order collapsed (Ghebali 2001, 83).

The OSCE's comprehensive and broad approach to conflict emphasizing early warning and prevention has undergone a shift from the immediate causes of conflict to finding ways of transforming the root causes (Chigas 1996). For example, the OSCE spillover mission to Macedonia, deployed in September 1992, was to monitor the borders of the host country and prevent the spillover of conflict from the former Yugoslavia until these functions were assumed by the United Nations. In January 1993, the OSCE mission began to give greater emphasis to identifying internal threats and maintaining a dialogue with government and civil society, gradually evolving into democratization and legislation to improve minority relations. Similar kinds of mission shift can be seen in Estonia, Moldova, Latvia, and Tajikistan. Democratization has added a layer of complexity and also raised difficult questions about how to evaluate the success of the OSCE. Democratization is a long-term process of social change, and there are not yet consensual norms about when to withdraw a mission (Abadjian 2000, 26–31).

In contrast to the early OSCE missions, which focused first on the immediate causes of conflict, a second generation of OSCE missions, starting with the mission to Bosnia and Herzegovina and including postconflict missions to Croatia and Kosovo and the OSCE presence in Albania, had an explicit democratization objective in their mandates from the outset. With experience has come the realization that elections are only one tool for promoting democratization, and many other efforts are needed even for elections to succeed, including the development of political parties, election laws, voter registration, fair and independent media, means of supervision and observance, and a nonviolent environment (von Grüningen 2001, xvi; Ducasse-Rogier 2001, 29; Everts 2001). The activities of the OSCE in the Balkans also underscore the multifaceted nature of building democracy and the many challenges facing such projects. In Kosovo, the OSCE has responsibilities for training thirty-five hundred police officers, judges, and prosecutors; monitoring human rights; creating an independent media; and organizing elections (Everts 2001). In Bosnia, the OSCE has faced considerable difficulties in fulfilling such a mandate. There the OSCE has been involved in elections (the first the OSCE has prepared), monitoring human rights, democratization, and military stabilization. Problems in the first round continued to plague subsequent elections. Technical problems, such as the lack of voters' registers in many polling stations, persisted. More important, the assumption that elections were a means to jump-start democratization was also flawed, since many of the preconditions for fair democratic elections were not in place. Perhaps most difficult of all, the nationalist parties that had started the war used the nascent democratic process as a way to gain a new legitimacy and continue to obstruct the implementation of the Dayton Accords (Ducasse-Rogier 2001, 24–26).

Interinstitutional Competition

The OSCE field missions have grown not only in size but also in bureaucratization, thus undermining to some extent the OSCE's comparative advantage as a flexible and highly adaptive organization (Abadjian 2000, 28–33). But the OSCE has not faced this growing complexity by itself. Not only the OSCE but also the Council of Europe, NATO, and the European Union have carved out mandates for preventive action, and the European Union has been developing a new policy on civil conflict management similar to the OSCE's REACT and the operation center mandated by the 1999 Istanbul summit. In the development of a conflict management regime, several institutions vie to fill the newly defined space as members of each organization negotiate their role among themselves and organizations negotiate their roles vis-à-vis one another.

The OSCE's approach to this situation has been to promote mutually reinforcing cooperation to make the OSCE "an integral part of the web of interlocking institutions which deal with European security, human rights and economic issues." These efforts have been under way since the mid-1990s, beginning with the 1994 Budapest Document, "Towards a Genuine Partnership," and the 1996 Lisbon Declaration on a Common and Comprehensive Security Model of Europe for the Twenty-First Century.[18] However, it was only at Istanbul, with the adoption of the Charter of European Security, that the OSCE elaborated a "Platform for Co-operative Security," committing itself to "further strengthen and develop co-operation with competent organizations on the basis of equality and in a spirit of partnership." Mechanisms for enhancing cooperation at the headquarters level include regular contacts and meetings, continuous dialogue, liaison officers, and cross-representation, among others (OSCE 2000, 13). Since Istanbul, the OSCE has opened contacts and negotiations with the United Nations and its agencies, the Council of Europe, the International Organization for Migration, the International Committee of the Red Cross, NATO, the European Union/European Commission, the Western European Union, and the Commonwealth of Independent States, among others (OSCE 2000, 14–15, 20). The Stability Pact for South Eastern Europe is an example of international organizations collaborating to deal with regional conflict-related challenges (Wisse Smit 2000; Hombach 2000).

At the field level, OSCE mechanisms for cooperation encompass information exchanges, joint needs assessment, secondment of experts, liaison officers, common projects and field operations, and joint training (OSCE 2000, 13–14). Since 1998 the OSCE has joined other international organizations in training mission members, and the Council of Europe seconded nine experts to the OSCE mission in Kosovo in 2000. Coordination allows different organizations to assume functional responsibilities for which they are best suited, as in the deployment of civilian police monitors in Croatia on the expiration of the UN Police Support Group mandate.

Albania provides a good example of the complexity of collaboration among international institutions in conducting democratization missions. The OSCE launched a process of mediation by Austrian chancellor Franz Vranitzky to create a government of national reconciliation and prepare parliamentary elections, in collaboration with the European Parliament and the parliamentary assemblies of the OSCE and Council of Europe. The OSCE then deployed a presence to provide electoral assistance, accompanied by an eleven-nation protection force to provide security. The OSCE mission also established a network of offices and representatives along Albania's borders to monitor refugee flows, cross-border traffic, and trafficking in humans and weapons (Borchgrevink 1998, 17; Huisinga 1998, 23). The OSCE also helped draft a new constitution, advance the rule of law and human rights, and develop election assistance. In addition, the OSCE provided a platform for coordinating and evaluating international economic assistance. However, that part of the regime space covering disarmament and control of emerging criminal bands remained unimplemented, resulting in two thousand deaths by summer 1997 (Huisinga 1998, 22).

Negotiating the shape of an emerging regime and various organizations' roles in it is, according to Daan Huisinga, "enhanced when the international community is able to work together and speak with one voice, as was illustrated by the TPM. Nobody, however, likes to be coordinated. Bilateral agendas, institutional jealousies, the staking out of turf, incompatible personalities, and individual professional ambition all hamper effective cooperation. . . . Through its flexible coordination framework the OSCE Presence has identified gaps in international assistance and has facilitated efforts aimed at filling these gaps" (Huisinga 1998, 29). Such operations are not likely to provide quick fixes, not least because democratic practices involve not only institutional change but, more fundamentally, a shift in underlying norms and principles (Huisinga 1998, 29). These are long-term processes of social change that will continue to demand labor-intensive efforts and multifaceted support by the international community, whether in Kosovo or in many of the other transitional countries where the OSCE is engaged. There is now a need to negotiate coordinated, concerted efforts under a focused regional strategy rather than sectoral ad hoc initiatives in the various countries (Ahrens 2001, 34).

Conclusions

Since the initiation of negotiations in Dipoli in 1972, the OSCE has passed through a dynamic process of regime building, governance, and adjustment. The CSCE commitments and the CSCE process helped in important ways to stimulate and legitimize the emergence of dissent in the Eastern bloc while at the same time providing a degree of stability and continued dialogue between East and West. The CSCE benefited substantially from the cybernetic processes that the Helsinki monitoring groups generated as a result of their activities. The ties that developed between civil societies in Eastern Europe and the West emerged out of the conviction of dissidents in the East that in order to end the Cold War, one had to act as if the bloc divisions no longer existed. They thus joined in the pursuit of fundamental freedoms and security and infused the Helsinki process of recurrent negotiations with a greater purpose and relevance than it might otherwise have had. The N+N countries within the CSCE played significant roles in promoting agreements that furthered the continuity of the process. If the human rights movement breathed life into the Final Act during the tense periods of renewed Cold War between East and West, the N+N facilitated the achievement of agreements that kept the CSCE process alive.

The interstate principles as enumerated in the Helsinki Final Act have remained largely intact and their meaning in relation to OSCE commitments and practices was further developed in follow-up and other special meetings. The universality of commitments made under international law has rendered obsolete absolute state sovereignty over human rights questions and has introduced new complexities in state prerogatives vis-à-vis international monitoring, preventive action, and intervention in case of significant threats to humanity. OSCE attention to conflict prevention, crisis management, and postconflict rehabilitation must negotiate its course through these new practical and normative challenges.

Since the end of the Cold War, the OSCE has helped transitional states develop democratic institutions and processes rather than practicing a diplomacy of shaming in regard to human rights abuses. But overlapping mandates and bureaucratic interests among such organizations as NATO, the Council of Europe, the European Union, and the OSCE in particular also create competition in the field and pressure to negotiate with competing organizations to define the new conflict management and democratization regime. These problems also underscore the need for more effective division of labor and use of resources among international organizations, an objective that figured in the 1999 OSCE Charter for European Security under its Platform for Security. Creative task sharing between international and regional organizations will be the major challenge for regional organizations around the world well into the new millennium.

What began in 1973 as a complex set of diplomatic negotiations that turned on a bargain between principles of state security and human rights and humanitarian concerns has evolved into an innovative international organization. Along the way, ideological confrontation and the bloc-based struggle for security were superseded by new commitments to norms and principles of common and comprehensive security. This normative consensus, integrally related to the promotion of democratic peace, has been challenged, however, by new security threats that have emerged as the communist bloc vanished—transnational networks of crime and violence involving human trafficking, drugs, the illicit arms trade, and ethnic violence. The core rule of governance in the twenty-first century cannot focus only on the nation-state monopoly of violence; it must take a transnational perspective. Such a broad approach has come to define the OSCE in the 1990s, which has emphasized such principles as transparency and accountability in interstate relations and the responsibility of states to uphold the rights and dignity not only of their own citizens but of citizens of other states as well. The OSCE has helped to expand this protective shield, however rudimentary it remains at this stage, by negotiating cooperative frameworks among regional and international organizations alike. But since state structures have weakened in the transitional period to the postcommunist era, international organizations will need to continue to negotiate their cooperation in defining the new European regime to promote security and fundamental freedoms and their roles in it, as well as how these responsibilities can be effectively assumed by domestic authorities and members of civil society. Only then will the new European regime be fully in place.

Notes

1. The OSCE was originally called the Conference on Security and Cooperation in Europe, or CSCE. I will use CSCE to refer to the pre-1994 period and OSCE generally to cover events after 1994.

2. "Suomen hallituksen Euroopan turvallisuuskonferenssimuistio 5. 5. 1969," *Englanninos, Ulkopoliittisia Lausuntoja ja Asiakirjoja* (1969), 65–66.

3. The Conference on Security and Cooperation in Europe was initially composed of all the member-states of NATO and the Warsaw Pact, the European Community, and the European neutral and nonaligned states. Albania was the only state not to participate, but it joined after the Cold War ended, along with the Soviet successor states and the newly independent states from the former Yugoslavia. Presently the number of OSCE participating states stands at fifty-five, although one of these states—the former Yugoslavia (that is, Serbia-Montenegro)—was suspended from 1992 to 2000 because of Serbian violations of OSCE commitments. The Former Yugoslav Republic of Macedonia's entry was initially blocked by Greece over objections to the country's name. The significance of the term "participating states" in CSCE practice stems from the political rather than legal character of the CSCE agreements. This is in contrast to legally binding treaties, which typically refer to the "High Contracting Parties."

4. The Decalogue is composed of Principles: I, Sovereign Equality, Respect for the Rights Inherent in Sovereignty; II, Refraining from the Threat or Use of Force; III, Inviolability of Frontiers; IV, Territorial Integrity of States; V, Peaceful Settlement of Disputes; VI, Non-intervention in Internal

Affairs; VII, Respect for Human Rights and Fundamental Freedoms, Including the Freedom of Thought, Conscience, Religion or Belief; VIII, Equal Rights and Self-Determination of Peoples; IX, Co-operation among States; and X, Fulfillment in Good Faith of Obligations under International Law.

5. Principle X reads that "in exercising their sovereign rights, including the right to determine their laws and regulations, they will conform with their legal obligations under international law; they will furthermore pay due regard to and implement the provisions in the Final Act" (§2). It states further that "[a]ll the principles set forth above [that is, all the ten principles] are of primary significance and, accordingly, they will be equally and unreservedly applied, each of them being interpreted taking into account the others" (§4). Hence the overall equality and interdependence of the Final Act's provisions.

6. For example, the European Community took an independent stance during the first CSCE follow-up negotiations in Belgrade in 1977–78, distancing itself from the more polemical position of the United States, led by Ambassador Goldberg, in an attempt to fashion a compromise between Soviet and U.S. positions on human rights questions and to provide a basis for a final substantive agreement to the Belgrade meeting (see Leatherman 2003; Kirk Laux 1984).

7. The first CSCE expert meeting to be held in a communist bloc country, the 1985 Budapest Cultural Forum, was only the second CSCE meeting open to nondiplomats. As Lehne observes, the participation of leading cultural figures from across the CSCE states "gave the meeting a unique atmosphere." Over nine hundred persons were accredited, a CSCE record. Parallel to the Cultural Forum, the International Helsinki Federation organized its own forum held in private apartments to bring together leading Eastern and Western intellectuals. Lehne argues that it had an "impact on the international debate on reform in Eastern Europe that equalled or even exceeded that of the official forum" (1991a: 31).

8. See the Helsinki Final Act, Followup to the Conference, §2(a).

9. The final text was called the Concluding Document of the Belgrade Meeting 1977 of Representatives of the Participating States of the CSCE—despite its communiqué-like character.

10. Because they are politically, not legally, binding, there is no ratification process as part of the implementation procedures, and thus the CSCE commitments are not subject to domestic legal and constitutional constraints. This also facilitates a more flexible approach to modifying agreements and interpretive rule making. However, the political character of the endeavor also carries certain risks, in that the CSCE may also be subject to the vagaries of political opportunism and posturing. Whether the political nature of human rights commitments makes them more vulnerable to noncompliance than legally binding commitments cannot, however, be easily judged (Buergenthal 1993, 7).

11. Final Act, Follow-up to the Conference, §2a.

12. The Final Act foresaw two such events, a meeting to discuss the Swiss proposal for the peaceful settlement of disputes to take place after the Belgrade follow-up (Basket I, Principle X: [b] Matters related to giving effect to certain of the above principles [ii]); and a Scientific Forum (Basket III: 4 Cooperation and exchanges in the field of education: [c] Science), also convened subsequent to the Belgrade follow-up.

13. Stressing the importance of Principle III over the other principles was a violation of the obligation to hold all principles of the Final Act of "primary significance," to be "equally and unreservedly applied." Moreover, the Soviets followed this pattern in the Soviet-GDR treaty of October 7, 1975, and also "described the GDR's borders as immutable," Soviet terminology that had been specifically rejected in Helsinki in favor of inviolability. *First Semiannual Report by the President to the Commission on Security and Cooperation in Europe* (December 1976), 16.

14. *First Semiannual Report*, 16 n. 28.

15. See Eduard A. Shevardnadze, *Vienna Meeting 1986 Verbatim Record of the Opening Statements, November 4–7, 1986,* CSCE/WT/VR.3.

16. See *Human Rights and Democratization in Bulgaria: Implementation of the Helsinki Accords.* Report Prepared by the Staff of the Commission on Security and Cooperation in Europe, Washington, D.C. September 1993, 2.

17. See also the Commission on Security and Cooperation in Europe, *The Helsinki Process and East West Relations: Progress in Perspective. A Report on the Positive Aspect of the Implementation of the Helsinki Final Act, 1975–84* (March 1985), 12. The New York–based Helsinki Watch Committee is one of ten such monitoring groups located in the United States, Canada, and Western Europe.

18. OSCE's *Annual Report 2000 on Interaction between Organizations and Institutions in the OSCE Area.*

References

Abadjian, Vahram. 2000. "OSCE Long-Term Missions: Exit Strategy and Related Problems." *Helsinki Monitor* 11 (1): 22–36.

Ackermann, Alice. 2000. *Making Peace Prevail: Preventing Violent Conflict in Macedonia*. Syracuse, N.Y.: Syracuse University Press.

Adler, Emanuel. 1998. "Seeds of Peaceful Change: The OSCE's Security Community-Building Model." In *Security Communities*, ed. Emanuel Adler and Michael Barnett. Cambridge: Cambridge University Press.

Ahrens, Geert-Hinrich. 2001. "Albania: A Status Report." In *The Operational Role of the OSCE in South-Eastern Europe*, ed. Victor-Yves Ghebali and Daniel Warner. Aldershot, England: Ashgate.

Anderson, Norman. 1999. "OSCE Preventive Diplomacy in the Former Yugoslav Republic of Macedonia." *Helsinki Monitor* 10 (2): 49–64.

Bloed, A. 1993a. "Monitoring the CSCE Human Dimension: In Search of Its Effectiveness." In *Monitoring Human Rights in Europe*, ed. Arie Bloed et al. Boston: Martinus Nijhoff.

———. 1998. "OSCE Involvement in Albania." OSCE Chronicle. *Helsinki Monitor* 9 (1): 40–47.

———, ed. 1993b. *The Conference on Security and Co-operation in Europe. Analysis and Basic Documents 1972–1993*. Boston: Kluwer.

Borchgrevink, Aage. 1998. "Albania's Second Transition." *Helsinki Monitor* 9 (4): 9–17.

Brown, J. F. 1991. *Surge to Freedom: The End of Communist Rule in Eastern Europe*. Durham, N.C.: Duke University Press.

Buergenthal, Thomas. 1991. "The CSCE Rights System." *George Washington Journal of International Law and Economics* 25: 333–386.

———. 1993. "The CSCE Rights System (Excerpt)." *CSCE ODIHR Bulletin* 1 (3): 5–7.

Chigas, Diana, with Elizabeth McClintock and Christophe Kamp. 1996. "Preventive Diplomacy and the Organization for Security and Cooperation in Europe: Creating Incentives for Dialogue and Cooperation." In *Preventing Conflict in the Post-Communist World*, ed. Abram Chayes and Antonia Handler Chayes. Washington, D.C.: Brookings.

Commission on Security and Cooperation in Europe. 1997. *The OSCE after the Lisbon Summit*. Washington, D.C.: CSCE.

Ducasse-Rogier, Marianne. 2001. "The Operational Role of the OSCE in the Field of Peace-Building: The Case of Bosnia-Herzegovina." In *The Operational Role of the OSCE in South-Eastern Europe*, ed. Victor-Yves Ghebali and Daniel Warner. Aldershot, England: Ashgate.

Everts, Dan. 2001. "Kosovo: Status Report." In *The Operational Role of the OSCE in South-Eastern Europe,* ed. Victor-Yves Ghebali and Daniel Warner. Aldershot, England: Ashgate.

Flynn, Gregory, and Henry Farrell. 1999. "Piecing Together the Democratic Peace: The CSCE, Norms, and the Construction of Security in Post–Cold War Europe." *International Organization* 53 (3): 505–535.

Ghebali, Victor-Yves. 1989. *La Diplomatie de la détente: La CSCE, d'Helsinki à Vienne (1973–1989).* Brussels: Établissements Emile Bruylant.

———. 1996. *L'OSCE dans l'Europe post-communiste, 1990–1996: Vers une identité paneuropéene de sécurité.* Brussels: Établissements Emile Bruylant.

———. 2001. "The 1999 Istanbul Charter for European Security: A Critical Assessment." In *The Operational Role of the OSCE in South-Eastern Europe,* ed. Victor-Yves Ghebali and Daniel Warner. Aldershot, England: Ashgate.

Hoedt, S., and Lefeber, R. 1991. "Europe: Divided We Stand." In *The Changing Political Structure of Europe: Aspects of International Law,* ed. R. Lefeber, M. Fitzmaurice, and E. W. Vierdag. Boston: Martinus Nijhoff.

Homans, George. 1961. *Social Behavior.* New York: Harcourt, Brace and World.

Hombach, Bodo. 2000. "Stability Pact Receives Vital Boost: Interview with Bodo Hombach, Special Co-ordinator of the Stability Pact." *European Security* 8 (1): 1, 10–11.

Huisinga, Daan. 1998. "Consolidation of Democracy and the Rule of Law in Albania: OSCE Assistance Efforts." *Helsinki Monitor* 9 (4): 18–29.

Jakobson, Max. 1983. *38 Kerros: Havaintoja ja Muistiinpanoja vuosilta 1965–1971.* Helsinki: Otava.

Kirk Laux, Jeanne. 1984. "Human Contacts, Information, Culture, and Education." In *Canada and the Conference on Security and Co-operation in Europe,* ed. Robert Spencer. Toronto: University of Toronto.

Lähelma, Timo. 1999. "The OSCE's Role in Conflict Prevention: The Case of Estonia." *Helsinki Monitor* 10 (2): 19–38.

Leary, Virginia A. 1980. "The Rights of the Individual to Know and Act upon His Rights and Duties: Monitoring Groups and the Helsinki Final Act." *Vanderbilt Journal of Transnational Law* 13: 375–395.

Leatherman, Janie. 1993. "Conflict Transformation in the CSCE: Learning and Institutionalization." *Cooperation and Conflict* 28 (3).

———. 2003. *From Cold War to Democratic Peace: Third Parties, Peaceful Change, and the OSCE* (working title). Syracuse, N.Y.: Syracuse University Press.

Leatherman, Janie, et al. 1999. *Breaking Cycles of Violence.* West Hartford, Conn.: Kumarian Press.

Lehne, S. 1991a. *The CSCE in the 1990s: Common European House or Potemkin Village?* Vienna: Braumüller.

———. 1991b. *The Vienna Meeting of the Conference on Security and Cooperation in Europe, 1986–1989.* Boulder, Colo.: Westview.

Leurdijk, Dick A. 1999. "Kosovo: A Case of 'Coercive Diplomacy.'" *Helsinki Monitor* 10 (2): 8–18.

Lundin, Lars-Erik. 2000. "The Charter for European Security from a European Union (EU) Perspective." *Helsinki Monitor* 11 (1): 8–10.

Maresca, John J. 1985. *To Helsinki: The Conference on Security and Cooperation in Europe, 1973–1975.* Durham, N.C.: Duke University Press.

Milinkovic, Branislav. 2001. "The OSCE and the FRY: The Beginning of a New Relationship." *Helsinki Monitor* 12 (1): 21–29.

Mychajlyszyn, Natalie. 1998. "The OSCE in Crimea." *Helsinki Monitor* 9 (4): 30–43.

OSCE. 2000. *Annual Report 2000 on Interaction between Organizations and Institutions in the OSCE Area (November 1, 1999–October 31, 2000).* Vienna: OSCE.

Pentikäinen, Merja, and Martin Scheinin. 1993. "A Comparative Study of the Monitoring Mechanisms and the Important Institutional Frameworks for Human Rights Protection within the Council of Europe, the CSCE, and the European Community." In *Monitoring Human Rights in Europe,* ed. Arie Bloed et al. Boston: Martinus Nijhoff.

Perry, Valery. 1998. "The OSCE Suspension of the Federal Republic of Yugoslavia." *Helsinki Monitor* 9 (4): 44–54.

Rotfeld, Adam Daniel. 1997. "Europe: In Search of Cooperative Security." In *SIPRI Yearbook 1997: Armaments, Disarmament, and International Security.* Oxford: Oxford University Press.

Schoutheete, Philippe. 1980. *La Coopération politique européenne.* Brussels: Éditions Labor-Nathan.

Skilling, Gordon. 1984. "The Belgrade Follow-Up." In *Canada and the Conference on Security and Co-operation in Europe,* ed. Robert Spencer. Toronto: University of Toronto Press.

van Santen, Hans. 2000. "The Istanbul Summit: A Moderate Success." *Helsinki Monitor* 11 (1): 11–21.

von Grüningen, Marianne. 2001. "Introductory Remarks." In *The Operational Role of the OSCE in South-Eastern Europe,* ed. Victor-Yves Ghebali and Daniel Warner. Aldershot, England: Ashgate.

Walker, William G. 2001. "OSCE Verification Experiences in Kosovo: November 1998–June 1999." In *The Kosovo Tragedy,* ed. Ken Booth. London: Frank Cass.

Ward, Benjamin. 2000. "The Failure to Protect Minorities in Post–Cold War Kosovo." *Helsinki Monitor* 11 (1): 37–47.

Weitz, Richard. 1993. "Pursuing Military Security in Eastern Europe." In *After the Cold War: International Institutions and State Strategies in Europe: 1989–1991,* ed. Robert O. Keohane, Joseph S. Nye, and Stanley Hoffmann. Cambridge, Mass.: Harvard University Press.

William, Abiodun. 2000. *Preventing War: The United Nations and Macedonia.* Lanham, Md.: Rowman and Littlefield.

Wisse Smit, Mabel. 2000. "The Jury Is Still Out on the Stability Pact for South Eastern Europe." *Helsinki Monitor* 11 (2): 7–19.

6

The
Ozone Depletion
Regime

Pamela S. Chasek

THE 1987 MONTREAL PROTOCOL on Substances That Deplete the Ozone Layer is widely seen as the basis for one of the more successful international environmental regimes. The Montreal Protocol has shown how an environmental treaty can thrive as a result of a unique collaboration between scientists and policymakers based on continually evolving theories; state-of-the-art computer models; and satellite, land-, and rocket-based monitoring of remote gases. This chapter examines the way in which this collaboration has led to the evolution and strengthening of the ozone regime.

While much attention has been given to the formation of the ozone regime—specifically, negotiation of the 1985 Vienna Convention for the Protection of the Ozone Layer and the subsequent Montreal Protocol—less consideration has been given to the way in which the regime has evolved. As I. William Zartman points out in chapter 1, the dominant element of regime evolution is negotiation, a process that is "too little considered in the study of regimes." As with all regimes, the difficult work of bringing the agreement back home and implementing it began after the Montreal Protocol was adopted. This implementation process has involved everything from ratification of the agreement to changing domestic laws and regulations, revising standards, modifying targets, devising enforcement mechanisms, and building new institutional structures. In other words, regime creation does not stop when the initial agreement is signed. Negotiation continues as regimes evolve. As Bertram I. Spector points out in chapter 2, regimes operate in a "postagreement" negotiation mode that certainly bears some resemblance to its forebears but also demonstrates many unique characteristics as well. The prevalence of negotiation activities extends from immediate regime implementation to governance and expansion of the regime over time. These negotiations take place not only at the international level but also at the national level since governments must embark on their own negotiations to ratify and implement the protocol at home.

National-level negotiations involve participation by various stakeholders, including government ministries and agencies, political parties, business, nongovernmental organizations (NGOs), and the public.

They usually take the form of both formal negotiations in institutional settings such as national parliaments and informal negotiations and debates within the bureaucracy and in the public media. At the international level, negotiations are often aimed at both the operational implementation of the agreement and tightening loopholes. Negotiations aimed at implementation concern the way in which agreement provisions are operationally defined, formalized, and implemented to create a regime. Issues in such negotiations can include membership rules, voting rules, development of institutions, and relationships between regime members and external entities. In this case, the negotiations aimed at tightening loopholes focused primarily on adjusting and amending the original protocol to keep up with the ever-increasing scientific evidence on the role of anthropogenic chemicals in the depletion of the Earth's ozone layer as well as addressing previously unforeseen problems.

Although many of the key actions that, in the long run, will actually determine the implementation and effectiveness of the protocol take place at the national level, the analysis that follows focuses primarily on the postagreement negotiations at the international level that play the largest role in regime formation and governance. These negotiations can be divided into three subprocesses: regime creation, regime adjustment, and regime operation/governance. This analysis looks first at the history of the treaty and then examines each of these three subprocesses to determine the functions of postagreement negotiations and how these negotiations differ from negotiation of the protocol itself.

The History of the Initial Agreement

The objective of the negotiations that resulted in the Montreal Protocol was to protect the ozone layer by taking precautionary measures to control global emissions of substances that deplete it. Ozone is an unstable molecule composed of three atoms of oxygen and has the property of being able to absorb certain wavelengths of ultraviolet radiation in the Earth's stratosphere, approximately six to thirty miles above the Earth's surface. These ultraviolet rays could damage and cause mutations in human, animal, and plant cells if they were not absorbed by the ozone layer.

In 1974, Mario Molina and Sherwood Rowland at the University of California, Irvine, discovered that the Earth's stratospheric ozone layer is at risk from a family of widely used anthropogenic chemicals known as chlorofluorocarbons (CFCs). Unlike most other gases, CFCs are not chemically broken down or rained out quickly in the lower atmosphere but instead persist and migrate slowly up to the stratosphere because of their exceptionally stable chemical structure (Benedick 1991). Molina and Rowland argued that the chlorine in CFC emissions reacts with and breaks down ozone molecules in the thin layer of stratospheric ozone and thus hinders the ozone layer's ability to prevent harmful ultraviolet rays from reaching the Earth (Molina and Rowland 1974).

In 1975, the United Nations Environment Programme (UNEP) first introduced the issue of ozone depletion to the UN system when it funded a study by the World Meteorological Society on the Molina/Rowland theory. In 1977, the United States, Canada, Finland, Norway, and Sweden urged UNEP to consider the international regulation of CFCs, a move based on the same theory. In March 1977, UNEP held a conference with experts from thirty-two countries that adopted the World Plan of Action on the Ozone Layer. Although international action to regulate CFC use was suggested as a policy option, there was still much scientific uncertainty and the idea was dropped. UNEP did, however, establish a Coordinating Committee on the Ozone Layer to determine the extent of the problem as a guide for future international action (Porter, Brown, and Chasek 2000).

In May 1981, the UNEP Governing Council authorized negotiations toward an international agreement on protecting the ozone layer. The Ad Hoc Working Group of Legal and Technical Experts for the Elaboration of a Global Framework Convention for the Protection of the Ozone Layer, which included representatives from twenty-four nations, began meeting in 1982. By March 1985, when representatives from forty-three nations convened in Vienna to finalize the convention, they were able to agree to cooperate only on monitoring, research, and data exchanges. The resulting Vienna Convention for the Protection of the Ozone Layer imposed no specific obligations on the signatories to reduce production of ozone-depleting chemicals and did not even specify what chemicals caused ozone depletion (Porter, Brown, and Chasek 2000; Benedick 1991).

At the last minute in Vienna, however, the United States and other members of the Toronto Group introduced a resolution authorizing UNEP to reopen diplomatic negotiations with a 1987 target for arriving at a legally binding control protocol. As a result of this resolution, two workshops were held in 1986, one in Rome and the other in Leesburg, Virginia, that enabled the negotiators to reassess the ozone/CFC problem.[1]

The first round of negotiations took place in Geneva in December 1986. Nineteen industrialized countries and six relatively advanced developing nations attended the week-long session. The negotiating parties appeared to be divided into three major camps, basically unchanged from the Vienna Conference twenty months earlier. Officially, the European Community, negotiating as a bloc, followed the industry line and reflected the views of France, Italy, and the United Kingdom. The European Community continued to advocate some form of production capacity cap but argued that there was time to delay actual production cuts and wait for more scientific evidence. Japan and the Soviet Union shared this perspective. In contrast, Canada, Finland, New Zealand, Norway, Sweden, Switzerland, and the United States publicly endorsed strong new controls. Despite gaps in knowledge, these governments were convinced that further delay would increase health and environmental risks to an unacceptable degree. A third group of active participants, including Australia, Austria, and a number of developing countries, were initially uncommitted.

At the second session, which met in Vienna from February 23–27, 1987, representatives from thirty-one countries debated the issues. Canada, the Nordic states, Egypt, Mexico, New Zealand, and Switzerland supported the U.S. text, which called for an initial freeze followed by cutbacks until CFCs were eliminated by the year 2000. Important gaps continued to separate the United States and the

European Community on virtually every substantive issue. An important step forward was the setting of a firm September date for the final plenipotentiaries' conference in Montreal, which "both turned up the pressure and eradicated any lingering doubts or wishful thinking about the seriousness of the intent to push forward to a protocol" (Benedick 1991, 71).

The third negotiating session took place in Geneva in April 1987. Thirty-three nations participated, including eleven developing countries. UNEP executive director Mostafa Tolba attended for the first time and organized a series of closed meetings of key delegation heads,[2] away from the formality of the large plenary sessions, to focus on the crucial control measures. This group was able to produce an unofficial draft by the end of the session (Benedick 1991).

In June 1987, Tolba reconvened his group of key delegation heads in Brussels to consider the controls and other major provisions. In July a small number of legal experts met in The Hague to analyze the entire protocol text as it had emerged from various working groups in order to produce a relatively uncluttered and consistent draft for the final negotiating session.

The parties reconvened in Montreal on September 8, 1987. Sixty governments, of which more than half were developing countries, sent delegations. The first six days were devoted to attempts in various working groups to reach greater convergence on the many bracketed portions of the text. On September 14, the plenipotentiary conference was convened to complete the negotiations. A number of factors have been credited with forging the final compromise, including disunity within the European Community (with the Federal Republic of Germany, Denmark, Belgium, and the Netherlands all urging stronger regulation), the personal role played by Tolba, relentless diplomatic pressure by the United States, and a certain reluctance to be blamed for the failure of the conference (Porter, Brown, and Chasek 2000). The final compromise included a pledge by industrialized countries to reduce CFC production by 50 percent of 1986 levels by 1999. Developing countries were permitted to increase their use of CFCs substantially for the first decade up to 0.66 pound (0.3 kilogram) per capita annually. The Montreal Protocol on Substances That Deplete the Ozone Layer was adopted on September 16, 1987.

Regime Formation: September 1987 to May 1989

After the adoption of the protocol, a new process began—the regime creation process, impelled by exogenous events, usually more scientific information. With the negotiated agreement as a guide, the regime formation process, as defined by Spector in chapter 3, involves the implementation and institutionalization of the agreed-upon rules and procedures. Many partial or imprecise agreements must be further elaborated through negotiation among signatories after they have entered into force. Thus, international negotiations during this phase of post-agreement negotiations concern how agreement provisions are operationally defined, formalized, and implemented. These negotiations actually create the regime out of the initial agreement. Issues in such negotiations can include membership procedures, voting procedures, institutional development, and relationships between regime members and external entities.

During the period after the protocol's adoption and before its entry into force and the first meeting of the parties in 1989, several factors can be credited with laying the path for efficient regime building: growing scientific evidence, national ratification and implementation programs, and the role of UNEP executive director Tolba.

The Role of the Scientific Community

The rapid ratification process (fifteen months) and the effectiveness of the regime-building process were a direct result of the scientific evidence on ozone depletion and the chemicals that cause it. On September 30, 1987, just two weeks after the signing of the Montreal Protocol, the U.S. National Aeronautics and Space Administration (NASA) and the National Oceanic and Atmospheric Administration (NOAA) released interim findings from an international scientific expedition in Antarctica. The data revealed a substantial worsening of the seasonal ozone depletion. The initial report did not, however, attribute the Antarctic ozone hole solely to CFCs (NASA/NOAA 1987).

On March 15, 1988, the report of the Ozone Trends Panel was released—a sixteen-month comprehensive scientific exercise involving more than one hundred scientists from ten countries. The panel found that human activities were causing atmospheric concentrations of chlorine to increase on a global scale. Depletion of the ozone layer was occurring not only over Antarctica but also over heavily populated regions of the Northern Hemisphere (NASA 1988). The implications of these new scientific findings were "profoundly disquieting" (Benedick 1991, 111). The model projections underlying the control provisions in the Montreal Protocol had assumed a probable global average ozone loss of approximately 2 percent by the middle of the twenty-first century. Now it was revealed that more than this had already occurred and ozone depletion appeared to be accelerating with increased accumulation of atmospheric chlorine.

Thus, by the first meeting of the parties, which was held in Helsinki on May 2–5, 1989, the scientific community had established that CFCs and halons were a primary factor in the cause of Antarctic ozone loss. In Helsinki, NASA's Robert Watson reported that the majority of the approximately 3 parts per billion of chlorine in the atmosphere came from anthropogenic sources. Calculations indicated that, even with full global implementation of the regulatory measures of the Montreal Protocol, atmospheric chlorine concentrations would increase to more than 6 parts per billion during the next few decades. Under these conditions the Antarctic ozone hole could never fill up. He said that in order to reduce the atmospheric levels of chlorine, it would be necessary to phase out all the substances controlled under the protocol, and he recommended strict limitations on carbon tetrachloride and methyl chloroform (UNEP 1989).

Activities at the National Level

During this period most of the activity was taking place at the national level. The Montreal Protocol would not enter into force until at least eleven countries, accounting for at least two-thirds of the world's

CFC consumption, formally ratified it. In March 1988 Mexico became the first country to ratify, followed three weeks later by the United States. By the end of July, Canada, New Zealand, Norway, and Sweden had all ratified. By the end of November ten more countries had ratified (Byelorussian SSR, Egypt, Japan, Kenya, Luxembourg, Nigeria, Portugal, Uganda, Ukrainian SSR, and the USSR). However, without at least two of the large European nations joining, the protocol could not enter into force. In mid-December 1988 the European Commission together with eight of its twelve member-governments ratified. Thus the Montreal Protocol entered into force on January 1, 1989, with twenty-nine countries, plus the European Commission, ratifying, accounting for an estimated 83 percent of global consumption of CFCs and halons.

Activities of the UNEP Executive Director

In January 1988, UNEP executive director Mostafa Tolba convened a meeting in Paris of about a dozen senior advisers from governments, environmental organizations, and industry to consider practical details of implementing the protocol. They agreed that the main goal was the early entry into force of the treaty and the broadest possible participation. The group created an implementation timetable, which included the following:

1. A meeting of experts in Nairobi in March 1988 to determine procedures for governments to report production and consumption data on CFCs and halons to UNEP.
2. Three meetings in October 1988 in The Hague: a scientific symposium to update findings on the state of the ozone layer, a meeting of legal and technical experts to develop recommendations for the first meeting of parties; and a technical workshop for industry on the status of research into substitutes and alternative technologies.
3. The first meeting of parties was rescheduled from November 1988 to May 1989.
4. Scientific, environmental, economic, and technological assessments would be completed not in 1990, as originally scheduled, but in 1989.

Thus, even before the protocol formally entered into force, the scientific community, national ratification processes, and Tolba and UNEP played a lead role in keeping governments focused on ozone depletion. These actions kept the issue on the international agenda and helped to ensure that the ratification schedule would be met.

First Meeting of the Parties

The first Meeting of Parties (MOP) to the Montreal Protocol was convened on May 2, 1989, in Helsinki. Delegates from more than eighty nations attended, even though only thirty-one were actually parties to the protocol. The protocol, which had been in force for only five months, could not legally be revised at this meeting, since any proposed amendments and adjustments must be submitted to UNEP, in its role as the secretariat, for communication to all parties at least six months before the meeting of parties that would consider them (Article 2, paragraph 9). Nevertheless, growing scientific evidence spurred the Helsinki Conference to renegotiate a political agreement to strengthen international controls. This agreement—the Helsinki Declaration on the Protection of the Ozone Layer—encouraged all states that had not done so to join the Vienna Convention for the Protection of the Ozone Layer and its Montreal Protocol. The Helsinki Declaration also stated the parties' agreement to

◆ phase out the production and consumption of CFCs controlled by the protocol as soon as possible, but not later than the year 2000, and, for that purpose, to tighten the timetable agreed upon in the Montreal Protocol;

◆ both phase out halons and control and reduce other ozone-depleting substances as soon as feasible;

◆ accelerate the development of environmentally acceptable substituting chemicals, products, and technologies; and

◆ facilitate the access of developing countries to relevant scientific information, research, and training, and seek to develop appropriate funding mechanisms to facilitate the transfer of technology and the replacement of equipment at minimum cost to developing countries.

The MOP also made a number of decisions at this meeting aimed at regime building or formation. Without the establishment of such rules, the provisions of the agreement could not be effectively implemented or monitored by the international community. The preparatory work organized by Tolba greatly facilitated agreement on such issues as

◆ the Rules of Procedure for Meetings of the Parties;

◆ the composition of the bureau;

◆ the establishment, in accordance with Article 6, of four review panels: Panel for Scientific Assessment, Panel for Environmental Assessment, Panel for Technical Assessment, and Panel for Economic Assessment;

◆ elements for the workplans required by Articles 9 and 10;

◆ the establishment of an Open-Ended Working Group to review the reports of the four panels, prepare draft proposals for amendments, and develop the workplans;

◆ the establishment of an Open-Ended Ad Hoc Working Group of Legal Experts to develop proposals for procedures and institutional mechanisms for determining noncompliance and for the treatment of parties that fail to comply with its terms;

◆ reporting guidelines; and

◆ the establishment of an Open-Ended Working Group to develop modalities for an adequate funding mechanism to enable developing countries to meet the requirements of the protocol.

After making the necessary decisions to ensure that the regime-building process was set in motion, the postagreement negotiation process shifted to a new phase: regime adjustment.

Regime Adjustment—Part I: June 1989 to June 1990

As Spector defines it in chapter 2, in the postagreement negotiation process, regime adjustment is the process in which the rules, procedures, and targets originally established in the negotiated agreement might be modified in conjunction with new information collected on the effects of compliance and, especially in the case of environmental issues, as science learns more about the problem. If significant changes to a regime are required, renegotiation may be called for. Otherwise, adjustments may be reflected in the need for additional domestic rule making. In many cases, regime adjustment may not take place at all or may occur only some years after a treaty has entered into force.

In the case of the Montreal Protocol, regime adjustment took place even before many of the regime-building decisions on administration, monitoring, reporting, and compliance had been set in place. Due to growing scientific evidence about the depletion of the ozone layer and its causes, the first series of postagreement negotiations aimed at strengthening the protocol took place between August 1989 and May 1990. At the national level, a number of new governments ratified the protocol and others started their own processes to enact laws and regulations to conform to the stipulations of the agreement. The regime adjustment negotiations at the international level encompassed two areas: strengthening the protocol's control measures and the treatment of developing countries. In the former, the negotiations were influenced by the latest scientific research, lobbying activities by the environmental community and industry, and Mostafa Tolba. The industrialized parties to the protocol continued to be the major actors at the negotiating table. In the latter, the negotiations assumed the traditional North-South focus that has characterized many international negotiations on environmental and development issues. In this case, the developing countries wanted to ensure that they were able to receive the necessary financial and technological assistance to enable them to phase out their use of CFCs and other ozone-depleting chemicals. The industrialized countries supported this goal but were concerned about their obligations and the mechanisms by which this transfer of funds and technology would take place.

Negotiations on Strengthening the Controls

The four assessment panels established in Helsinki completed their work in the summer of 1989. The summary of the panels' conclusions (the Synthesis Report) became the basis for the negotiations of the Open-Ended Working Group to prepare recommendations for revising the protocol. The Synthesis Report declared that a complete and timely phaseout of all major ozone-depleting substances with worldwide compliance was of paramount importance in protecting the ozone layer (UNEP 1989a). The longer the delay in implementing such measures, the longer the recovery time for the ozone layer, stated the working group. In addition to the substances already controlled by the protocol (CFCs and halons), the following ozone-depleting chemicals should also be controlled: hydrochlorofluorocarbons (HCFCs), methyl chloroform, and carbon tetrachloride.

The working group also noted that the accelerating pace of industrial research, testing, and technological innovation in 1988 and 1989 had considerably increased the options for replacing and conserving CFCs. While most of industry was by this time generally reconciled to the inevitability of eliminating all substances that threaten the ozone layer, the large chemical companies continued to stress the costs and difficulties of phaseout and appeared to want to postpone it as long as possible (Benedick 1991).

With these considerations in mind, during the course of seven meetings in late 1989 and early 1990, representatives from more than fifty countries participated in the Open-Ended Working Group. No distinction was made between parties and nonparties; however, only parties were eligible to propose new language. Industry was also well represented at the sessions. According to Benedick (1991:140–141),

> Although these negotiations had approximately the same nine-month duration as those preceding the original treaty, there were many more meetings, and they were in many ways more complicated and difficult, reflecting the much higher number of participants and the increasing complexity of the issues. The broad consensus of the Helsinki Declaration proved unexpectedly difficult to render into legally binding provisions. Indeed, so many widely varying proposals for protocol revisions were presented that the evolving draft texts threatened to become unmanageable. It soon became apparent that the working group would not be able to agree on specific recommendations that, according to the terms of the Vienna Convention and the Montreal Protocol, had to be

delivered by the UNEP secretariat to governments six months before a meeting of parties.

With unaccustomed indulgence, government legal experts determined that this requirement did not mean that negotiators could not look at proposals presented after December 1989, "as long as such proposals are sufficiently related to proposals communicated to the Parties." ... Accordingly, the working group's recommendations were submitted in December in the form of a single text with dozens of bracketed options and alternative formulations; governments were thus able to continue the necessary deliberations . . . right up to the June 1990 meeting of parties.

At the first meeting of the working group in August 1989, Mostafa Tolba offered the following "cautious" recommendations: (1) a phaseout of currently controlled CFCs by the end of the century; (2) a 50 percent reduction of currently controlled halons by 1995; (3) the inclusion of carbon tetrachloride and methyl chloroform as controlled substances, with unspecified phaseout schedules; and (4) a requirement to report data on production and trade in HCFC substitutes (UNEP 1989b).

A month later, the Bureau of the Parties to the Montreal Protocol met with Tolba in Geneva and formulated more detailed recommendations for consideration by the working group. Benedick (1991) notes that use of the bureau in this manner had "no analogue in the less complex process leading up to Montreal." The bureau met with Tolba four times in 1989 and 1990 and played an important role in defining issues for the larger group. The bureau's proposals on new control measures included (1) a 50 percent reduction in CFCs by 1994 or 1995, an 85 percent reduction by 1998, and phaseout by 2000; (2) development of more information on "essential needs" as a basis for the working group to recommend phaseout targets for halons; (3) a 50 percent reduction in carbon tetrachloride and methyl chloroform by 1992 or 1993, an 85 percent reduction by 1998, and phaseout by 2000; and (4) HCFC controls that permit only use in "critical" products as decided by the parties (UNEP 1989c).

In November 1989, the European Community, Australia, Austria, Canada, Finland, New Zealand, Norway, Sweden, and Switzerland went beyond the bureau's recommendation and proposed advancing the protocol's target date for CFC reduction. The United States and Japan, however, wanted more time for the interim reductions. Australia, Canada, Finland, New Zealand, Norway, Sweden, Switzerland, and the United States advocated a complete phaseout of all halons by the end of the century. In contrast, the European Community, Japan, and the Soviet Union were concerned about the continuing unavailability of alternatives in some critical uses (Benedick 1991).

With regard to the chemicals not yet covered by the protocol, there was general consensus that carbon tetrachloride should be phased out by the year 2000, with various proposals for interim reduction steps. Methyl chloroform proved to be more contentious, however, because of the strong position taken by industry. There was also divergence of opinion within the working group over HCFCs. Australia, Finland, New Zealand, Norway, Sweden, and Switzerland wanted to phase them out completely between 2010 and 2020. The United States proposed a later timetable, with a total phaseout by 2035–2060. The European Community, Japan, and the Soviet Union still opposed including these compounds in the protocol (Benedick 1991).

A month before the final session of the working group on June 20, 1990, Tolba circulated a "personal" proposal for revisions to the protocol's control measures. Tolba's compromise package attempted to reach a balance among the many contending proposals that were embedded in the heavily bracketed text produced by the working group (UNEP 1990). Japan, the Soviet Union, and the United States were the strongest advocates of Tolba's compromise package in the working group. Australia, New Zealand, and the Nordic countries, often joined by Austria, Canada, and Switzerland, supported tighter regulations and earlier phaseouts. Developing countries were generally bystanders in the debates over controls.

It was not until the ministers arrived and the second Meeting of Parties convened in London from June 27, 1990, that a final agreement was reached. The key to many of the compromises was the findings of the special assessment panels, reinforced by some sophisticated bargaining (Benedick 1991). The London Amendments to the protocol on control measures included

- ◆ CFCs: (1) the 20 percent cutback targeted in the Montreal Protocol for 1993 was dropped as no longer relevant; a 50 percent reduction by 1995 was introduced in its place; (2) 85 percent reduction by 1997; and (3) phaseout by 2000.
- ◆ Methyl chloroform: (1) freeze in 1993; (2) 30 percent reduction in 1995; (3) 70 percent reduction in 2000; (4) phaseout in 2005; and (5) a commitment to review by 1992 the feasibility of earlier reductions and phaseout.
- ◆ HCFCs: Due to EC opposition, the only mandatory requirement was an obligation to report on production, imports, and exports; there was also a nonbinding resolution providing for regular review of the situation with a phaseout by 2040.
- ◆ New halons and carbon tetrachloride: a request for further study, and a phaseout in 2000, respectively (UNEP 1990a).

Negotiations on Treatment of Developing Countries

In the text of the Montreal Protocol as adopted in 1987, developing countries were given a ten-year grace period during which they could expand their use of CFCs and halons before moving to newly developed technologies and following the original reduction schedule. But with industrialized countries moving toward a complete phaseout, rather than the original 50 percent reduction, the grace period for developing countries was becoming almost irrelevant. As a result, these countries were now interested in moving as rapidly as possible to new technologies and wanted to ensure that help was available to accomplish this.

According to Benedick (1991, 152), "the creation of a financial mechanism and the related questions of modalities for the transfer of technology proved to be the most difficult issue in the entire treaty revision process." At the first meeting of the working group in August 1989, developing country representatives outlined four initial basic concepts: (1) a discrete multilateral trust fund should be established within UNEP to meet all incremental costs to developing countries of complying with the protocol; (2) the fund should be financed by "legally enforceable obligations" from industrialized countries, on some agreed-upon burden-sharing basis; (3) such contributions should be additional to, rather than a diversion from, existing aid flows; and (4) free access and nonprofit transfer to developing countries of safe technologies should be guaranteed (UNEP 1989d). The donors understood the concerns of developing countries but were not predisposed to create a new funding mechanism or to accept the suggestion that donor contributions should be mandatory rather than discretionary. The donors also balked at the proposed guarantee of technology transfer, which raised issues of intellectual property rights and patents (Benedick 1991). Yet another sticking point concerned the amount of funds actually required.

At the February 1990 working group meeting, the United States proposed and the working group accepted the idea of a three-year rolling fund with a budget subject to periodic revision. Tolba proposed that a new multilateral fund be established with mandatory assessed contributions by industrialized countries on a principle of "additionality" (funds additional to existing aid flows). While there was still considerable resistance on the part of donor countries to additionality and the creation of a new institution at the end of the meeting, progress was made because there was growing recognition that something new and different was required, that such a mechanism should be under the control of the parties, and that funding assistance could be provided in the form of both concessional loans and grants.

During the week leading up to the next working group meeting, in May 1990, Tolba took the lead again and held informal consultations on both funding and transfer of technology with small groups of government representatives and with various intergovernmental and nongovernmental organizations. A shift in the U.S. position resulted in a call for a World Bank fund for ozone protection with no additional donor contributions (Weisskopf 1990), but under Tolba's leadership the working group reached agreement on the list of incremental costs eligible for support; the concept of a tripartite division of responsibilities among the World Bank, UNDP, and UNEP; and the concept of voluntary contributions on an assessed basis (Benedick 1991).

Agreement was finally reached at the second MOP. With regard to the funding mechanism, the United States agreed to accept the concept of additionality if it could be guaranteed that the fund would not turn into an open-ended commitment. The United States wanted the fund to be operated and administered by the World Bank, with oversight vested in an executive committee established by the parties, on which the United States, as the largest prospective donor, would have a permanent seat. The other parties were able to accept this condition in exchange for U.S. acceptance of additionality. As a result, the executive committee would have fourteen members, equally divided among developed and developing countries, and a two-thirds majority would be required on all votes. Based on studies of the cost of phasing out CFCs and halons, delegates agreed that for the initial three years of the fund, the budget would be $160 million (if China and India were to become parties the budget would increase by $80 million).

However, technology transfer proved to be a more difficult issue to resolve. Developing countries wanted to build into the protocol an assurance that they would not be obligated to implement the reduction schedules if they did not receive sufficient financial and technical assistance. The donor countries, however, would not agree to a blank check or to a situation in which any party could unilaterally claim that it had received insufficient aid and would therefore not fulfill its obligations under the treaty. The resolution of the impasse came on the last day of the London meeting. Industrialized countries affirmed their commitment to "take every practicable step . . . to ensure that the best available, environmentally safe substitutes and related technologies are expeditiously transferred to Parties under paragraph 1 of Article 5 . . . under fair and most favorable conditions" (UNEP 1990a, 36).[3] In addition, the amended protocol text acknowledged that "developing the capacity to fulfil the obligations of the Parties operating under [Article 5] paragraph 1 . . . will depend upon the effective implementation" of the financial mechanism and technology transfer (UNEP 1990a, 32). The London Amendment entered into force on August 10, 1992.

Negotiations during the first regime adjustment phase were similar to the negotiations of the protocol in a few notable ways: governments continued to be the primary actors, Tolba played a mediating/facilitating role, and the scientific and industrial communities provided supporting data and information. Yet there were also some marked differences. Whereas developing countries had not played a major role in negotiating the protocol or the amendments to the control measures, they did play a central role in the negotiations on the financial mechanism and technology transfer. This shift highlighted a growing trend in environmental negotiations of Northern recognition of the importance of developing country participation in and compliance with international environmental treaties as well as a Southern recognition that participation in environmental regimes is inevitable and it is in the South's best interest to negotiate the most favorable terms to govern its participation.

Regime Operation/Governance: July 1990 to November 1992

After the adoption of the London Amendment, the MOP and its subsidiary bodies shifted focus from regime adjustment to regime operation/governance. Negotiations during regime operation/governance involve the collection of information concerning actions of the parties—monitoring, verification, and enforcement—and the resolution of disputes. Negotiation is the process by which problems with compliance, enforcement, and interpretation are worked out. In many environmental treaties, there are few, if any, measurable performance standards, mechanisms, monitoring compliance controls, or even reporting procedures. Where these governance issues are spelled out, the provisions of the treaty are not always implemented, and so the parties must adjust and amend the language to ensure that the procedures work in practice as they had been intended to work in theory. This is usually an ongoing process that takes into consideration changes in the treaty as well as changes in the international system.

During the period after the 1990 London meeting and through the third MOP, which was held in Nairobi on June 9–21, 1991, a number of regime adjustment and strengthening issues were still on the table, and the MOP and its assessment panels and working groups continued to discuss the most recent scientific evidence, industrial developments, and new or improved control measures under the protocol. However, the parties also examined a number of governance issues, including the operations of the multilateral fund, the problems faced by developing countries, noncompliance procedures, and reporting. So, while the scientists and technological experts continued to play a role, it was the legal experts who stepped to the forefront in preparation for the third MOP.

Noncompliance

At the Helsinki meeting, the parties agreed to establish an Open-Ended Ad Hoc Working Group of Legal Experts to develop and submit to the secretariat appropriate proposals for consideration and approval by the MOP on procedures and institutional mechanisms for determining noncompliance with the provisions of the protocol and for the treatment of parties that fail to comply. At the London meeting, the parties adopted interim procedures and institutional mechanisms for determining and handling noncompliance. Under these procedures, an Implementation Committee was established to review charges of noncompliance and recommend to the party the steps necessary to bring about full compliance with the protocol. In Decision II/5, adopted in London, the parties agreed to extend the mandate of the Working Group of Legal Experts so it could further elaborate these procedures as well as the terms of reference for the Implementation Committee (UNEP 1990a). The Working Group of Legal Experts held meetings in December 1990 and April 1992 to fulfill this mandate.

At the third MOP, the parties adopted the recommendations of the Working Group of Legal Experts thus far and made some further requests. In Decision III/2, the working group was requested by the year's end to identify possible situations of noncompliance; develop an indicative list of advisory and conciliatory measures to encourage full compliance; reflect on the possible need for legal interpretation of the provisions of the protocol; and draw up an indicative list of measures that might be taken by the MOP with respect to parties that were not in compliance. The MOP adopted the detailed noncompliance procedures at its fourth meeting, in Copenhagen in November 1992 (UNEP 1992).

Reporting

In addition to addressing matters of noncompliance, the Working Group of Legal Experts also gave the Implementation Committee responsibility for examining the data reported in accordance with Article 7 of the protocol and, in its report to the third session of the MOP, the Implementation Committee concluded that reporting was not satisfactory. Of the seventy-one parties to the protocol at that time, only thirty-one had reported complete data for 1986. Of the remainder, nineteen had reported incomplete data, six had reported no data available and/or had requested assistance; and fifteen had not reported. Of the forty-eight parties required to report data for 1989, only twenty-three had complied by May 1991, and only twenty of these had submitted complete data. Some developing countries experienced serious reporting problems due to lack of technical and economic resources. The Implementation Committee stressed the need for technical and financial support to countries to enable them to comply with the data-reporting provisions of the protocol. Establishing noncompliance when the only resource was the lack of such support would only hurt the developing countries (UNEP 1991). Thus, Decision III/7 invited any party experiencing difficulties in data reporting to inform the secretariat so that suitable measures could be taken to rectify the situation (UNEP 1991).

Although this decision acknowledged the problem of reporting, it did little to rectify the situation. At the fourth MOP, in Copenhagen in November 1992, the Implementation Committee noted once again that developing countries were still having serious problems fulfilling their data-reporting requirements. The committee recommended that they seek help from the Multilateral Fund to do so. In addition, the Ad Hoc Group of Experts on the Reporting of Data had identified several technical and administrative problems and their possible solutions (UNEP 1992).

Multilateral Fund

In January 1991, the Montreal-based Interim Multilateral Ozone Fund began operation. By November 1992, sixty projects had been approved for the phaseout of more than 30,000 tonnes of ozone-depleting substances, which represented 20 percent of the total consumption of the developing countries party to the protocol (UNEP 1992). During this period, the parties continued negotiations on the establishment of the Permanent Fund, its executive committee, the level of contributions, and a list of categories of incremental costs. In Decision IV/18, of November 25, 1992, the MOP decided to establish the Financial Mechanism, including the Multilateral Fund provided for in Article 10 of the protocol. The fund was to be operative as of January 1993 and the total contributions for 1993 were set at $113.34 million.

The nature of the negotiations on noncompliance, reporting, and operation of the Multilateral Fund was quite different from that of the regime adjustment negotiations as well as the negotiations of the protocol itself. Most of the work on reaching acceptable compromises was done within the context of expert groups. Although in many cases the participants in the work of the expert groups were the same government delegates who attend the MOPs, the negotiating forum is quite different. There is none of the publicity that accompanies the MOP, even though there is still time pressure to reach an agreement prior to the MOP. Developing countries participated actively in these negotiations —particularly the negotiations on the operation of the Multilateral Fund—whereas their participation was marginal prior to the adoption of the protocol. Finally, these negotiations did not generate the same amount of attention from the scientific community as did the original negotiations or the regime adjustment negotiations because they did not address what chemicals should be phased out and by how much but focused instead on the mechanics of successful regime operation.

Regime Adjustment—Part II:
June 1990 to November 1992

Although regime governance activities were the primary focus of the third MOP, in Nairobi in 1991, work continued through the period from June 1990 to November 1992 to make additional adjustments and further strengthen the protocol. As has been the case throughout the development of the ozone regime, endogenous inputs provided by scientific findings sparked the political process. In January 1992, researchers discovered ozone losses of up to 20 percent in the Northern Hemisphere and a maximum depletion over Russia of between 40 and 45 percent below normal for a few days. Because this depletion was not only severe but also unexpected, many argued that the need to preserve the ozone layer demanded a reconsideration and renegotiation of the terms of the Montreal Protocol (Rowlands 1993).

The Scientific Assessment Panel reported that the latest satellite and ground-based ozone data demonstrated that the rates of ozone depletion at mid- and high latitudes were greater than previously measured and that there was increased evidence of a chlorine-induced effect. The panel suggested that the following measures be undertaken to minimize peak chlorine loading and ozone depletion: a reduction in the emissions of long-lived CFCs, carbon tetrachloride, methyl chloroform, and halons as soon as possible; the recycling of HCFCs to the maximum extent possible; and a phaseout of HCFCs sometime during the next century (UNEP 1991).

This report led the Open-Ended Working Group of the Parties to prepare a new set of amendments and adjustments to the protocol for consideration at the fourth MOP, in Copenhagen on November 23–25, 1992. The working group, which met twice in 1992, easily reached consensus on strengthening the controls on chemicals already covered in the protocol, largely because the majority of the developed countries had already met or exceeded their production and consumption reduction targets. Most parties therefore agreed that CFCs should be eliminated by January 1, 1996, but there were still questions about intermediate targets before the conference began. Some delegations wanted 80 percent reductions (compared to 1986 levels) by 1994, while others did not want any intermediate obligations. In the end, both the phaseout date and a 75 percent reduction by January 1, 1994, were agreed upon (UNEP 1992; Rowlands 1993).

But the exogenous input was tempered by the cybernetic process of domestic involvement. There was less scientific evidence for, and thus political acceptance of, the need to add new chemicals, and this question became the focus of work in Copenhagen. HCFCs were the subject of much debate. Those supporting some use of HCFCs argued that society's primary goal must be to eliminate CFCs as quickly as possible. Although there are problems associated with the use of HCFCs,[4] they were considered to be one of the most attractive alternatives to CFCs. Thus, the argument continued, it is better to use the lesser of the two evils while more appropriate alternatives are being developed and tested. Others, however, challenged this assertion by arguing that suitable alternatives to CFCs and HCFCs do exist. They argued that international regulation could both encourage the scientific development of suitable substances and add to the commercial attractiveness of such alternatives, as has been the case with CFCs (Rowlands 1993).

Industry representatives maintained that an impending ban on HCFCs would destroy the commercial incentives for producers to make the chemicals and for manufacturers to use them in their products and processes. They claimed that a slower phaseout was appropriate so that businesses would be able to recoup their research, development, and capital investments. Without this reprieve, companies would continue to use ozone-damaging CFCs while waiting for more suitable alternatives (Rowlands 1993).

In the end, the negotiators agreed to cap their use of HCFCs in January 1996 at a level equal to the sum of their HCFC use in 1989 and 3.1 percent of their use of CFCs in 1989. This formula acknowledges both the considerable existing uses of HCFCs and their role as transition substitutes for CFCs. Subsequent to that, the parties agreed to reduce their use of HCFCs by 35 percent by 2004, by 65 percent by 2010, by 90 percent by 2015, by 99.5 percent by 2020, and by 100 percent by 2030 (UNEP 1992, 37).

Methyl bromide was one substance about which there was difficulty in achieving a balance between damage to the environment and the vital applications for which it was needed.[5] The debate about methyl bromide revolved, to a significant extent, around the North-South axis. Industrialized states, led by the United States, called for a substantial cutback in the use of this chemical. They were persuaded by the scientific evidence and also believed that a 25 percent reduction could be achieved by more efficient use of the chemical (Rowlands 1993). Developing countries, however, were adamant in their opposition to any regulation. Not only did they maintain that the science was still marked by too many uncertainties, but they also noted that the preamble to the protocol ensured that any measures take "into account technical and economic considerations and [bear] in mind the developmental needs of developing countries" (Rowlands 1993). In the end, a compromise was reached that developed countries would freeze their methyl bromide production at 1991 levels by 1995 (UNEP 1992). However, further action would await the publication of a more complete assessment report.

In summary, by the time the parties left Copenhagen they had renegotiated on the following amendments to the protocol:

- a phaseout of CFC production and consumption in 1996 (formerly 2000);
- a phaseout of halon production and consumption (the original three halons contained in the 1987 protocol) by 1994 (formerly 2000);
- a phaseout of production and consumption of other halons by 1996 (new);
- a phaseout of production and consumption of carbon tetrachloride in 1996 (new);
- a phaseout of production and consumption of methyl chloroform in 1996 (formerly 2005);
- a complicated formula for the reduction of HCFCs, with an eventual phaseout by 2030 (new);
- a phaseout of hydrobromofluorocarbons by 1996 (new); and
- a freeze on methyl bromide at 1991 levels in 1995 (new).

The parties also focused on strengthening controls and agreed on stronger import/export controls, a new list of controlled substances, noncompliance procedures, and an indicative list of categories of incremental costs to be covered under the Multilateral Fund (UNEP 1992). The Copenhagen Amendment entered into force on June 14, 1994.

Like the London Amendment negotiations before it, the negotiation of the Copenhagen Amendment featured the increasing role of developing countries in the governance and expansion of the protocol, the continuing relationship between scientific and technological advances and the development of international policy, and, perhaps most notably, the flexibility inherent in the original text of the protocol that has facilitated the continuing expansion negotiations.

Regime Adjustment and Governance: 1992–2002

While the first five years of the ozone regime were characterized by an intense period of regime building and adjustment, the subsequent ten years focused on governance, in combination with continuing regime adjustment to take into account the latest scientific knowledge and technical advances. As Gunnar Sjöstedt notes in chapter 3, the first two years of the ozone regime were spent developing rules, norms, and principles, which represented a necessary prerequisite for adoption of rules with teeth in the form of the London and Copenhagen Amendments. However, the regime has continued to undergo a number of procedural and rule changes in the period since Copenhagen that included both implementation negotiations and expansion negotiations, as defined by Spector in chapter 2 of this volume.

In preparation for the fifth MOP, which was held in Bangkok on November 17–19, 1993, the various components of the Montreal Protocol regime (the Assessment Panels, the Working Group of Legal Experts, the Open-Ended Working Group of Parties, the Preparatory Committee, and the Multilateral Fund) worked within their mandates on both regime adjustment and governance. Thus, as scientific evidence continued to mount, the regime also had to reexamine the situation of the former Soviet bloc countries with economies in transition and the needs of developing countries with regard to implementation.

When the fifth MOP opened, Elizabeth Dowdeswell, the new executive director of UNEP, noted a number of important governance issues before the parties.[6] The average reduction of ozone-depleting substances by developed countries was 45 percent, but of the developing countries only nine had reduced their consumption of controlled substances and three had shown an increase of more than 80 percent. Three other issues were also inhibiting the full and effective implementation of the protocol:

◆ The status of ratification: although 129 parties had ratified the Montreal Protocol, covering 90 percent of the world's population and nearly 99 percent of ozone-depleting substances, only 69 parties had ratified the London Amendment, and only 9 the Copenhagen Amendment.
◆ The delay in reporting data by parties: for 1992 only 23 of 99 parties had reported data.
◆ The requirement for replenishment of the Multilateral Fund for the years 1994–96: it was in the interest of the donor countries to contribute the maximum possible resources now to reverse the trend of increasing consumption of ozone-depleting substances in developing countries (UNIS 1993).

Among the substantive issues on the agenda for the Bangkok meeting were the replenishment of the Multilateral Fund and the scheduled 1994 phaseout of halons. With regard to the fund, the Preparatory Committee had endorsed the estimate that $510 million would be needed for the period 1994–96. Although most delegates supported this figure to ensure that developing countries met the requirements of the protocol, some thought that the size of the fund was not large enough, given the larger number of parties operating under paragraph 1 of Article 5. Others noted that in view of the international economic situation, the fact that the size of the fund was increased at all was a notable achievement. A number of representatives from countries in transition to market economies commented that they were unable to pay their contributions to the fund and asked the secretariat and the parties to look more closely into this matter. One stated that his government would have to seek assistance from the Global Environment Facility (GEF) in order to meet the phaseout schedule required by the protocol since his country was not eligible for assistance from the fund (UNEP 1994). Within the framework of their discussion of the fund, the parties also addressed its operation, the time lags between the approval of projects, and the disbursement of funds and the assessment of contributions.

With regard to halons, the parties accepted the recommendation that it was technically and economically feasible to eliminate the use of halons in some applications for which exemption had been requested. Decision V/14 (UNEP 1993,15) states

> that no level of production or consumption is necessary to satisfy essential uses of halon in Parties not operating under paragraph 1 of Article 5 of the Protocol, for the year 1994 since there are technically and economically feasible alternatives and substitutes for most applications, and since halon is available in sufficient quantity and quality from existing stocks of banked and recycled halon.

The parties also adopted decisions that cleared up ambiguities in the protocol, such as the feasibility of banning or restricting the import of products produced with, but not containing, controlled substances from states not party to the protocol; the application of trade measures under Article 4 to controlled substances listed in Group I of Annex C and in Annex E; and new forms for reporting of data.

Implementation negotiations continued at the sixth Meeting of the Parties to the Montreal Protocol, in Nairobi on October 6–7, 1994. Some of the major issues before the MOP included the need to prepare a new scientific assessment of the state of understanding of ozone depletion, the nomination of essential uses of controlled substances, continuing problems in data reporting, and the alarming trend in contributions still outstanding to the Multilateral Fund and the Trust Funds for the Vienna Convention and the Montreal Protocol (UNEP 1994a).

Many of the decisions made at this meeting dealt with regime governance issues. These included the status of developing country parties in regard to Article 5; nominations for essential uses of controlled substances; clarification of "quarantine" and "preshipment" applications for control of methyl bromide; the provision of information; the budget; nominations for officers and committee memberships; and additional research in some areas, including further controls on ozone-depleting substances and essential uses (UNEP 1994a).

When government delegates met in Vienna on December 5–7, 1995, for the seventh MOP and the tenth anniversary of the Vienna Convention, they agreed to further adjustments to the regime in the form of new commitments. Governments agreed that industrialized countries would phase out methyl bromide by the year 2010. They also agreed on interim targets, including a reduction by 25 percent for 2001 and by 50 percent for 2005. In addition, exemptions would be permitted for certain trade-related applications ("preshipment" and "quarantine") and for "critical agricultural uses." Although it was generally understood that the latter exemption should be defined as narrowly as possible, its exact definition was set to be considered in 1997 based on work to be carried out by the Technical and Economic Advisory Panel (TEAP). The agreement also banned trade in methyl bromide with countries that were not parties to the protocol's 1992 Copenhagen Amendment (UNEP 1995).

Developing countries, which previously faced no controls at all, agreed to freeze methyl bromide use by 2002 at average 1995–98 levels, with a phaseout schedule to be determined by 1997. Delegates also agreed on new controls for HCFCs, including a phaseout by the year 2020 (the previous commitment was to a phaseout by the year 2030). Developing countries, which had not had any HCFC controls before, agreed to a freeze for the year 2016 (on the basis of consumption levels in 2015) and to a phaseout as of 2040. Delegates also reaffirmed the 2010 CFC phaseout deadline for developing countries (UNEP 1995).

Other important implementation-related issues discussed by the parties included technology transfers and additional funding from industrialized countries to developing countries, the problem of possible noncompliance with treaty obligations by a number of countries with economies in transition, continuing problems with data reporting, including reporting failures and data discrepancies, illegal trade in controlled substances, and budgetary matters (UNEP 1995).

The eighth MOP took place in San José, Costa Rica, on November 25–27, 1996. Continuing the MOP's pattern of shifting focus each year between regime governance and regime adjustment, the eighth meeting focused primarily on governance-related issues to improve implementation of the protocol and its amendments and adjustments. Delegates in Costa Rica continued to praise the effectiveness of the protocol and noted an improvement in data reporting, but a number of implementation problems continued to surface. These included the low number of ratifications of the London and Copenhagen Amendments, the lack of financial support for essential research and monitoring activities, significant arrears in the trust funds for the Vienna Convention and Montreal Protocol, arrears in contributions to the Multilateral Fund, and illegal trade in ozone-depleting substances. In addition, baseline data were still outstanding from a number of parties despite a considerable improvement in the number fulfilling their reporting requirements (UNEP 1996).

Delegates addressed many of these issues at the meeting and made a number of procedural decisions, including replenishment of the Multilateral Fund and a three-year rolling business plan for 1997–99; a call for ongoing research and development of alternatives to CFC metered-dose inhalers, which are used to control asthma and other respiratory illnesses; illegal imports and exports of controlled substances; revised formats for reporting data under Article 7 of the protocol; compliance problems in countries with economies in transition; and the scale of contributions and other budgetary matters (UNEP 1996).

The tenth anniversary of the Montreal Protocol was marked in Montreal at the ninth MOP, which took place on September 15–17, 1997. Returning once again to expansion negotiations, the parties adopted the Montreal Amendment and Adjustments, tightening restrictions on several ozone-depleting substances. For example, the parties agreed to move up the phaseout of methyl bromide to 2005 from 2010, with exemptions for "critical uses" and interim reductions of 25 percent by 1999, 50 percent by 2001, and 70 percent by 2003. Developing countries, previously committed only to a freeze by 2002, agreed to a 20 percent reduction by 2005 and a phaseout by 2015. They agreed to use the four-year average of 1995–98 usage as the base for calculating the phaseout; the interim reduction schedule would be reviewed in 2003. In addition to the $10 million agreed upon in 1996 for funding demonstration projects to test the feasibility of alternatives to methyl bromide, the Multilateral Fund would make $25 million per year available in 1998 and 1999 for phasing out methyl bromide in developing countries (UNEP 1997).

Delegates also agreed to a new licensing system for controlling trade based on licenses issued by parties for each import and export, and on regular information exchange between parties. This enables customs and police officials to track trade in CFCs and to detect unlicensed trade. The system became effective in 2000. In previous years, the MOP had agreed to study this problem, and this was the first time that any concrete action had been taken to address the growing problem of illegal trade in controlled substances (UNEP 1997). The Montreal Amendment entered into force on November 10, 1999. Proposals by the European Community and Switzerland to accelerate the phaseout of the consumption of HCFCs and to introduce production controls were not accepted. These countries made a declaration urging that the issue be revisited at a future meeting (UNEP 1997).

The tenth MOP was held in November 1998 in Cairo. Parties focused on governance issues, including the challenge of how to develop policies to protect the ozone layer consistent with ongoing efforts to reduce emissions of the greenhouse gases that cause climate change. Several gases with lower ozone-depleting potential that are used as replacements for CFCs (notably hydrofluorocarbons [HFCs] and perfluorocarbons [PFCs]) contribute to global warming. MOP-10 agreed on a process for coordinating the work on ozone of the Scientific Assessment Panel and the Technology and Economic Assessment Panel with that of similar bodies linked to the United Nations Framework Convention on Climate Change. MOP-10 also recommended that measures to close CFC production facilities be strengthened; that the Global Environment Facility continue to assist parties with economies in transition to adhere to their phaseout benchmarks; that national management strategies for reducing halon emissions be adopted; and that new measures be taken to limit the export of new and used products and equipment that require CFCs or other ozone-depleting substances (ENB 1999, 2).

The parties returned to expansion negotiations in Beijing at their eleventh meeting, from November 29 to December 3, 1999. Delegates adopted the Beijing Amendment, which provides for a freeze in the level of HCFC production in 2004 for developed countries and in 2016 for developing countries; the phaseout of bromochloromethane by 2002; a ban on trade in HCFCs with nonparties beginning in 2004; and reporting on annual consumption of methyl bromide for quarantine and preshipment applications. The Beijing Amendment entered into force on February 25, 2002. The adjustments stipulate the phaseout of production allowances to meet the basic domestic needs of developing countries for CFCs, halons, and methyl bromide (ENB 2000, 2). The MOP also adopted the Beijing Declaration and decided on the replenishment of the Multilateral Fund with $477.7 million for 2000–02.

The twelfth MOP, which took place in Ouagadougou, Burkina Faso, in December 2000, returned again to governance issues. The meeting was notably low-key and quiet, with delegates adopting seventeen decisions covering a wide range of topics, including disposal of controlled substances, monitoring of international trade and prevention of illegal trade in ozone-depleting substances and products containing such substances, measures to facilitate the transition to CFC-free metered-dose inhalers, and financial and budgetary matters (ENB 2000).

At the thirteenth MOP, in Colombo, Sri Lanka, in October 2001, the parties continued to focus on governance and the implementation of existing commitments, rather than on the negotiation of new provisions. This meeting also marked the first time that the parties reviewed compliance by developing countries, thus quietly launching a new era in the regime. Delegates also evaluated the Multilateral Fund, adopted procedures for assessing the ozone-depleting potential of new substances, and expedited the procedures for adding new substances to the protocol and monitoring illegal trade in ozone-depleting substances (ENB 2001).

The fourteenth MOP, which took place in Rome, Italy, in November 2002, continued the emphasis on governance, focusing primarily on the replenishment of the Multilateral Fund. Delegates also addressed a number of issues relating to the future effectiveness of the protocol, including the phaseout of methyl bromide, the illegal trade in ozone-depleting substances, compliance procedures, the destruction of ozone-depleting substances, and synergies between ozone depletion and climate change (ENB 2002).

Continued annual MOPs that alternated focus between governance issues and strengthening control measures thus characterized the ozone regime between 1992 and 2000. Since 2000, governance and compliance issues have taken center stage. Scientific and technical assessment panels continued their work during the periods between MOPs, and their recommendations for strengthening the protocol's control measures were acted upon as necessary. This period was also characterized by increased participation by developing countries in all areas of the protocol's governance and implementation. Although their priorities continued to be financial and technical assistance—as has been the case in all international environmental regimes over the past five years—their participation in the ozone regime is notable because of their lack of participation in the negotiations leading up to the Montreal Protocol. Thus, increased participation in the ongoing negotiations has produced changes in the shape and provisions of the regime. As the participation of developing countries increased, the negotiations themselves adopted an increasingly North-South focus—a contrast to the pre-1987 period, when the negotiations were often between the Toronto Group and the European Community, supported by the Soviet Union and Japan. Furthermore, the breakup of the Soviet Union created an entirely new set of issues, notably the inability of some of the former Soviet states to comply with their obligations under the protocol.

The executive director of UNEP has played a smaller role as the regime has matured. Even though the secretariat for the Vienna Convention and the Montreal Protocol is administered by UNEP and is housed at UNEP's headquarters in Nairobi, the regime has not seen the level of activism demonstrated by Mostafa Tolba during the negotiation of the protocol and the early years of its implementation. This could be due to a number of factors, most notably Tolba's departure from UNEP at the end of 1992 and the strengthening of the capacities of the secretariat itself. Although Tolba's successors, Elizabeth Dowdeswell and Klaus Töpfer, have made a point of attending most meetings, they have not played an activist or mediating role. But this type of role has not always been necessary because regime negotiations (including the MOP, the subsidiary bodies, and the secretariat) have developed a momentum of their own.

Finally, the most consistent characteristic of the ozone regime during its first fifteen years has been the fact that the parties have consistently based their efforts on the latest scientific, technological, and economic assessments. The work of the various assessment panels, and the ability of the parties to take appropriate action based on this work, has been key to the success of the protocol. Furthermore, although industry has not always supported strengthening the control measures and expanding the number of chemicals addressed by the protocol, its continued response in developing alternative technologies has been central to the effective implementation of the protocol.

Summary and Conclusions

Over its first fifteen years the evolution of the ozone regime has been characterized by a comprehensive postagreement negotiation process that has addressed regime building, regime adjustment, and regime governance issues, often on an alternating basis. From September 1987 through May 1989 the focus was on regime creation. Prior to the first MOP, in Helsinki in May 1989, the major actors were the scientific community, which continued to increase its knowledge of ozone depletion and the anthropogenic chemicals that cause it; national governments, particularly of industrialized countries, which had to ratify the protocol so it could enter into force on schedule; and UNEP, in particular its executive director, Mostafa Tolba, who convened meetings and workshops to ensure that the issue of ozone depletion remained at the forefront of the international environmental agenda and that proper groundwork was laid for continuing negotiations in the MOPs.

The first MOP, while consisting of many of the same delegates who had negotiated the protocol, and using many of the same procedures, had a different character due to the issues under negotiation. The issues were primarily procedural in nature—adoption of rules of procedure, establishment of the bureau and of working groups and panels, creation of reporting guidelines, and arrangement for funding of the secretariat. Nevertheless, the parties demonstrated sufficient political will to adopt the Helsinki Declaration, which pledged them to further strengthen the protocol at their next session. The focus on procedural rather than substantive issues allowed the MOP to get off to a good start and launched the next phase—regime adjustment.

From June 1989 through June 1990 the focus was on regime adjustment. The primary negotiating forum was the Open-Ended Working Group, established to address strengthening the control measures in the protocol and assisting the developing countries with financial and technical assistance. In the negotiations on strengthening control measures, the industrialized countries were the primary actors, and they relied heavily on the work of the assessment panels established in Helsinki. As the scientific evidence continued to mount, the policymakers deferred more to the scientists' recommendations. This had not been the case in the initial negotiations, where scientific uncertainty was an excuse for inaction on the part of some industrialized countries.

In the negotiations on the needs of developing countries, the atmosphere was quite different. Developing country parties and nonparties played a leading role in elaborating their needs under the protocol. Unlike the initial negotiations, these negotiations took on the air of many North-South debates within the UN system on finance and technology transfer. Issues such as additionality, preferential transfer, intellectual property rights, the role of the World Bank, and donor commitments, which characterize so many UN debates, made their appearance during meetings of the working group. Since the control measures under the convention can only be effective with the participation of developing countries, this group carried a lot of weight during these negotiations.

In these regime adjustment negotiations, Tolba continued to play an active role as mediator and facilitator. He convened special meetings, prepared option papers for consideration by the governments, and proposed compromises. It is not certain whether the leverage he enjoyed was the result of his active participation throughout the initial negotiations, the fact that he is from a developing country, his negotiating skills, or a combination of these. Clearly, however, his involvement in the postagreement negotiating process, while occasionally controversial, was another key to its success during the first five years.

After the London meeting, the MOP and its subsidiary bodies shifted their attention to consideration of issues related to regime operation and governance. The legal advisers played a primary role in this process as they helped the Implementation Committee and the Open-Ended Working Group to address a number of issues related to the effective operation of the protocol, including how to determine noncompliance, how to deal with states that are not in compliance, how to deal with reporting problems, and the operation of the Multilateral Fund. Although the MOP made the necessary political decisions with regard to these governance matters, most of the issue definition was the responsibility of the legal experts, and negotiations were the responsibility of the working group. This was another example of effective cooperation among the various bodies within the regime.

In 1992, after a series of regime expansion negotiations, the parties met in Copenhagen and amended and adjusted the protocol again to reflect the latest scientific evidence about ozone depletion and the chemicals that cause it. As the Montreal Protocol regime entered its fifth year, however, the nature of the postagreement negotiation process began to change. Although the MOP had been successful in amending and strengthening the protocol, a number of other governance problems began to surface and characterized the development of the regime from 1993 to 2000. For example, problems with noncompliance and reporting continued to show up on the agenda. The MOP had still not been able to determine how to define and implement some of the monitoring provisions of the protocol. Furthermore, developing countries were faced with a decrease in options for CFC and other chemical replacements as the industrialized countries phased out their production. The Multilateral Fund has not proven to be sufficient to address all of the perceived needs of developing countries to enable their implementation of the control and reporting provisions of the revised protocol. As the number of parties, and hence the number of developing country parties, has increased, the MOP has begun to resemble the UN General Assembly in its size and perhaps even in its North-South character.

Furthermore, the situation of the countries with economies in transition also came to the surface. Under the terms of the protocol, they are considered developed countries and as such must comply with the control provisions without the delay afforded to developing countries. They must also contribute to the Multilateral Fund. These countries have found it difficult to fulfill these obligations and, as a result, have been the subject of a number of decisions made by the MOP in an effort to facilitate their compliance.

Amid these governance issues, the protocol's technological and scientific assessment panels have continued to evaluate the latest scientific findings and technological advances and bring further exogenous agents into the regime. As a result, the MOP has continued to strengthen the protocol's control provisions by speeding up the phaseout of some chemicals and by adding new chemicals to the list of substances controlled by the protocol. It is this integration of the scientific, technological, and economic assessment panels and legal experts into the work of the MOP that many believe has contributed to the strength and the success of the regime.

The pattern that has emerged since 1993 is characterized by parallel work on regime adjustment and regime governance. On the regime adjustment side, the Environmental Effects Assessment Panel, the Scientific Assessment Panel, and the other scientific and technical subsidiary bodies continue to meet and discuss the latest science and technology and make recommendations to the Open-Ended Working Group of the Parties on strengthening the control provisions of the protocol. As a result, the protocol was amended in 1990, 1992, 1997, and 1999 and adjusted in 1993, 1995, 1997, and 1999. On the regime governance side, the Executive Committee of the Multilateral Fund, the Ad Hoc Working Group of Legal and Technical Experts on Non-Compliance, the Implementation Committee under the Non-Compliance Procedure for the Montreal Protocol, and other committees continue to meet and make the necessary recommendations to the Open-Ended Working Group of the Parties or the MOP. The parties and the secretariat have done their best to gaurantee that the relevant governance-related issues are dealt with on a timely basis to ensure that the protocol is implemented to the fullest extent possible.

While successful creation of an environmental treaty is heralded around the world, it is always important to note that this is only the beginning. The implementation phase—from ratification and entry into force through the various types of regime-building negotiations —is what really makes or breaks a treaty. Nevertheless, many scholars of regimes and multilateral negotiations tend to ignore this crucial aspect in the development of an effective regime. When the Montreal Protocol was first adopted in 1987, many criticized it for being too weak and predicted that it would be ineffective in protecting the ozone layer. Fifteen years later, the ozone regime was heralded as the most successful environmental regime to emerge out of the UN system. This change is largely the result of the role that a continuing postagreement negotiation process has played in the ozone regime.

Notes

1. For information about the workshops and the negotiation of the Montreal Protocol, see Benedick 1991, 40–97.

2. This group consisted of the heads of delegation of Canada, Japan, New Zealand, Norway, the Soviet Union, the United States, and the European Commission, plus Belgium, Denmark, and the United Kingdom (the European Community presidential troika).

3. Paragraph 1 of Article 5 reads: "Any Party that is a developing country and whose annual calculated level of consumption of the controlled substances is less than 0.3 kilograms per capita on the date of the entry into force of the Protocol for it, or any time thereafter within ten years of the date of entry into force of the Protocol shall, in order to meet its basic domestic needs, be entitled to delay its compliance with the control measures set out in paragraphs 1 to 4 of Article 2 by ten years after that specified in those paragraphs."

4. Because it has a shorter atmospheric lifetime, the chlorine in one HCFC molecule will destroy a much smaller amount of stratospheric ozone than will one CFC molecule. This shorter lifetime, however, means that the HCFC's destruction of ozone will also take place much sooner.

5. Methyl bromide is used as a fumigant for soils, structures, and storage and is in use in many countries for fumigation of horticultural produce.

6. Elizabeth Dowdeswell served as UNEP's executive director from 1993 to 1997.

References

Alliance for Responsible CFC Policy. 1990. "Realistic Policies on HCFCs Needed in Order to Meet Global Ozone Protection Goals." Washington, D.C.

Benedick, R. 1991. *Ozone Diplomacy*. Cambridge, Mass.: Harvard University Press.

ENB. 1999. "Summary of the Eleventh Meeting of the Parties to the Montreal Protocol and the Fifth Conference of the Parties to the Vienna Convention: 29 November–3 December 1999." *Earth Negotiations Bulletin* 19 (6), December 6.

———. 2000. "Summary of the Twelfth Meeting of the Parties to the Montreal Protocol on Substances That Deplete the Ozone Layer: 11–14 December 2000." *Earth Negotiations Bulletin* 19 (12), December 15.

———. 2001. "Summary of the Thirteenth Meeting of the Parties to the Montreal Protocol on Substances That Deplete the Ozone Layer: 16–19 October 2001." *Earth Negotiations Bulletin* 19 (17), October 22.

———. 2002. "Summary of the Fourteenth Meeting of the Parties to the Montreal Protocol and the Sixth Conference of the Parties to the Vienna Convention: 22–29 November 2002." *Earth Negotiations Bulletin* 19 (24), December 2.

Molina, M., and S. Rowland. 1974. "Stratospheric Sink for Chlorofluoromethanes: Chlorine Atom Catalyses Destruction of Ozone." *Nature* 249 (June): 810–812.

NASA. 1988. "Ozone Trends Panel: Press Conference." Washington, D.C. March 15.

NASA, NOAA, National Science Foundation, and Chemical Manufacturers Association. 1987. "Initial Findings from Punta Arena, Chile, Airborne Antarctic Ozone Experiment." Fact sheet. September 30.

Porter, G., J. W. Brown, and P. S. Chasek. 2000. *Global Environmental Politics*. 3d ed. Boulder, Colo.: Westview.

Rowlands, I. H. 1993. "The Fourth Meeting of the Parties to the Montreal Protocol: Report and Reflection." *Environment* 35 (6): 25–34.

UNEP. 1989. "Report of the Parties to the Montreal Protocol on the Work of Their First Meeting" (UNEP/OzL.Pro. 1/5). May 6.

———. 1989a. *Synthesis Report* (UNEP/OzL.Pro.WG.II(1)/4). November 13.

———. 1989b. "Open-Ended Working Group of the Parties to the Montreal Protocol, Second Session of the First Meeting, Final Report" (UNEP/OzL.Pro.WG.I(2)/4). September 4.

———. 1989c. "Report of the First Session of the Bureau of the Parties to the Montreal Protocol" (UNEP/OzL.Pro.Bur.1/2). September 29.

———. 1989d. "Open-Ended Working Group of the Parties to the Montreal Protocol, First Session of the First Meeting, Final Report" (UNEP/OzL.Pro.WG.I(1)/3). August 25.

———. 1990. "Proposed Adjustments and Amendments to the Control Measures of the Montreal Protocol—Revised Note by the Executive Director" (UNEP/OzL.Pro.WG.IV/2/Rev.1). June 20.

———. 1990a. "Report of the Second Meeting of the Parties to the Montreal Protocol on Substances That Deplete the Ozone Layer" (UNEP/OzL.Pro.2/3). June 29.

———. 1991. "Report of the Third Meeting of the Parties to the Montreal Protocol on Substances That Deplete the Ozone Layer" (UNEP/Oz.L.Pro.3/11). June 21.

———. 1992. "Report of the Fourth Meeting of the Parties to the Montreal Protocol on Substances That Deplete the Ozone Layer" (UNEP/Oz.L.Pro.4/15). November 25.

———. 1993. "Report of the Fifth Meeting of the Parties to the Montreal Protocol on Substances That Deplete the Ozone Layer" (UNEP/Oz.L.Pro.5/12). November 19.

———. 1994. "Copenhagen Amendment on Ozone Layer to Enter into Force." UNEP News Release 1994/9, March 22.

————. 1994a. "Report of the Sixth Meeting of the Parties to the Montreal Protocol on Substances That Deplete the Ozone Layer" (UNEP/Oz.L.Pro.6/7). October 10.

————. 1995. "Report of the Seventh Meeting of the Parties to the Montreal Protocol on Substances That Deplete the Ozone Layer" (UNEP/Oz.L.Pro.7/12). December 27.

————. 1996. "Report of the Eighth Meeting of the Parties to the Montreal Protocol on Substances that Deplete the Ozone Layer" (UNEP/Oz.L.Pro.8/12). December 19.

————. 1997. "Report of the Ninth Meeting of the Parties to the Montreal Protocol on Substances That Deplete the Ozone Layer" (UNEP/Oz.L.Pro.9/12). September 25.

UNIS. 1993. "Towards Better Protection of the Ozone Layer." UNIS News Release G/35/93, November 17.

Weisskopf, M. 1990. "US Intends to Oppose Ozone Plan." *Washington Post*, May 9.

7

The Regimes against Torture

Anna R. Korula

T HE PRESENT-DAY PROSCRIPTION OF TORTURE has its origins in the development of humanitarian law on armed conflict. It was first encoded in the annexes of 1907 to the Hague Peace Conferences of 1899, stipulating that prisoners of war must be treated humanely. In response to the atrocities of World War II, legal norms were established and the prohibition of torture was embodied in the Universal Declaration of Human Rights (1948, Article 5).

Several other influential documents also recognize freedom from torture, among them the American Declaration of the Rights and Duties of Man (1948, Article 26), the Geneva Conventions (1950, Common Article 3), the United Nations International Covenant on Civil and Political Rights (1976, Article 7), the European Convention on Human Rights (1950, Article 3), the American Convention on Human Rights (1969, Article 5), the African Charter on Human and Peoples' Rights (1981, Article 5), and the Charter of Fundamental Rights of the European Union (2000, Article 4). However, despite the existence of such declarations, conventions, and charters, members of the international community have still felt the need to establish regimes to govern and suppress the practice of torture.

As with the horrors of genocide and war, torture evokes concern throughout international society. However, the majority of states still resort to torture in one form or another,[1] even though they may publicly deny it or decry the use of torture by other states. The use of torture as a systematic means of repression and control by totalitarian states and even by so-called democracies continues unabated, as evidenced by sheaves of witness and victim statements, by media reports, by case files of the International Criminal Tribunal for the Former Yugoslavia (ICTY), the International Criminal Tribunal for Rwanda (ICTR), and the South African Truth and Reconciliation Commission, and by the mass graves found in conflict zones in the Balkans and in parts of Africa, Asia, Oceania, and South America. Given the ubiquity of torture, it is only fitting that its regulation has been encoded and institutionalized, extended and refined at the international, regional, and national levels.

Today, protection from torture is regarded as a fundamental human right to which all individuals are entitled, regardless of nationality or ethnic origin. The evolving regimes on torture now include specific conventions and mechanisms at both the universal level—that is, at the level of the United Nations—and the regional level—through such institutions as the European Convention for the Prevention of Torture and Inhuman and Degrading Treatment or Punishment (ECPT), the Inter-American Convention to Prevent and Punish Torture, and the African Special Rapporteur on Prisons and Conditions of Detention. This chapter concentrates mainly on the regimes set up under the United Nations and the Council of Europe. It illustrates how these regimes—some "formal," others "informal"[2]—have developed through a series of postagreement negotiations.

The concept of torture was defined in 1984 in Article 1 of the United Nations Convention against Torture as "any act by which severe pain or suffering, whether physical or mental, is intentionally inflicted on a person for such purposes as obtaining from him or a third person information or a confession, punishing him for an act he or a third person has committed or is suspected of having committed, or intimidating or coercing him or a third person, or for any reason based on discrimination of any kind, when such pain or suffering is inflicted by or at the instigation or with the consent or acquiescence of a public official or other person acting in an official capacity. It does not include pain or suffering arising only from, inherent in or incidental to lawful sanctions."[3] This instrument has been ratified by 132 countries (as of December 2002) and is increasingly referred to by international and regional human rights courts, as well as by national courts. Some countries that have not yet ratified the Convention against Torture also refer to it, thereby extending both its legal force and its reach.

Efforts to contain torture and regulate its use, at least at the universal level, have been aimed mainly at torture practiced by states—perhaps because in the past international legislation to curb the behavior of states was limited by concerns about domestic jurisdiction and national sovereignty. However, there is increasing awareness that perpetrators are not always state organs and can include nonstate actors such as rebel groups; paramilitaries; vigilantes; criminal elements; commerical enterprises; ethnic, political, and religious factions; and individuals. Human rights regimes are only beginning to extend international instruments (for example, the May 2002 optional protocol to the Convention on the Rights of the Child) to cover some of these nonstate perpetrators.

The objective of using torture is to bring about, even if only temporarily, the disintegration of personality and the shattering of mental and emotional equilibrium in order to crush the will of the individual subjected to torture. Schmid (1993) classifies the functions of torture as follows:

- torture for purposes of extortion;
- torture to establish domination (over the victim);
- torture as individual punishment and for revenge;
- torture for information and (self-)incrimination;
- torture for terror and intimidation;
- torture for sadistic and sexual pleasure;
- torture as training for schooling torturers;
- torture for scientific experimentation;
- torture as a method of destruction (for example, destruction of the will or physique of the victim);
- torture for purposes of indoctrination;
- torture as forced obedience; and
- torture for irrational, idiosyncratic motives.

Torture apparently fulfills a dozen human "needs" that a small but powerful part of mankind seems to have. Until some functional equivalents can be found to offset these needs, the fight against torture may have to concentrate on combating symptoms rather than root causes (Schmid 1993).

The Interdisciplinary Research Program on Root Causes of Human Rights Violations (PIOOM 1994) identified fifteen modes of torture:

- psychological torture (generating states of anguish or stress through, for example, mock executions and false reports about the victim's family or friends);
- torture by means of deprivation (of water, food, sleep, vision);
- forced postures (for example, manacling a victim's hands behind his or her back for prolonged periods);
- cuts, punctures, wounds, rupture, extractions (for example, of teeth, nails, hair);
- forced ingestion (of water and unpalatable substances);
- hanging, throwing, stretching;
- beating;
- application of electrical charges or special implements of torture;
- application of drugs or nontherapeutic medicines or substances;
- burns;
- immersion ("submarine");
- unnerving or terrifying noises, light, or darkness;
- rape;
- obligation to sign statements under threat or coercion; and
- inhuman, degrading treatment and abuse or ill treatment in general (for example, solitary confinement, unsanitary prison conditions, lack of access to adequate medical aid).

Sieghart (1983) discusses what constitutes inhuman treatment and punishment as evident from case law stemming from the experience of the European Convention for the Prevention of Torture. Customary law and case law stemming from the ICTY, the ICTR, the International Criminal Court, and national courts will further extend the interpretation of torture while keeping regime norms alive at international and domestic levels and supporting the development of a regime against torture through interlinked institutional structures, mechanisms, procedures, and rules.

In the current regimes against torture, the main actors are obviously states. Other players such as nongovernmental organizations (NGOs), existing institutions such as the UN secretariat and field missions, and experts and other individuals also feed into the processes of negotiation and implementation. Courts, treaty bodies, experts, opposition parties in repressive states (where they manage to survive), IGOs, and NGOs have been involved in the processes surrounding implementation and enforcement. The media play a role in opinion building, as do NGOs, although the media are rarely present during the actual negotiation of conventions or at the meetings that constitute the review process during regime operation.

The current mandate of the institutions and bodies set up under the international conventions is to ensure that states comply with the prohibition of torture and with the ensuing implementation obligations. The regimes against torture seek to achieve this goal by closely examining the implementation behavior of states and by propagating international decision-making procedures through formal international review of state practices, as well as by continuing refinement of the regime through postagreement activities. Such action falls under the rubric of international monitoring, as categorized by Donnelly (1986a); it also corresponds to the activities described by Zartman (chapter 1 in this volume) as regime operation and evolution, and to Spector's description of behavioral regime dynamics (chapter 2). As Donnelly notes, declaratory regimes readily evolve into promotional regimes. Once states perceive a norm to be sufficiently important or appealing that they accept it as more than just a guideline, they can hardly argue against promoting it. Most states, however, are reluctant to make the qualitative leap from declaration and promotion to implementation and enforcement. Hence, international human rights regimes typically have experienced relatively smooth initial growth but thereafter have made at best only incremental and gradual progress toward a real commitment by states to implement and enforce regime norms.

Broad postnegotiation talks can have prenegotiation-type consultations embedded in them, constituting feedback loops essential to the dynamics and development of the regime. They may have differing actors (NGOs, for example) and influences (media coverage, for instance) that contribute to consensual decision making during postnegotiation phases, which may lead to pluri-sequential rule generation and observance (see Sjöstedt, chapter 3 in this volume) and to overlapping or nested postagreement negotiation processes and/or regimes.

At the universal level, regime responses have evolved from declaratory to promotional to enforcement and implementation activities. As the basic agreement has been reinforced, postagreement negotiations have added new provisions, which in turn have reinforced the initiating agreement. The movement has been from political to legal, oscillating between the two at times, or from declaration to implementation and enforcement. For example, after the UN Voluntary Fund for Torture was established in 1981, due to the efforts of Amnesty International and various other international NGOs, the next steps were to initiate negotiations on the declaration and then to proceed to encode the norms established by the declaration in a convention, based on initiatives taken by Sweden and propelled by key individuals and NGOs. Some of these features of regime evolution are discussed further below.

The Regimes against Torture under the United Nations

The descriptive analysis that follows briefly touches on the initiating negotiations and agreements of UN instruments and mechanisms. Implementation is reviewed from the perspective of postagreement negotiations—for example, the involvement of the Special Rapporteur on Torture (see below, p. 247) in such postnegotiation activities as on-site inspection, reporting, and good offices; the work of the UN Committee against Torture; and the adoption of the Optional Protocol to the UN Convention against Torture in December 2002, which establishes a preventive mechanism and an enforcement regime.[4]

Preregime Agreements

UNIVERSAL DECLARATION ON HUMAN RIGHTS. The first UN prohibition against torture was contained in the Universal Declaration on Human Rights in 1948, but it did not feature an implementation mechanism. Pursuant to the UN Charter of 1945, in 1946 the Economic and Social Council of the United Nations (ECOSOC) set up the Commission on Human Rights (CHR, which today consists of fifty-three states, elected for three-year terms).[5] After the drafting of the Universal Declaration, the commission's mandate was extended to examine the implementation of the Universal Declaration as well as to draft other human rights standards and treaties as necessary.

DECLARATION ON THE PROTECTION OF ALL PERSONS FROM BEING SUBJECTED TO TORTURE AND OTHER CRUEL, INHUMAN OR DEGRADING TREATMENT OR PUNISHMENT. This declaration was drafted by the CHR in the early 1970s and adopted without a vote by the General Assembly in 1975. Although this text was only a declaration and therefore did not contain any legally binding provisions, it had the merit of containing a first attempt to define torture in legal terms and to lay out the ensuing obligations of states.[6]

UN VOLUNTARY FUND FOR VICTIMS OF TORTURE. In December 1981, the UN General Assembly agreed to set up a voluntary fund to assist victims of torture. This initiative was taken in response to the systematic use of torture against political opponents by military dictatorships, mainly in Latin America. Because it was reluctant to infringe on state sovereignty, the General Assembly felt that the only thing the international community could do was to give assistance to the victims. Today, the fund receives voluntary contributions and maintains a strict interpretation of its mandate for the rehabilitation of victims of torture; it declines engagement in projects that have to do with the prevention of torture.

Negotiating the Regime

In December 1977, as a follow-up to the declaration of 1975, the General Assembly requested that CHR draw up a draft convention. The negotiations on the convention were complicated by political and ideological rifts, but unofficial and informal talks, education of adamant parties, strong chairmanship, problem-solving approaches, and informal mediation led to success some seven years later. These negotiations, described in Burgers (1989) and in Burgers and Danelius (1988), are summarized below. The UN Convention against Torture, and Other Cruel, Inhuman, or Degrading Treatment or Punishment (CAT) was adopted unanimously by the General Assembly in December 1984 and entered into force on June 26, 1987. The convention is open to all states.

The CAT was the first UN treaty specifically against torture and forms the foundation of the universal torture regime. Although the process from declaration to convention—that is, the movement from declaratory regime to promotional regime (Donnelly, 1986a)[7]—and its final passage into law proceeded relatively smoothly, the preagreement negotiation process leading up to it was far from easy because the treaty contained international legal—and thus compelling—obligations. The progression from a rule-based promotional regime to a rule-directed implementation and enforcement regime was further hindered by a complex array of process factors and feedback loops that have characterized the governance dynamics of the regime.

The CAT is a standard-setting instrument and primarily illustrates implementation negotiations as well as the expansion negotiations that occur in the postagreement negotiation period (Spector and Korula, 1993). It represents codification of norms and decision-making procedures accepted by international actors to regulate an issue area, a definition suggested by Donnelly (1986a), after Krasner (1982) and Haas (1980). The organizational structure of the regime against torture at the universal level is shown in figure 1, together with the phases of regime formation, evolution, and governance. Within the human rights world, it is considered a treaty sui generis, because it contains not only a human rights norm (the prohibition of torture) but also standards pertaining to criminal procedure (Articles 4 and 5), international extradition (Article 8), and administrative norms (Articles 10 and 11), as well as elements of refugee law (Article 3).

To draft the convention, the CHR set up a working group in 1977, which met for a week prior to each of the next six annual sessions of the CHR and held additional meetings during CHR sessions. The working group was open to all members of the CHR, but fewer than half the members took an active part. However, observer delegations

Figure 1. The Regime against Torture at the Universal Level

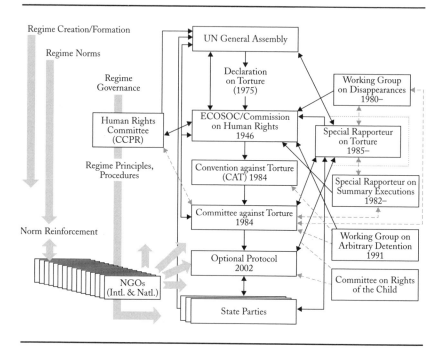

from several states that were not CHR members participated on what was essentially an equal footing with CHR members, as did several NGOs with consultative status with ECOSOC, such as Amnesty International and the International Commission of Jurists (IcJ). NGOs actively lobbied delegates in corridors, helped define issues, formulated drafts, built coalitions among like-minded states, and tried to win over fractious delegates. Because participation was open to all CHR members, decisions could be made only by consensus.

In 1981, the negotiations became deadlocked because of wide divergence on two issues that were not covered by the declaration of 1975. The first issue was the system of universal jurisdiction suggested in a Swedish draft of 1978, by which torturers could be tried in all countries adhering to the convention, whether or not they were nationals of that state and whether or not the act of torture had taken place in the state initiating criminal proceedings. Most Western governments and NGOs favored universal jurisdiction. Some Latin American states, especially Argentina and Uruguay, opposed the system and therefore took active part in the deliberations even though they probably did not intend to adhere to the convention. The second controversial issue concerned the implementation provisions, in particular the identity and functions of the body that would be mandated to supervise implementation.

Progress on these issues was made only after J. H. Burgers, who assumed the chairmanship in 1982, decided to stop seeking consensus on competing approaches and instead to explore the degree of support for specific solutions. These would then be passed on to the CHR or the General Assembly for definitive decisions. This formula-detail approach, recognized early in the literature on negotiations (Zartman and Berman 1982), produced results. A clear majority among CHR members was finally achieved on the question of universal jurisdiction, partly due to the influence of NGOs, especially in the case of France and the Netherlands. More and more states gave their consent, until only Argentina and Uruguay were left in the opposition camp. At the end of 1983 the new Argentine government of President Alfons declared its support, and Uruguay, unable to stand alone, gave its assent.

Resolution of the stalemate on implementation came in the form of general agreement to create a new organ, the Committee against Torture, although the Soviet Union rejected the proposed competence of the committee to initiate inquiries into systematic torture, and Australia pressed for a provision for publication of the findings of such an inquiry. A reformulated version (Article 20) was accepted by even Brazil and Uruguay, which had initially opposed it. The Soviet Union then proposed that the entire implementation system be made optional but was vigorously opposed by all Western delegations. In 1984, the Soviet Union withdrew this proposal but insisted that Article 20 should be optional. (The proposal as finally adopted stipulated that if reliable information is received containing well-founded indications that torture is systematically practiced in the territory of a state party, the committee may invite that state party to cooperate in the examination of the information and to this end submit observations with regard to the information. Further, a confidential inquiry may be made by the committee and may even include a visit to the territory of the state party, with its agreement.)

In 1982 and 1983, the working group concentrated its efforts on the clarification of issues rather than on the formal adoption of texts. This approach proved successful, for in 1984 consensus was reached on almost the entire draft, and the working group was able to place before the CHR a draft of thirty-two articles, of which only Article 20 and half of Article 19 (as adopted: "The States Parties shall submit . . . reports on the measures they have taken to give effect to their undertakings under this Convention") were still in brackets, awaiting consensus. The CHR had to decide what action to take, which was essentially whether to settle the outstanding issues by voting or, as suggested by the Soviet Union, to renew the mandate of the working group and to request that it reach full consensus in 1985. The CHR chose a third option, however, which was to transmit the draft as it stood to the General Assembly. A draft resolution submitted by Argentina, Finland, India,[8] the Netherlands, Senegal, and Yugoslavia was adopted without a vote and by this resolution the UN secretary-general was requested to bring to the attention of all states the report of the working group, as well as the records of the CHR's debate, and to invite these governments to submit their comments on it.

From September through November 1984, several informal consultations on the draft convention took place in New York among delegates to the General Assembly. The Dutch delegation chaired four informal meetings representing all geographical regions. However, support for the draft among the full membership of the United Nations was not as strong as among the members of the CHR, not least because many African and Asian states were not prepared to take a definitive stand on the draft convention and expressed misgivings about the inquiry system of Article 20. A number of other problems were raised regarding other provisions—for example, some Islamic states were concerned about the implications of the convention for certain forms of punishment prescribed by Islamic law.

On November 23, fourteen states submitted a draft resolution to the Third Committee suggesting adoption of the convention as it stood.

The Soviet Union submitted amendments to Articles 19 and 20, but Byelorussia offered an alternative formulation of Article 20. Meanwhile, it became apparent that some delegations were preparing a proposal to postpone the decision on the draft convention until the next General Assembly session.

Those who favored the adoption of the convention now had to choose between two options, namely, confrontation and consensus. It was clear that if the draft convention were put to a vote it would be adopted with a great many abstentions on the part of Asian and African states and a number of negative votes from the Eastern bloc, which would, of course, reduce the chances of global adherence. Moreover, if the decision were deferred to the next session of the General Assembly, the discussion on several provisions of the draft would be reopened, threatening either a delay of several years or the adoption of a seriously weakened version. The decision was made to seek consensus on the basis of the Byelorussian proposals and the Soviet Union's requirements regarding Article 19. The principal concerns of Third World delegations with respect to Article 20 were taken into account and a compromise was struck. On December 5, 1984, the Third Committee adopted the draft without a vote, as revised orally by the sponsors of the draft, and on December 10, Human Rights Day, the plenary General Assembly finally adopted the CAT (Burgers 1989).

The CAT, as adopted, calls for submission of an initial state report within one year of entry into force of the convention for the state party concerned. It also stipulates that every four years each state party must issue a further report describing new measures. The convention attracted over two dozen signatures in just three months but entered into force with 20 ratifications or accessions only two and a half years later. By May 1992, 67 states had become parties to the convention, and by December 2002, 132 states had signed.[9]

It is evident from this description of the negotiations that a combination of process and content interventions, as discussed in Pruitt (1981), was used to draft and ratify the treaty. It was often the "third-party" experts—in this case, NGOs and experts working for NGOs— who facilitated concession making and problem solving. Typically, content intervention was used in the later stages of negotiations. Pruitt's goal/expectation model also appears to be characteristic of post-agreement negotiation processes, since the two necessary conditions—having the goal of achieving coordination and trusting the other party—are likely to be default settings because building an agreement indicates the parties' intent to cooperate and at least some degree of trust. Norms and principles, especially those related to justice and fairness, therefore legitimize or strengthen rules and may even facilitate their implementation through opinion building and subsequent education (as suggested by Sjöstedt in chapter 3).

Several national and international NGOs also provided input to the drafting process by formulating drafts, lobbying, and helping to build coalitions. A number of human rights NGOs, in conjunction with the experts (usually lawyers) who served in an individual capacity on the committees or as special rapporteurs under specific human rights regimes, fed the process of regime evolution through norm-driven opinion building.

In the negotiations that create single-issue regimes such as the CAT, a good deal of the agenda formation has already occurred, so negotiators begin with issues that have already been defined and build upon them. In postagreement negotiations it is highly likely that these processes continue, although the complexity of an issue area and increasing scientific knowledge (as in the case of environmental issues) can cause postagreement negotiations to splinter into subissues. In general, the negotiations do not appear to proceed from the abstract to the concrete, because the issues are fairly clearly defined at the outset. As is shown later, there is little or no progression from competitive to coordinative tactics because the predominant goal in most human rights postagreement negotiations is cooperation, once agreement has been reached. This does not, of course, include cooperation on implementation and monitoring. However, the end-game phase is largely negated in postagreement negotiations, as are asymmetric power positions. Further, accommodation or consensus strategies rather than confrontation or coalition strategies (Dupont and Faure, 1991) typify the process in postagreement negotiations at the universal level in particular, presumably because the stakes for most governments are not as high in human rights regimes as in trade and security regimes. Communication and culture variables also appear to be symptomatic of postagreement negotiation processes in the regime against torture.

Enforcing the Regime

The Committee against Torture was set up under Article 17 of the CAT to monitor and review the implementation of the convention. Its functions, powers, and procedures are modeled on those of other treaty bodies, especially the Human Rights Committee (HRC) under the UN Covenant on Civil and Political Rights, but it is one of the smallest of the independent treaty bodies. It is serviced by the same secretariat as the HRC, together with several other bodies. The committee complements the functions of the Special Rapporteur but has a more limited mandate that offers relatively little room for shaping the implementation process.[10]

In November 1987, in what may be viewed as the first important step toward regime governance, the state parties to the convention elected ten members to the committee. The committee held its first session in Geneva on April 18–22, 1988, at which it adopted all the rules of procedure, with the exception of those relating to the inquiry procedure established by Article 20.

Disagreement with regard to this treaty focused mainly on methods of control and implementation (Kooijmans 1986). The four implementation procedures, based on drafts proposed by the Swedish government (Articles 19–22), provided ample opportunity for the committee to induce governments to abstain from practicing torture (Nowak 1988). The convention clearly spells out the committee's structure and mandate.[11] The committee has four main functions:

♦ to examine reports submitted to it under Article 19 by the state parties on the measures they have undertaken to give effect to their obligations under the convention;

♦ to conduct visits to countries, under Article 20, if the committee has received "reliable information which appears to it to contain

well-founded indications that torture is being systematically practiced,"[12] provided the state has not made a reservation to this article
and that the state under examination actually agrees to the visit by
issuing an invitation;[13]

◆ to receive and consider communications under Article 21 from other
state parties that consider that a state is not fulfilling its obligations
under the convention, provided the state in question has explicitly
accepted the committee's competence;[14] and

◆ to receive and consider communications under Article 22 "from or
on behalf of individuals . . . who claim to be victims of a violation by a
state party of the provisions of the Convention,"[15] provided the state
in question has explicitly recognized the committee's competence.

Ten independent experts examine the reports presented by state
parties to the CAT. This activity constitutes the bulk of the committee's work. The states submit an internally consolidated report, which
requires input from several ministries, such as justice, interior, defense,
and foreign affairs. The report is sent to the secretariat of the committee at the Office of the High Commissioner for Human Rights in
Geneva, translated if necessary, and then sent to the committee members themselves. The committee then designates one of its members as
a rapporteur and another as co-rapporteur, and they take the lead on the
questions to the state that may arise out of the report and are responsible for formulating the committee's observations and recommendations. On the date of the examination of the report, the state can send a
delegation to present the report.[16] After the state's oral presentation, the
rapporteurs ask their questions, usually keeping to the various articles
of the UN convention, followed by other members of the committee.
The state receives the committee's comments and recommendations
(called "Concluding Observations"), which may be specific to the state or
cover issues in general, much in the same manner as the annual reports
of the UN Special Rapporteur on Torture or other human rights treaty
bodies.[17] The aim of these legal inputs is to help form an *opinio iuris*
and thus consolidate the general prohibition of torture, as well as to
assess compliance. At present, the secretariat has only an advisory role.

The committee, although created by virtue of an international treaty, does not have an enforceable mandate. States that do not submit their reports or that do not implement the committee's recommendations are not subject to any kind of international sanction. At present, the committee has a small internal working group that is considering what can be done about the various states that have not submitted reports for over ten years. The options being considered are international condemnation, in the form of lists submitted to the General Assembly, or cooperation, in conjunction with the Technical Cooperation and Advisory Services of the Office of the High Commissioner for Human Rights.

The effectiveness of the committee's work stems from its ability to publicize infractions of regime norms and its capacity to offer advice and recommendations that have added value for the governments in terms of technical expertise. However, several governments have serious doubts as to the technical added value and see the reporting exercise and actual presentation to the committee as a necessary evil.[18]

It is also worth pointing out that the examinations of the reports are held in public sessions. The committee does not allow NGOs to take the floor, but NGOs may be present and are permitted to submit information ahead of time for the committee members to consider in conjunction with the official state reports. Furthermore, NGOs have initiated country briefings, to which the committee members are invited *ad personam*.[19] The effectiveness of these inputs is evident in the questions put to the state delegations by the committee members. The presence of NGOs also means that there are public witnesses to what the state delegation has said in a UN forum, as well as to what the committee's recommendations have been. The posting of both the official state reports and the committee's findings on the Internet has further publicized the information.

In practice, numerous obstacles have prevented effective implementation. Donnelly (1986b), in an article written before the convention entered into force, assessed the mandatory implementation system as exceedingly weak, because it involves only the review of reports on national implementation and thus depends entirely on the good faith of states. The only mandatory procedure in the committee is the consideration of periodic reports by states, since the other three implementation procedures are either optional or can be opted out by states upon ratification (Nowak 1988). The reports submitted are of varying standards and are generally overdue at the time of the meeting, and discussion of them can be summarily postponed at the request of the submitting state.[20]

Byrnes (1992) points out that the committee provides NGOs with a greater degree of formal involvement in its work than any other UN committee; provision has been made (Rules of Procedure 1989) for the committee to invite NGOs to furnish it with relevant information under all its procedures. The fact-finding activities of the NGOs are vital to the governance of the regimes, at both the universal and regional levels, because data from and lobbying by NGOs contribute extensively to opinion building and thus serve to reinforce regime norms, activities that are vital to continuing commitment to the regime.

Although the regime against torture is characterized by the acceptance of norms, the regime falls under the typology suggested by Zartman (p. 24 above) of an international standard with self-selected national exemptions. The UN convention permits reservations, unlike the European convention, and many declarations and reservations to the CAT have been deposited. However, there have also been several withdrawals of reservations, indicating a willingness to comply, reinforcement of norms, and adjustment to the regime.

Under the universal regime itself there seems to be an overlap between the functions of the Special Rapporteur and the Committee against Torture. In practice, however, there is little overlap and any resulting problems can be overcome through an exchange of information (Byrnes 1992). So far there have been only informal links and an irregular flow of information. For example, the committee requests and reads the reports of the SR on occasion, and the SR may read committee reports out of personal interest. If the links between the universal and regional and subregional regimes were more clearly defined and the information flow more closely supervised, perhaps governance in these regimes could be improved. For example, the SR and the different working groups could regularly read and review one another's reports to increase awareness of one another's work and avoid duplication of efforts.

The UN Special Rapporteur against Torture

To ensure compliance with the prohibition of torture, the Commission on Human Rights established a Special Rapporteur against Torture in its Resolution 1985/33. This is a separate but parallel structure for enforcement. The Special Rapporteur (SR) is to "seek and receive credible and reliable information from Governments, as well as specialized agencies, intergovernmental organizations and non-governmental organizations" and to "respond effectively." The SR is an independent expert in the area, serving in an individual capacity, and is not a full-time staff member of the United Nations. The incumbent spends a few weeks a year on this assignment and reports to the CHR.[21] The SR has a universal mandate; in other words, the SR can investigate any country about which allegations have been received, regardless of whether or not the country has ratified the CAT. The SR at present carries out this mandate by visiting countries to assess the situation firsthand. Since the mode of operation has not been defined in the convention, there is room for flexible and dynamic evolution of implementation over time. The SR reports to the fifty-three member-states of the CHR, which are expected to take the necessary steps to ensure compliance. However, the record suggests that, since the mid-1990s, the debate about compliance has been subject to political considerations that have little to do with the reality of the practice of torture.[22] Nevertheless, despite the weak implementation, SRs have in practice managed to carve out an important role under their mandate.

The original broad formulation of the mandate has enabled SRs to establish working practices that no state has queried per se. These practices include the transmission of urgent appeals, dispatching fact-finding missions to countries upon invitation, making surprise visits to sites not listed by the state concerned, and submitting annual reports on their activities, as well as general recommendations and considerations. Countries may disagree with the findings and have their responses included in the appendices of the annual report, but the report may not be changed. An indication of the evolving mandate of the SR may be gleaned from the report submitted by SR Sir Nigel Rodley in 2002, which shows that Rodley had initiated and undertaken nineteen visits in twelve years, considerably more than the committee had managed in the same amount of time.[23]

This evolution is mainly due to two factors: initiatives taken by the SRs themselves and initiatives by the main sponsor of the resolution on torture (in this case, Denmark, which has consistently tried over the years to enlarge the resolution against torture and the mandate of the SR).[24] Every year, a resolution condemning the practice of torture is adopted by the CHR. Like any other resolution, it can be adopted either by vote or by consensus. Over the past ten years, the practice of preparing resolutions has changed. In order to ensure consensus, the Danish delegation has held open-ended consultations on the text of the resolution,[25] enabling countries to voice their opinions and preferences before the resolution is acted upon. This process in itself constitutes ongoing postagreement negotiations and has certainly contributed to strengthening the prohibition of torture. Finally, it is worth noting that the examination of the question of torture is also included in the mandates of the country rapporteurs, as well as in that of some of the thematic rapporteurs.[26]

The act of investing authority in an SR has itself triggered postagreement negotiation activities and processes and ultimately spurred governments to participate in regime development and governance, with the SR acting as an accepted interface. The work of the SR provides an example of informal implementation negotiations that constitute an important feature of postagreement negotiation at the universal level.

A key difference between the SR and the Committee against Torture is that the SR has a universal mandate and can investigate allegations in any country, whereas the committee can operate only within the framework of the convention and only when cases are brought to its attention. The postagreement negotiations in which the SR engages constitute a special, even a unique, approach: they are not formal negotiations but a one-on-one process intended to translate, explain, defend, and apply the agreement to the parties. The SR acts as a go-between, mediator, and active proponent of the agreement. This is a characteristic UN approach to postagreement negotiations in the case of torture and other thematic rapporteurs. States appear to be willing to accept this independent mediator/facilitator role to clarify issues and to move ahead with implementation. Needless to say, the effectiveness of this office could be greatly increased if SRs could devote more than a few weeks a year to this role.

Such results, it may be noted, were achieved even before the regime was formally in place through entry into force of the convention, suggesting that norms and principles can in themselves have an impact on a problem even before the procedures crystallize (see Sjöstedt, this volume, chapter 3). Whether this leads to greater effectiveness remains uncertain. The SR, however, does appear to be a causal link between international review and domestic implementation, especially since his or her mandate has universal jurisdiction.

The SR's functions can also be viewed as the operationalization of the cooperative processes that are typical of postagreement negotiations and seek to sustain dialogue and establish continuities (see Spector, this volume, chapter 2). The SR transmits knowledge, facilitates opportunities to design innovative, mutually acceptable solutions, and bridges the gap between negotiated texts and negotiated settlements that are the key aspects of implementation. In these ways, the SR's efforts primarily revolve around regime governance and the interface between the domestic and international levels of monitoring and enforcement. They exhibit characteristics of facilitative mediation, especially in the role of fact-finder and counselor (Spector and Korula 1992), and appear to have served the purposes of regime governance.

Human rights negotiations have hitherto been low-key initiatives, sometimes on a one-to-one basis, such as that evidenced by the interventions of the SRs in cases of torture, disappearances, and so on. Postagreement negotiation processes that impinge on implementation touch on an extremely sensitive issue central to human rights practices, namely, how a state behaves within its own borders, and particularly how it treats its own citizens. Therefore, state sovereignty and attendant lack of political will, in combination with budgetary constraints, have made human rights negotiations, especially those effected by SRs, less amenable to interventions on a grand scale, such as those characteristic of environmental or trade negotiations. Human rights have invariably retained a low priority on the agendas of states. Because of some of these factors, large-scale, high-impact negotiations such as those chaired by Mostafa Tolba in the environmental domain have not been center-stage in the evolution of the human rights regime, though the situation is changing gradually.

The Istanbul Protocol

In 1999, the General Assembly in its Resolution 55/89 against torture strongly encouraged states to "reflect upon the [Istanbul] Principles as a useful tool in efforts to combat torture." These evolved during the drafting of a Manual on the Effective Investigation and Documentation of Torture and Other Cruel, Inhuman or Degrading Treatment or Punishment—also known as the Istanbul Protocol—by a coalition of experts representing forty NGOs and institutions outside the UN structure. The principles were annexed to the report of the SR to the CHR and to the General Assembly's Resolution 55/89, thus ensuring a degree of international recognition by states. They are declaratory insofar as they describe the steps to be taken by states, investigators, and medical experts to ensure the prompt and impartial investigation and documentation of complaints and reports of torture.[27] However, any state in breach of the protocol is in de facto breach of the CAT and the Universal Declaration on Human Rights.

Negotiating Adjustment and Expansion: The Optional Protocol to the UN Convention for the Prevention of Torture

Protocols are clear examples of norm reinforcement and help maintain interest in and the momentum of regime governance. They are also formal expansion negotiations that constitute a critical part of post-agreement negotiations. Negotiations on a Draft Optional Protocol to institute an effective system for the prevention of torture culminated in December 2002 after eleven years of discussion. These negotiations constituted the adjustments necessary to the regime already in place under CAT and reflect a combination of new and old initiatives as well as fresh thinking based on feedback from ongoing practices.

The need for adjustment of the regime was recognized early. The idea for a system of preventive visits to places of detention was proposed in 1976 by Jean-Jacques Gautier, a Swiss banker, who was in turn inspired by the "preventive visits" of the International Committee of the Red Cross. A draft convention was drawn up even before the United Nations began to consider a convention against torture and was adopted by the International Commission of Jurists as a draft optional protocol to the draft CAT, so as not to impede progress on the latter. This move can also be viewed as a reinforcement of regime norms.

In 1980, the government of Costa Rica officially submitted a text to the CHR that came to be known as the Costa Rica Protocol. The CHR deferred discussion on the protocol until spring 1989, recommending that "interested regions where a consensus exists should consider the possibility of a draft Convention containing ideas similar to those set out in the draft optional protocol." In 1989 the CHR further postponed consideration of the draft optional protocol, "which could represent a major step forward towards the effective prevention of torture," until 1991, because it felt it "advisable to take note . . . of the experience of the European Convention for the Prevention of Torture."

By this time, the Costa Rica Protocol could no longer be used as it stood. The Swiss Committee against Torture (SWAT), an NGO, organized a colloquium in 1990 during which a draft optional protocol was drawn up. A new draft was formulated by December 1990 based on this renewed NGO initiative. This draft was submitted to the CHR in 1991, which one year later set up an open-ended, intersessional working group to develop the draft. Although the time frame was open-ended, the fact that the results of the intersessional meetings fed into the agenda of the regular sessions of the CHR did generate some pressure.

The real negotiations on the draft protocol took place in the working group beginning in October 1992. NGOs could participate and take the floor. Most of the NGOs—for example, SOS Torture—were based in the North but had universal jurisdiction. Not all the negotiators at the governmental level were experienced negotiators or knowledgeable on the subject; the NGOs were in general more knowledgeable, better briefed, and more committed.

SWAT (now an international NGO known as the Association for the Prevention of Torture, or APT), the International Commission of Jurists, and subsequently the Austrian Committee against Torture (ACAT) were the NGOs most active in the process, not only in putting the discussion on the agenda and reopening the issue of an optional protocol but also in drafting the protocol itself. The CHR extended the mandate of the working group in 1993, but it ultimately failed to achieve a suitable agreement.

Several obstacles were encountered at the domestic level. In the Austrian case, for instance, individuals in the Ministry of Justice and the Ministry of Foreign Affairs blocked progress because they lacked either knowledge of or interest in the issues. They had to be persuaded through extensive correspondence, telephone calls, formal and informal meetings, and encounters with visiting dignitaries or bureaucrats who favored the protocol. The official Austrian position was that the Council of Europe's regional system (see below) was extensive and more than sufficient, so no real need existed for a system whereby non-Europeans would examine the performance of Europeans. Great Britain held a similar view.[28] The predominant perception in Austria, as elsewhere, was that the Austrian government did not practice torture, so it needed to do no more than support affirmative or declaratory statements. It was difficult to persuade bureaucrats of the need to examine the practices of police officers, for example, and to institute criminal liability in the event of evidence of torture.

Since 1993, the working group has met at regular intervals to negotiate the text of an optional protocol to the CAT, one that would establish a system of preventive visits. The existing mechanisms and interventions for the prevention of torture at the international level are largely reactive; they respond to acts of torture after they have taken place. The optional protocol was envisaged to be a proactive mechanism that would focus on preventing torture through regular visits to places of detention, both established state institutions and unauthorized ones identified by NGOs.

At a meeting of the working group in January 2002, a breakthrough was achieved with the presentation of a new draft text by the chairperson from Costa Rica. The compromise text envisioned a two-pillar system of torture prevention: in addition to establishing an international visiting mechanism, state parties would be required to establish an independent visiting mechanism at the domestic level. This domestic mechanism was to ensure that places of detention within a state would be visited or reviewed regularly, thus neatly extending the sphere of influence of the regime into the domestic arena. The CHR adopted the draft text of the optional protocol in April 2002. The text was then submitted for consideration by ECOSOC as well as the General Assembly and was adopted by the General Assembly on December 18, 2002. The optional protocol is open for signature and ratification beginning February 4, 2003, and requires twenty ratifications to enter into force.

The Regional Regime under the Council of Europe

The Council of Europe's European Convention on Human Rights (ECHR) was signed in November 1950 and entered into force in 1953. Article 3 of the convention guarantees freedom from torture and inhuman treatment or punishment. The human rights regime under the Council of Europe has several implementation systems: one under the charter of the Council, another under the ECHR, and a third under the European Convention for the Prevention of Torture and Inhuman or Degrading Treatment or Punishment (ECPT). The Council of Europe system is based on one set of interlocking principles but has at least three sets of rules and decision-making procedures.

These principles and norms have been reinforced and extended in scope by the European Union's Charter of Fundamental Rights of December 2000 (Article 4). This instrument is more far reaching in its coverage because it does not delimit the context in which torture takes place. It stipulates that the methods by which confessions are extracted must be documented and also covers trade in the instruments of torture, adding further important dimensions to the regime. This echoing of norms at the regional level strengthens the overall regime through adjustment and expansion.

The UN Universal Declaration was used to formulate the ECHR and was viewed as the first step toward the collective enforcement of some of the rights in the declaration. However, with the ECHR the unique idea of protecting individuals, not states, became the primary objective and became firmly embedded in international human rights law.

The ECHR entered into force in September 1953 with ten ratifications; twenty-nine states were parties by the mid-1990s. The two bodies that administer it are the European Commission on Human Rights and the European Court of Human Rights. The right of individuals to lodge complaints with the commission was made conditional on the express acceptance of the procedure by the state concerned and, if the case were to reach the court, its acceptance of the jurisdiction of the court.

The ECPT was adopted on November 26, 1987, to strengthen the implementation of the ECHR and entered into force in 1989 with seven ratifications. The European Committee for the Prevention of Torture and Inhuman or Degrading Treatment or Punishment (generally referred to as the CPT) was established by Article 1. It allows for a system of "preventive visits" to places of detention and is the first international instrument to incorporate the concept of prevention into human rights law and practice. The convention is open to all European states that are members of the Council of Europe, and it was debated whether it should be opened to nonmember-states.

The CPT comprises independent experts from member-countries and has as many members as there are parties; they serve for a period of between four and eight years. The committee meets in camera. It drew up its rules of procedure in November 1989; these have since been revised five times, indicating a willingness to adjust procedures to the exigencies of the situation and to learn from experience.

The CPT has also encouraged states to publish their reports, and, as the APT in its 1993 annual report notes, the states that do not do so attract attention. Reports are published together with the response of the CPT and, where available, the follow-up report. In the absence of reports or in the face of evidence of the systematic use of torture, the CPT has used the unorthodox and forceful measure of making a public statement. The statement on Turkey in the mid-1990s elicited considerable reaction from the Turkish government and may well encourage Turkey to improve its record, if only to avoid public censure.

The secretariat of the Council of Europe is swamped with petitions and is overburdened. The ECPT, however, is a stronger instrument than the UN convention, even though it is not a standard-setting instrument, in part because it does not allow states to make any reservations to the provisions of the convention (Article 21). Its system of on-site visits makes it one of the most effective of existing systems for the prevention of torture. It appears that the members of the CPT are more actively engaged in the activities of the committee. Moreover, Protocol No. 2 allows for continuity in membership by ensuring that, as far as possible, one-half of the membership of the committee is renewed every two years. In addition, the expertise of the members reflects a number of disciplines, and whenever the CPT makes on-site inspections a team of additional experts (for example, psychologists, translators, and medical personnel) accompanies the CPT members. Article 9 does allow states to postpone the visit of the CPT, but most states have not tried to prevent such visits from taking place. The effectiveness of the ECPT appears to depend on the relative homogeneity of the group of participating states, especially in terms of their acceptance of norms and principles.

The CPT also appears to be better informed than the UN Committee against Torture. The CPT consistently makes it a point to contact NGOs in a country that it is preparing to visit. For example, during the CPT's visit to Austria in 1991, the members met with Austrian

NGOs before they talked to Austrian bureaucrats and were exceedingly well informed on the situation in Austria (Nowak and Suntinger 1993; Nowak, interview). In the view of one NGO representative, the diplomats who attend the meetings of the Consultative Assembly or the Council of Ministers rely on trusted NGOs for data and advice because they are unable to invest the time and effort required to gain insights into the problem area.

The Council of Europe's human rights regime is generally regarded as being the most effective of the regional regimes. The Council of Europe system is also recognized for its underlying political commitment to respect human rights (Forsythe 1991). Donnelly (1986a) attributes the Council of Europe's success above all to national commitment, but also to such factors as the existence of a cultural community that supports human rights. The fact that regional enforcement is more successful than enforcement at the universal level underscores the importance of cultural community. Despite numerous outstanding problems, it appears from this case that postagreement negotiations can bring parties closer to the overall norms of the regime.

Conclusions

Negotiations at the UN level relating to the regime on torture appear to have been more cooperative than conflictual, possibly because there is an implicit need to cooperate on implementation once an agreement has been adopted and has entered into force. By and large, postagreement negotiation processes are more open than are the initiating negotiations. Moreover, as in most other UN negotiations, lack of agreement during negotiations means only postponement of the issue to the next session and reversion to the status quo in the meantime. This momentum brings pressure on the parties to conclude negotiations and avoid postponement and seems to increase the effectiveness of the postagreement negotiation process.

In the regimes against torture, norms appear to remain relatively stable, with rules and procedures changing in response to external factors. For example, the opening of the Soviet archives after the Cold War provided evidence of the extent of the atrocities committed under Stalin, and the June 1993 World Conference on Human Rights galvanized the General Assembly to institute the office of High Commissioner for Human Rights, as well as to give the go-ahead for the Draft Optional Protocol to CAT. Further, shifts in power—for example, those caused by the disintegration of the Eastern bloc—have brought about changes in the attitudes of certain states as well as greater willingness to adhere to conventions and to comply with them.

Donnelly (1986a) notes that idealists correctly stress the remarkable degree of normative consensus in human rights regimes but err in ignoring the weakness of most decision-making procedures and the substantive disagreement on interpretation of regime norms. Realists, on the other hand, correctly stress the place of power and sovereignty in the actual operation of such regimes but ignore the consensus on norms, which does demonstrably alter state behavior in some cases. However, counterpressures to limit regime effects by the opponents of regime formation (discussed by Zartman, this volume, chapter 1) are invariably present in the formative phases of human rights regimes. Zartman emphasizes that how a problem is conceptualized, as well as the norms governing conflict and cooperation, can significantly influence state behavior. The present analysis of regimes against torture corroborates these assumptions.

The intersection of regimes discussed by Zartman is clearly evident in the maintenance of the regional and universal human rights regimes discussed in this chapter, as are the purposive and recursive nature of pre- and postagreement negotiations. Formulas as well as consensuation are also clearly evident.

The institutions and bodies set up under the CAT and by the Council of Europe are capable of acquiring a life of their own and, although modest in scope, play constructive roles in the operation of governance systems. They are often entangled in the complex, and sometimes contradictory, processes of maintaining separate organizational identities and jurisdictions. In addition, the NGOs that actively lobby and even help draft the treaties constitute epistemic communities of knowledge-based experts. They conform to the roles suggested by

Haas (1990, 1992) in that they articulate cause-and-effect relationships, help states identify their interests, frame the issues for collective debate, propose specific policies and solutions (thereby generating cybernetic learning loops), and identify salient points for negotiation; they also crystallize the issues in drafts of legal documents. Exogenous factors such as new information and shifting values also influence regime operation and maintenance. The behavioral flux of redefinition, adaptation, and restructuring precipitated through the process of negotiation (see Spector, this volume, chapter 2) is also much in evidence in human rights regimes, especially in their postagreement phase.

The regulation of torture practiced by states can be addressed only at the international level, where norms and standards are set. When these norms and standards are assimilated and implemented at the regional level as well, they appear to be more effective and seem to reinforce agreements made at the universal level. However, a dichotomy in the levels of implementation is evident in states that are parties to the agreements at the universal as well as regional levels, as illustrated by the Austrian case discussed above.

The continuities as well as the evolutionary nature of postagreement negotiations suggested by Spector (this volume, chapter 2) are very much in evidence in the regimes analyzed in this chapter; so, also, are the progressions from uncertain expectations to established relationships in postagreement negotiations and the movement from the initial creation of formulas to their transformation into detail, especially with regard to negotiations on reporting and protocols. Postagreement negotiations enable new information and scientific developments to be incorporated in the progression from regime formation to regime operation. Intellectual and entrepreneurial leadership has also played a major role in shaping the agreements and the postagreement negotiation processes (Young 1991).

Processes in multilateral negotiations and postagreement negotiations appear to be similar, although the special roles played by, for example, the SR or the Committee against Torture in the development and governance of the regime are unique to postagreement negotiations. Leadership, specifically entrepreneurial and intellectual, is clearly evident in the postagreement negotiation processes where the SR is active and where NGOs (and specific individuals in particular) have made significant contributions. An example of intellectual leadership is provided by the World Medical Association's adoption of the Tokyo Declaration (October 10, 1975), which serves as a guideline for the medical profession concerning torture and other cruel activities related to detention and imprisonment. (The UN definition was adopted two months later.) In 1973, Amnesty International had hosted a conference in Paris that called for the abolition of torture and raised the issue of the role of medical personnel in torture. The first Amnesty medical group was formed in 1974, and in 1986 a forum was created by the Danish Medical Association and the International Rehabilitation and Research Centre for Torture Victims to discuss the issues and to generate momentum toward the abolition of torture. Several recommendations stemming from the conferences sponsored by these organizations are directly relevant to postagreement negotiation processes —for example, the inclusion of medical personnel on fact-finding missions (DBM 1987, 1990).

The UN system is viewed as relatively weak in practice, contrary to initial expectations and in comparison with the Council of Europe's regime against torture. This weakness has many causes, among them lack of knowledge (border guards, for example, are often unaware of their right to remand to custody any person who has been universally recognized as a torturer, such as Gen. Augusto Pinochet), fear of creating politically sensitive international incidents, and a dearth of commitment on the part of governments. Other reasons for the relative weakness of the UN regime on torture are the small size of the Committee against Torture, which has only ten members and can count on only a handful of them to be fully engaged in a specific set of deliberations (Dormenval 1990); the low quality of state reporting; and neglect of the mechanism for interstate complaints.

In practice, the issue areas within the regime are weakly linked, but it is conceivable that other related issue areas, such as disappearances, arbitrary detention, and summary executions, will be gradually included as logical extensions to the present structure, resulting in more complex interdependencies and a stronger overall regime, and allowing more logical patterns of governance to emerge. Information flows between the expert committees and ad hoc groups need to be improved, since there has been a dearth of cross-checking and information-sharing.

Further, it is evident that states may agree (for example, at the European level) to sign an agreement without realizing its full implications, may sign without intending to comply, or may simply lack the capacity to implement the provisions. The diplomats who were involved in the negotiations for the European regime were under the impression that as stable, Western democracies they were in no danger of noncompliance. It was only when on-site visits began that they realized the CPT was in earnest about its mandate and that they were required to report on measures taken—for example, to improve deplorable prison conditions, to reduce the use of prolonged solitary confinement, to record the methods used to extract confessions, and to rectify the lack of sanitary facilities in specific prisons (which was viewed as being tantamount to degrading and inhuman treatment or punishment).

Governments often lack the will to enforce the agreements that they sign, despite those governments' implicit acknowledgment of the erosion of sovereignty by participation in pre- and postagreement negotiations. Numerous tactics, such as delays in the submission of reports or claims of insufficient funds and a lack of infrastructure, are employed in the postagreement phase. Unstable implementation paths are therefore evident in human rights regimes (see Spector, this volume, chapter 3). A major obstacle to implementation of the CAT is that it constitutes international criminal law: its main thrust is to punish perpetrators. Governments are generally reluctant to implement a convention that makes a human rights offense a criminal offense (Nowak, interview). Different value systems also play a role; for example, Peter (1993) and Cobbah (1987) suggest that there is a preference for arbitration over litigation in some African countries.

Budgets present another difficult issue. The CAT's Optional Protocol will be an extremely expensive system to implement because it involves on-site visits by groups of ten to twenty experts and support staff. If one hundred countries ratify this instrument, and if only two or three countries can be visited in a year (making for a ponderously slow review process), the costs could be considerable and would limit implementation. There is a move to follow the approach of the Racial Discrimination Convention, where the parties make contributions to the budget. At present, money for the activities under the CAT comes from the overall budget. These issues will have to be examined more carefully and feasible solutions designed if postagreement negotiation processes are to be made more effective. To avoid bias the Office of the High Commissioner for Human Rights or UN headquarters could authorize contract research on these issues.

With regard to the question of whether the regional regime replaces the international regime or whether they are different manifestations of the same process, the experts seem to suggest that it is necessary to have both systems and that they work in synergy, even though one (the European) appears to be more effective than the other. This difference is due, in the view of one expert, to the nature of the instruments and the composition of the bodies directly responsible for implementation. The Council of Europe actors are fewer in number, the baseline conditions in Europe are decidedly higher than in the Third World, the legal and administrative machinery is better established, and the regional process is more amenable to criticism and change. The regional and universal regimes inevitably have a push-pull effect on each other, because the actors at the regional level also participate in the universal regime. However, at present the process of learning and knowledge transfer appears to be haphazard and ad hoc.

In practice, governments find ways to avoid monitoring and control, and the regimes against torture are hard-pressed to find ways to induce compliance, inasmuch as the regimes have instituted formal international review of state practices but no authoritative enforcement procedures. Further, states that are averse to compliance adapt by crafting loopholes that are not within the purview of the regime against torture. One cruel mechanism, termed maladaptation, is the use of "disappearances": instead of torturing and then releasing individuals who may live to tell the tale and provide evidence, persons simply disappear without a trace.[29]

In March 1992, the United States became the first nation to pass legislation—the Torture Victim Protection Act—offering torture victims the legal right to sue their oppressors (Drinan, Kuo, and Kuo 1993). This act strengthens the international conventions and goes one step beyond them by providing a remedy in national courts. If other nations follow suit, the international torture regime will be enhanced by strong implementation at the national level.

Have the regimes against torture ameliorated the problem? The answer, it would seem, lies along a continuum. Efficiency, equity, and sustainability may be unattainable norms as yet, and the use of torture is hardly on the verge of extinction. But state behavior is changing and there is increased awareness of the problem and of the remedies available, even though they are limited in scope and number. The expert bodies' activities and the review processes provide continuities in post-agreement negotiations and in themselves increase awareness of the problem within states. And states are embarrassed when international attention is drawn to alleged violations in their jurisdiction: they are concerned about how human rights standards and violations are perceived internationally, even if they do little to remedy the situation. Clearly, states are not going to volunteer information about their misdeeds, and therefore monitoring and assessment of human rights transgressions have to be strengthened. If incidents of torture appear to be on the rise, it is partly because more incidents are now reported. This in itself indicates that awareness of the problem has increased, but also that more resources should be invested in combating torture.

Furthermore, landmark postagreement negotiations such as the World Conference on Human Rights held in 1993 and its follow-up meetings have increased public attention on implementation, leading to a subsequent slight increase in the budget of the UN Office of the High Commissioner for Human Rights. The attendant international awareness, as well as the publicity given large-scale human rights violations in places such as the Balkans, Rwanda, Sierra Leone, and East Timor, has also served to bring human rights issues and negotiations to the forefront. In recent years, there has been growing acceptance—albeit mostly in the democratic countries—of the need to adhere to international monitoring and reporting requirements, as well as increased state willingness to take human rights obligations more seriously. All of these developments may be viewed as behavioral shifts triggered by postagreement negotiation processes.

Notes

The author gratefully acknowledges the assistance of Claudine Haenni, who undertook the unenviable task of updating this chapter.

1. See, for example, the discussion on use of "moderate physical force" by Israel when it was being examined by the UN Convention against Torture, and Other Cruel, Inhuman, or Degrading Treatment or Punishment (CAT) in 1999 and the subsequent rulings of the Israeli Supreme Court.

2. A "formal" regime is one based on an official text, whether a treaty or a resolution. An "informal" regime is based on the working practices of the formal bodies and agencies of a body such as the United Nations.

3. There have been several discussions about the drawbacks of this definition. See M. Evans, "Coming to Grips with Torture," *International Law Quarterly* 4 (2002). Although it is theoretically binding only for the states party to the UN Convention against Torture, this definition is being increasingly used by both the UN Special Rapporteur against Torture and regional human rights courts such as the European Court of Human Rights.

4. The analysis is based on interviews conducted on November 19, 1993, and February 12 and May 20, 1994, with Manfred Nowak, University of Vienna, who is director of the Boltzmann Institute of Human Rights. Nowak is an active member of the Austrian Committee against Torture (ACAT) and was involved in the negotiation and implementation processes surrounding the Convention against Torture as well as its Draft Optional Protocol, both as an NGO representative and in his capacity as a member of the Austrian delegation to the UN Human Rights Commission, which oversees the drafting of the Draft Optional Protocol. François de Vargas, secretary general of the Geneva-based Association for the Prevention of Torture (formerly the Swiss Committee for the Prevention of Torture) was interviewed on March 2, 1994. The author is grateful to Nowak and Vargas for granting interviews and for patiently and frankly answering numerous questions, many on sensitive issues.

5. For the current composition, see the website of the Office of the High Commissioner for Human Rights, www.unhchr.ch.

6. See, for example, Article 6: "Each State shall keep under systematic review interrogation methods and practices as well as arrangements for the custody and treatment of persons deprived of their liberty in its territory, with a view to preventing any cases of torture or other cruel, inhuman or degrading treatment or punishment."

7. Declaratory regimes involve international norms, but no international decision making; promotional activities may involve international information exchange, promotion, or assistance, and perhaps even weak monitoring of international guidelines. International enforcement activities include international decision making and the stronger forms of international monitoring. International implementation activities include weaker monitoring procedures, policy coordination, and some forms of information exchange.

8. Ironically, Amnesty International's 1992 report on India indicates that "torture is pervasive and a daily routine in every one of India's states, irrespective of whether arrests are made by the police, the paramilitary forces or the army."

9. For the complete list, see either the website of the office of the High Commissioner for Human Rights, www.unhchr.ch, or the UN press release, "Committee against Torture Concludes Twenty-ninth Session," November 22, 2002, 5.

10. A review of the committee's procedures and performance, as well as recommendations for strengthening the committee, is discussed in Bank (2000).

11. See Part II, Articles 17 to 24, UN Convention against Torture.

12. Article 20 §1, UN Convention against Torture.

13. To date this mechanism has not often come into play, although only nine states have made reservations to Article 20. In most cases the states and the committee could not agree on the terms of a visit and the states involved delayed issuing a formal invitation.

14. In fact, this provision has never been used by states. One of the reasons is probably that most states fear that another state may do the same to them, and there is no immediate self-interest, as there would be in the case of disarmament or environmental issues.

15. Article 22 §1.

16. In practice, given the lack of resources within the Office of the High Commissioner and the low number of committee members (ten), the delay between the reception of the report and its examination is between eighteen and twenty-four months.

17. See the General Comments on implementation made by the Human Rights Committee, especially General Comment 20.

18. Interviews with Danish and Russian delegations in Geneva conducted by M. Evans and C. Haenni in May 2002 in the context of research on the effectiveness of the CAT.

19. Not *in corporem;* the contrary would preclude the committee from participating.

20. See Dormenval 1990 and Byrnes 1992, who elaborate on the shortcomings of, and the problems faced by, the committee.

21. Since 1999, the Special Rapporteur also reports annually to the General Assembly.

22. Today, most NGOs consider that the resolutions coming out of the CHR do not mirror the human rights situation in the world but instead reflect what is currently politically feasible.

23. E/CN.4/2002/76.

24. Compare Res. 1986/33 and Res. E/CN.4/2002/31.

25. This practice started in 1996 and was followed shortly by the opening of the consultations to NGOs. Such consultations have become a fairly standard practice for most thematic resolutions at the CHR, but not for the country resolutions.

26. See, for example, the mandates of the Special Rapporteur on Violence against Women and the Special Representative for Human Rights Defenders.

27. For further information, see the Istanbul Protocol on the High Commissioner's website and the Human Rights Fact-Sheet 4/Rev.1, pp. 10ff.

28. In the debates and informal negotiations that led up to signature of the CAT by the United States in 1988, a combination of personal interventions, personalities, external events, and the timing of and position on the agenda at the congressional hearings served to bring reluctant senators and congressmen to closure on the issues. Winston Nagan, University of Florida, Gainesville, and Leiden University, personal communication.

29. A. P. Schmid, Leiden University, personal communication.

References

Bank, Roland. 2000. "Country-Oriented Procedures under the Convention against Torture: Towards a New Dynamism." In *The Future of UN Human Rights Treaty Monitoring,* ed. P. Alston and J. Crawford. Cambridge: Cambridge University Press.

Burgers, J. Herman. 1989. "An Arduous Delivery: The United Nations Convention against Torture (1984)." In *Effective Negotiation: Case Studies in Conference Diplomacy,* ed. J. Kaufmann. Boston: Martinus Nijhoff.

Burgers, J. Herman, and Hans Danelius. 1988. *The United Nations Convention against Torture.* Boston: Martinus Nijhoff.

Byrnes, A. 1992. "The Committee against Torture." In *The United Nations and Human Rights: A Critical Appraisal,* ed. P. Alston. Oxford: Clarendon Press.

Cobbah, Josiah A. M. 1987. "African Values and the Human Rights Debate: An African Perspective." *Human Rights Quarterly* 9: 309–331.

Crelinsten, R. D., and A. P. Schmid, eds. 1993. *The Politics of Pain: Torturers and Their Masters.* Leiden: COMT.

DBM. 1987. "Doctors, Ethics, and Torture." *Danish Medical Bulletin* 34 (4): 185–216.

———. 1990. "Medical Aspects of Torture." *Danish Medical Bulletin* 37 (1): 1–88.

Donnelly, J. 1986a. "International Human Rights: A Regime Analysis." *International Organization* 40 (3): 599–642.

———. 1986b. "The Emerging International Regime against Torture." *Netherlands International Law Review* 33 (1): 1–23.

Dormenval, A. 1990. "UN Committee against Torture: Practice and Perspectives." *Netherlands Quarterly of Human Rights* 8 (1).

Drinan, S. J., Robert F. Kuo, and Teresa T. Kuo. 1993. "Putting the World's Oppressors on Trial: The Torture Victim Protection Act." *Human Rights Quarterly* 15 (3).

Dupont, C., and G. O. Faure. 1991. "The Negotiation Process." In *International Negotiation: Analysis, Approaches, Issue,* ed. V. Kremenyuk. San Francisco: Jossey-Bass.

Forsythe, David P. 1991. *The Internationalization of Human Rights.* Lexington, Mass.: Lexington Books.

Gupta, Dipak K., Albert J. Jongman, and Alex P. Schmid. 1994. "Creating a Composite Index for Assessing Country Performance in the Field of Human Rights: Proposal for a New Methodology." *Human Rights Quarterly* 16 (1): 131–162.

Haas, E. B. 1980. "Why Collaborate? Issue Linkage and International Regimes." *World Politics* 36: 357–405 (April).

Haas, Peter M. 1990. *Saving the Mediterranean. The Politics of International Environmental Cooperation.* New York: Columbia University Press.

————. 1992. "Epistemic Communities and International Policy Coordination." *International Organization* 46 (1): 1–36.

Kooijmans, P. 1986. "Torture and Other Cruel, Inhuman or Degrading Treatment or Punishment. Report by the Special Rapporteur." ECOSOC, E/CN.4/1986/15. February 19.

————. 1987. "Question of the Human Rights of All Persons Subjected to Any Form of Detention or Imprisonment, Torture, and Other Cruel, Inhuman or Degrading Treatment or Punishment." ECOSOC, E/CN.4/1987/13. January 9.

Krasner, S. 1982. "Structural Causes and Regime Consequences." *International Organization* 36: 185.

Maran, Rita. 1990. "The Juncture of Law and Morality in Prohibitions against Torture." *The Journal of Value Inquiry* 24: 285–300.

McGoldrick, D. 1991. *The Human Rights Committee.* Oxford: Clarendon Press.

Nowak, M. 1987. "Recent Developments in Combating Torture." *SIM Newsletter* 19 (24).

————. 1988. "The Implementation Functions of the UN Committee against Torture." In *Progress in the Spirit of Human Rights*, ed. M. Nowak, D. Steurer, and H. Tretter. Festschrift für Felix Ermacora. Kehl am Rhein: N. P. Engel Verlag.

Nowak, M., and W. Suntinger. 1993. "International Mechanisms for the Prevention of Torture." In *Monitoring Human Rights in Europe*, ed. A. Bloed et al. Dordrecht: Kluwer.

————. 1994. *The Draft Optional Protocol to the UN Convention against Torture: A Cornerstone of the Human Rights Policy of Prevention.* Draft document.

Odio Benito, E. 1993. "Chairman-Rapporteur: Report of the Working Group on the Draft Optional Protocol to the Convention against Torture and Other Cruel, Inhuman, or Degrading Treatment or Punishment." ECOSOC, ECN.4/1993/28. December 2.

Peter, Chris Maina. 1993. "The Proposed African Court of Justice: Jurisprudential, Procedural, Enforcement Problems, and Beyond." *East African Journal of Peace and Human Rights* 1 (2): 117–136.

PIOOM. 1994. *Manual for Monitoring Human Rights*, ed. A. Schmid and A. Jongman. Leiden: Leiden University, PIOOM/LISWO.

Pruitt, Dean G. 1981. *Negotiation Behavior.* New York: Academic Press.

Rodley, N. S., et al. 1979. *Monitoring Human Rights Violations in the 1980s: Enhancing Global Human Rights.* New York: McGraw-Hill.

Schmid, A. P. 1993. "Twelve Functions of Torture." Paper presented at the workshop "The Crime of Torture: Causes, Consequences, Cures." World Congress, International Society for Criminology, Budapest. August 23.

Sieghart, Paul. 1983. *The International Law of Human Rights.* Oxford: Clarendon Press.

Spector, Bertram I., and Anna R. Korula. 1992. "Facilitative Mediation in International Disputes: From Research to Practical Application." WP-92-16. International Institute for Applied Systems Analysis, Austria.

————. 1993. "Problems of Ratifying International Environmental Agreements: Overcoming Initial Obstacles in the Post-Agreement Negotiation Process." *Global Environmental Change* 3 (4): 369–381.

Susskind, Lawrence E. 1994. *Environmental Diplomacy: Negotiating More Effective Global Agreements.* Oxford: Oxford University Press.

United Nations. 1992. "Report of the Committee against Torture. General Assembly. Official Records: Forty-seventh Session." Supplement No. 44 (A/47/44).

Young, Oran R. 1991. "Political Leadership and Regime Formation: On the Development of Institutions in International Society." *International Organization* 45: 281–308.

————. 1992. "International Environmental Governance: Building Institutions in an Anarchical Society." *Science and Sustainability.* Selected papers on IIASA's 20th Anniversary. Laxenburg, Austria: International Institute for Applied Systems Analysis.

Zartman, I. W., and M. R. Berman. 1982. *The Practical Negotiator.* New Haven, Conn.: Yale University Press.

Part III
Analysis

8

Regimes in Motion

Analyses and Lessons Learned

Bertram I. Spector and I. William Zartman

T HE USUAL PATTERN DISCERNIBLE in the construction of institutions, legislation, and other large endeavors begins with the elaboration through negotiation of a formula—a basic law, constitution, treaty, or other paradigmatic document—and then moves through corrective amendment toward more detailed measures of implementation, down to the "puzzle phase" of adjustment and application (Kuhn 1962). This is an ideal image, a concrete-lined irrigation canal rather than a free-flowing river. Some regime-building efforts follow such a smooth path, but most of them undergo major changes in course as they encounter new interests and resistance, absorb turbulence, and react to exogenous impacts. It is the struggle between these pressures and system-maintenance efforts to stay the course that characterizes the recursive negotiation of international regimes.

Postagreement negotiations are highly intricate, interactive, and multitheatered matters. The four case studies in this volume examine cases that embody a broad sample of regime-building dynamics. In many ways, the initiating preagreement negotiations set the stage for the subsequent negotiations and helped explain the progression of the talks. But so many new issues, actors, and conditions emerged in the postagreement negotiation theaters that the early themes did not always help to anticipate the middle movements, and by the nature of things, there is no finale. Regimes are living things, and in their lives negotiations matter.

From the point of view of the regime-building process, there are three kinds of regimes: (1) those rare and usually narrow ones that remain in force more or less as originally negotiated; (2) those more common ones that grow and evolve along a steady course through recurrent negotiations; and (3) those, equally common, that follow a jagged course, forward, backward, and sideways, from one negotiated encounter of parties to another. The fact that this collection contains no examples of the first kind of regime reflects their rarity.

The second type, marked by gradual evolution through negotiation, is represented by the Mediterranean Action Plan (MAP), ozone depletion regime, and, at a much slower pace, the regime against torture. Another striking example, at the edge of this category of regimes, is the evolution of Europe, from the Schuman Plan (ECSC) to the European Common Market to the European Community (EC) to the European Union (EU), showing that Europe is not (yet) a state but a peculiar regime in evolution.

The third type is seen in the C/OSCE regime, with its internal battles over its appropriate strength and direction and the change in mission occasioned by the shift from the Cold War. The most striking case of this type is the Climate Change Convention, which followed a contentious course through the passage of the Kyoto Protocol and then split into two groups, one larger in substance (the United States) and the other larger in numbers (all the other parties). In addition, these types may be mixed over the course of their life: The CSCE was relatively stable in its growth during its life as a conference but then launched into a new and contested career as an organization.

What explains differences between these types? What is the relation between negotiation processes and norms, on the one hand, and the evolution and stability of regimes, on the other? What is it in the negotiation process that fosters regime growth and dynamic stability? If regimes are moving courses, where are they going, and how can that course be stabilized in the process of getting there?

Stability from the Process

The first cut at an answer comes from the array of factors—maintenance, cybernetics, adjustment, and exogenous events. Where there is no exogenous disruption, the regime's evolution has a greater chance of proceeding on course from negotiation to negotiation than when unforeseen events deflect that course. In the C/OSCE regime, the end of the Cold War introduced massive changes not foreseen or foreseeable in the regime formation negotiations, setting the regime off in new—and arguably better—directions. The finding is removed from the obvious by the matter of foreseeability. Clearly, forces majeurs can disrupt any regime-building plans, but if they occur along lines already foreseen in the planning, they become a matter of intensity, not of direction. For example, exogenous inputs from the scientific community actually assisted the ozone regime negotiations, and accidents and incidents of varied importance pushed the MAP regime forward.

The cybernetic factor can also work both ways. A number of the regimes in question benefited from strong support in civil society, and some profited from a "coalition of interest and ideology" uniting private and public interest groups (Zartman 2001, 310). The ozone regime turned a corner when businesses seeing a profit in developing substitutes for chlorofluorocarbons (CFCs) joined Greens in support of the negotiations (Benedick 1991). The scientific findings and the technical feasibility of solutions at home were changing so fast that many of the subsequent agreements on thresholds and control schedules were obsolete before they came into effect, thereby propelling diplomatic activity toward further adjustments. Since many of the industrialized countries had unilaterally gone beyond the reduction targets on the table, they could easily accept these new provisions without incurring new obligations.

The CSCE also gave rise to support groups throughout member-countries—transnational coalitions, grassroots organizations, and monitor and watch groups—that enabled it to weather the end of the Cold War (Deng and Zartman 2002, chap. 3). MAP arose out of efforts by the scientific community and continued through engagement by NGOs and domestic stakeholders. The torture regime has ridden on the back of deep, organized popular pressure but has also run up against sharp opposition from the domestic groups whose behavior it seeks to outlaw. These instances stand as a reminder to negotiators—and above all their governments—to cultivate support from civil society, where norms are generated, as a necessary adjunct to their diplomatic work.

The adjustment factor is less easy to generalize. One aspect stands out, however, and that is the need for immediate benefits to outweigh the cost of concessions in regime building. Benefits are often reckoned in the future and so are hidden by the cost of current measures. Calculation of absolute costs under uncertainty is the prime element in determining parties' negotiation behavior in regime adjustment, and it has limited both regime formation and regime application in such diverse cases as the OSCE and ozone protocols. Negotiators need to devise positive cost-benefit balances to keep their regimes on course rather than count on the impelling power of the general sense of the problem and the need to solve it. The policy reversal of the United States toward the Kyoto Protocol under the Bush administration is a striking example of attempts to adjust the regime's course and of the thesis of this book in general.

Stability from the Stages

A second way of answering the questions about dynamic stability looks at the negotiation stages. The first stage of negotiations concerns regime initiation and formation. Fortunately, it appears—as initially suggested —that no particular form of initiation promises the best course for future regime growth. Regimes that begin with a broad formula— whether expressed in a framework agreement (the ozone treaty), an action plan (MAP), or a long-lasting legislative conference (Law of the Sea)—can start life on a sound footing and move to handle the challenges of governance and adjustment on that basis. But they may also be upset by later shifts of interest and power among the parties, or by exogenous shocks unforeseeable in the original formulation. Other regimes have begun in a more ad hoc way by putting together little pieces—substantive (acid rain), procedural (MARPOL), or parties (hazardous wastes)—where a broad frontal attack on the problem would only crystallize opposition.

The history to date of the ozone depletion regime is an intricately fashioned web of regime-building, governance, and adjustment negotiations based on the original formula, spurred on by rapidly mounting scientific evidence, a growing scientific consensus that facilitates political consensus, and dynamic shifts from substance to procedure. The process may be stagelike, but it certainly is not linear. Regime-building negotiations led to governance talks, then to adjustment and back to governance negotiations, all within short periods of time.

Initial negotiation of nonbinding instruments by the Organization for Economic Cooperation and Development (OECD) alerted domestic audiences to the need for control of hazardous wastes and reflected both early consensus and expert involvement. It presented a stagelike negotiation model that proceeds from principles and guidelines to details, and one that produces specific instruments from soft law beginnings. The initiating negotiations quickly turned from issue substance to political confrontation, pitting North (the waste generators) against South (the recipients). NGOs also put pressure on the industrialized countries to reach an accommodation, which in the end was a fragile compromise with many unanswered issues left over for the postagreement negotiations. Since the negotiation process continues to emphasize the North-South conflict, the fragile heritage of the initiating negotiations has not dissipated.

Not all problems are susceptible to the same strategy for institutionalized treatment. Whether the strategy is deductive, involving a broad basis with subsequent focus on adjustment negotiations, or inductive, involving a piecemeal approach with subsequent focus on bringing the pieces together in negotiations on a comprehensive formula, will depend on the nature of the problem and the array of parties' interests and power to take or oppose institutionalized action. Even though membership may be attainable only through a vague or inductive beginning, a solid beginning rooted in a problem-solving consensus is much to be preferred.

A particularly important procedural ingredient, especially in the initial negotiations, is the third-party mediator, who can keep the negotiations on track until the regime is actually created and its own dynamic can contain the parties. In the CSCE, the neutral and nonaligned (N+N) coalition played the essential role of sustaining the regime process and finding compromise during the initial period. As a coalition, these individually weaker nations were able to operate effectively as mediators and facilitators between the two superpowers, eliminating the effects of power differentials. Elsewhere, UNEP executive director Mostafa Tolba served as an active mediator in the negotiations for the Montreal Protocol and the MAP.

In the regime against torture, mediation practiced by a special rapporteur assumed the most visible role as stimulant. Created as an independent mechanism outside the convention itself, the special rapporteur has served all the roles of a classic mediator—as communicator, formulator, even manipulator—to review, cajole, seek compliance, and report to the international community. After the regime formation negotiations, governance can take place in the negotiation interface that the rapporteur creates between domestic and international levels to enhance monitoring and enforcement and to resolve grievances. Negotiators need to provide such procedural devices—catalysts, guides, monitors—to facilitate the creation of new regimes.

The second stage concerns regime governance negotiations. Where initiation and formation negotiations establish a good working relationship among the parties, the general acceptance of the regime and its problem-solving procedures changes the nature of the negotiating process from initial concessional bargaining to problem solving as a basis for governance. With this, the parties turn from a definition of the formula for dealing with their common problem to its application to realities. As in many organizations that evolve, and then stabilize and become established over time, the members quit competing and vying for advantage and begin to see the benefits of interdependence and coordination of effort as long as the stakes and problems remain relatively stable.

While the internal processes within the regime still maintain the attributes of a negotiation, it becomes transformed from one highlighting competition and exchange to one emphasizing cooperation and joint gains. There is a slow, steady adaptation of member perspectives toward accepting common obligations rather than defending individual interests. As one of the earliest regime cases in this volume, MAP had the time to mature to this point of governing regularity, but the same evolution is discernible, even if at an earlier stage, in the ozone regime.

The same evolution can lead away from integrative negotiation, however, when expert groups come to the fore and the political negotiators move to the background (Auer 1998). Attempts to address real issues within a bureaucratic, concessional bargaining atmosphere characteristic of ensconced organizational decision-making processes can take a toll on regime effectiveness. In the ozone negotiations, new thresholds and constraints tended to outpace the capacity of developing countries to implement the provisions and adjust their domestic activities appropriately. For effective measures to solve the initial problem, whatever it may be, the parties to a regime need to move their negotiations from competition to cooperation as soon as possible, establishing early on the basic formula for the distribution of costs and benefits and building on it before including new members and new issues (unless, of course, such new dimensions are necessary for the establishment of a basic formula).

Indeed, there is an economic or negotiating absolute about many governance and enforcement issues: Nothing happens unless there are provisions for an exchange of resources (usually funds or technology) or obvious benefits to offset the costs of cooperation, and the relation between the two sides' terms of trade determines the location of provisions for implementation. If minimum trade-offs are not present in a regime, it often remains merely a symbolic statement of abstract principles.

Such dimensions are the meat of the third stage, adjustment negotiations. Adjustment is the process that handles new information, process feedback, and shifts in the alignment of the parties' power and interests. Adjustment negotiations, like regime-building negotiations, can be contentious and often require more than an exchange of trade-offs to reach mutual accommodation. These are problem-solving negotiations that often aspire to major step-level changes, and successful reorientation of the regime requires creativity and flexibility. Regimes evolve and adjust, but usually not in linear movement; they follow jagged courses and oxbow loops instead. Just as a catalytic event was needed to begin negotiations to achieve the initial agreement, so, too, some catalytic occurrence is necessary to modify the regime in a major way. This can take the form of an external event, significant new information, a forceful personality, the push of the media, or simply the glaring inadequacy of the original formula. Sometimes negotiations to adjust a regime are stimulated by the unilateral actions of a powerful party that wants to go beyond the current provisions and take the next step.

The strength of scientific evidence over the course of negotiations for the ozone regime spurred the first conference of the parties to deal effectively with procedural and institutional issues, thus establishing the basis for further negotiations within the regime. This institutional base, spearheaded by UNEP with the involvement of the scientific community and the inclusion of NGOs and industry, provided the engine for dealing with more complicated issues, holding more frequent meetings, and making bolder revisions and adjustments to the initial agreements. Accommodations were developed in the financial mechanisms and technology transfer as the regime turned to expanding membership into the South; the parties negotiated a trade-off between those who would pay compensation to achieve adherence (the North) and those who would "pay" adherence in order to gain compensation (the South).

Adjustment negotiations for the CSCE saw a process of continual development of the regime through incremental progress on definitions and clarification of issues. In the midst of the Cold War, CSCE agreements based on trade-offs were sought, but they were hard to find because of the intransigence of the Eastern bloc. In a battle of the norms, the Soviets sought to maintain the status quo on the ground through immutable frontiers, while the West sought to inject change through the recognition of human rights and the free movement of peoples. A modus vivendi was found in weak CSCE institutionalization; with minimal structure, there was little chance for enforcement of the West's proposals.

Along with other regimes, the CSCE regime was forced to reconsider its raison d'être with the end of the Cold War. New adjustment negotiations targeted conflict prevention as the mission of the regime. A first step toward this new objective, with the removal of Soviet defensiveness, was the development of formal structures and institutions to go with the norms, leading the conference to become an organization. Despite the major changes negotiated in the regime, regime adjustments in this case are accomplished through a legislative approach to rule making and do not require domestic ratification negotiations.

Stability from the Depths

Regimes are affected by the turbulence they churn up from the bottom, but they are also strengthened by the effect of encasement, the existence of regional arrangements within global efforts, and both depend on domestic norms and activities. The more homogeneous normative base within a region can be a source of consensus in negotiating regional regimes that is absent when membership is expanded. While courts and interest/advocacy groups characterize the domestic regime, they operate within a consensual arena that does not exist on the international level.

Usually, regimes are self-enforcing by nature, with trade-offs for negotiation purposes but few sanctions or inducements to comply (Barrett 1998). Nonstate involvement in governance negotiations often contributes to self-enforcement. Not only can NGOs, citizen and advocacy groups, industry, and banks influence, lobby for, and advocate proposals; make demands within negotiations; and serve as watchdogs of government compliance; they are often the targets of compliance to regulation themselves. They are, after all, the ones who are charged by their national governments with "getting it done."

Domestic postagreement negotiations on hazardous wastes presented a formidable task of designing domestic laws, infrastructures, and competencies among national authorities. Especially among the developing countries, a clear consensus on the issue and the technical capacity to deal with the problem has been lacking. At the regime level, many of the initiating negotiation structures were still in place and operational during the postagreement period; scientific expert groups and diplomatic teams were effectively kept intact through successive meetings of the parties.

The multilevel interaction evident in the Mediterranean regime as well as in several of the other cases involves simultaneous subregional regimes and domestic implementation and adjustment negotiations in each country. In MAP, the major subregional negotiations are located within the European Union and serve to complicate the politics and the legal framework of the larger regime. Given overlapping memberships and loyalties, as well as conflicting and inconsistent commitments, the interaction among regimes creates a dynamic in which different levels can lead or restrain each other.

The regime on torture shares the same characteristic of encased regional or subregional and domestic regimes dealing with the same issue. A European regime on torture is but one of several regional agreements in effect that can be considered stronger than the global regime, in that the parties have accepted site visits. Global governance of the torture regime is, on the whole, weak due to a lack of institutional authority, poor state reporting, few developed mechanisms, and low political will to implement obligations nationally. It does draw some small strength from regime encasement.

Unilateral action within domestic regimes is one of the few options for strengthening an international regime; a country such as the United States can adopt strong national legislation that others will follow by example (Susskind 1994). But the growing universal reach of national courts, as in the Pinochet case in the torture regime, also strengthens the international regime. As in other cases, domestic groups of NGOs and experts working within the torture regime have been extremely important in fact-finding and reporting, drafting proposals, building coalitions, and developing the conditions for problem solving within the regime governance process. In fact, NGOs are often officially represented on national delegations. Regime effectiveness in problem solving must be viewed as the sum of successful international regime and domestic negotiations; one without the other may not produce the desired result.

At least two remedies to this vision of fragile regimes have emerged from the cases in this volume. First, high, sustained interest in an issue may not be universal but rather regional or subregional, leading to development of regional or subregional regimes that may mirror a broader regime but with the potential for greater effectiveness. Regionalization can enhance consensus on common interests and common approaches to solutions and thus make for easier trade-offs, generating stronger provisions, enforcement with teeth, and more effective regime institutions. With the prospect of greater local control over a regime and high interest, nations appear to be willing to retreat from their sovereignty claims.

Second, the countervailing force of nonstate actors rising from the bottom in the postagreement negotiation process is growing and can influence the formulation and operation of stronger and more potent regimes as these groups develop national political power bases, learn how to effectively negotiate or impact negotiations, form domestic and then transnational communities, and attract more media attention. As stakeholders and implementers in the regime, these nonstate actors often possess the power, if they can organize themselves, to make or break regimes. On the one hand, they can refuse to implement regime provisions or drag their feet, or, on the other hand, they can educate the public, direct the attention of political decision makers to new threats or reasons to strengthen the regime, lobby for enforcement, and monitor and report on compliance. To strengthen the mutual reinforcement that the three levels can give one another, negotiations need to focus on developing better linkages between them to facilitate learning, development of norms, and domestic ownership of the regime governance process.

Fear of relinquishing sovereign legal authority is obviously a very sensitive issue that constrains the evolution of any regime. International regimes constitute governing in the absence of government through the processes of negotiation. But they are certainly not spared the vicissitudes of government as a result. They are characterized by the lack of adequate institutions, authority, and enforcement over member-states. Most important, there has yet to be developed a successful formula that reduces the fears of independent countries of surrendering some of their national sovereignty. Postagreement negotiations can result gradually in a sustained recognition of superordinate goals but are much slower in the achievement of effective commitments to accomplish these objectives. Many regimes therefore operate on weak and ambiguous language, limited obligations, frail institutions, and minimal enforcement options. Typically, they can arrive at additional negotiated agreements that only mirror domestic actions already taken by the key parties; that is, the top of the current sinks to the bottom rather than the bottom rising to the top. Little progress is generated in this way; at best, the new provisions can be propagated to a wider audience. The typical absence of political will that is needed to make regimes vibrant and workable rests on two related problems: insufficient national interest in the issues, and a reluctance to surrender the required authority and control to international institutions, which in turn might be influenced strongly by opposing countries or coalitions.

In the weakest of cases, is regime building worth it? What are the benefits if a regime possesses little authority and enforcement capability? First, at a minimum, even weak regimes can keep an issue on the international agenda. Information is gathered and disseminated, exposing profligate practices as well as successful approaches. Most important, this monitoring offers a moving picture of progress on the problem: Is it getting better or worse and at what rate? Second, even weak regimes keep the parties that should be talking to one another in sustained dialogue. While much of this dialogue might be characterized as just "spinning wheels," some good can result in the form of sharing experiences and making new agreements to cooperate. Whatever the outcome, sustained dialogue at least maintains the opportunity of turning the idealism of regime principles into action, whereas the absence of dialogue does not. Third, the public exposure given an issue in even a weak regime can activate unofficial actors and stakeholders to lobby and possibly affect national policy.

Stability from Stakeholders

Regime dynamics and effectiveness are clearly affected by the interests, commitment, political will, and aversion to risk of leaders at the different levels at which postagreement negotiations occur. "Think globally, act locally" has become the hackneyed battle cry of the environmental movement, but it is not exclusive to environmentalists. Other regime arenas, such as human rights, energy, and economic reform, are governed by this principle as well. But are international regimes and postagreement negotiation processes, as currently configured, able to conceive globally and perform locally and effectively? As the cases in this volume suggest, regimes are in a continual struggle to achieve some degree of effectiveness and their achievements are sometimes questionable.

Perhaps regimes—as currently conceived and formulated by diplomats and policymakers—are not quite complete. Our analyses suggest that between domestic postagreement negotiations and international regime-based negotiations a layer of interaction may be missing that highlights transnational compliance and effective implementation. Broadly conceived, success in postagreement negotiation requires movement on three supporting layers. However, one of these layers is often inert or missing altogether. First is the international regime layer. Here, the problem is defined, the formula to resolve the problem is conceived, and recurring attempts are made to apply and adjust that formula or its replacements. International regimes gather and coordinate information needed to sustain this consensus on problem and formula and, sometimes, use peer pressure to persuade the parties to act on these principles. But it would be misleading to judge the success of a regime entirely by how well international institutions and procedures operate, nor can regimes operate effectively on the international level alone. Such success reflects only the effectiveness of bureaucratic mechanisms, not alleviation of the initiating problem.

Nor is it useful to judge success on the second, domestic, negotiation layer alone. The domestic level is where it gets done. The state actors are the ones that transform the abstract principles and commitments in treaties into concrete regulations and procedures. They establish the local infrastructure that can facilitate appropriate implementation and compliance. But this is not a very efficient process. For global accords, the domestic postagreement negotiation process must occur over 150 times—once in each state—to be accomplished! In each case it gets done separately, and perhaps differently. So in the end, compliance and effectiveness are very difficult to measure from this domestic layer; it is difficult to compare and aggregate apples, leaves, and blossoms.

The third layer is often the missing link. It concerns the interaction that should, but may not, be taking place between the singular international and the multitheater domestic negotiations. This interface is where the conceptual superstructure and the domestic undergirding of rules come together to be implemented. Guidelines that outline effective ways to pursue national implementation generally are not well established in treaties. International agreements often include only very general principles and approaches for implementers. Potentially important interfaces with regional and international agencies are left ad hoc; no specific procedures or structures to maintain practical communications or coordinate efforts are suggested. Yet upper-layer negotiations and decisions are thoroughly debated and adjusted at lower levels and the results sent up as inputs into the next international round. These interlevel interfaces are usually essential to achieve the interdependent goals outlined in the treaties. The lack of these interfaces can result in chaotic, uneven, and highly differentiated implementation. If cross-level interfaces are institutionalized, the sharing and reinforcing effect of experiences transnationally might help to overcome the absence of implementation guidelines and yield, not necessarily uniformity, but a more harmonious and efficient sense of direction to domestic compliance actions.

What form might such an interface take? The goals should be, one, to find a way to pass information and guidance from the international regime level to the implementers and from domestic forums to the official negotiators, and, two, to create networks at the multitheatered domestic level to enable experiences to be shared and successes to be reinforced. The objective would be to integrate efforts across national actors and multiply their effect. It could take the form of a transnational stakeholders network (TSN) or a global public policy network (GPPN) comprising both official and unofficial actors—state agencies responsible for rule enforcement and monitoring, as well as NGOs, industry, banks, community leaders, and other actors that have some stake in implementing the agreements (Reinecke 1999). They would form communities of interested parties—governmental and nongovernmental—that in some fashion participate in the implementation process. The purpose of their network would be to share ideas on domestic legislation and regulation, export capacity-building groups to countries that need them, foster regional coordination of implementation, and develop the analysis and arguments that can support the mobilization of governmental and nongovernmental machinery for effective implementation.

Operationally, TSNs and GPPNs could meet periodically, as do professional associations, to facilitate the sharing of ideas but would also communicate more frequently via facsimile, electronic mail, and websites. A clearinghouse of legislative materials, implementation mechanisms, enforcement options, policy research, and opportunities for coordination of efforts would also prove useful. The network would seek common, but differentiated, approaches and mechanisms to implement the agreement, based on the differing capacities and resources of the member-countries. The creation of such networks would become the responsibility of the international regime, but they should then be allowed to take on a life of their own. They should be considered official bodies but could operate as nongovernmental, nonpolitical networks, their sole function being to support effective implementation across national parties.

TSNs and GPPNs already exist in some fashion, though with limited membership, in unofficial capacities and on selected issues (Reinecke 1999). For example, the Earth Council and the International Environmental Negotiation Network focus not only on monitoring but also on support implementation activities in the areas of sustainable development among countries that participated in the United Nations Conference on Environment and Development. The International Helsinki Federation began as a watch group to monitor human rights violations under the CSCE regime but grew to support implementation across Eastern bloc countries.

The growing international call to fight corruption is a case in point. Regional conventions to reduce corruption over the past decade and a growing movement to develop an international agreement against corruption have served to put the issue on national agendas, mobilize many diverse stakeholder groups, and initiate some meaningful reforms in the direction of transparency, accountability, integrity, and good governance practices. However, there was a demand from all of these stakeholders and national entities for something more, some way to share experiences and legal and programmatic approaches to speed the reform process and avoid the mistakes of others. With the help of the OECD and other donor organizations, several networks of stakeholders—governmental and nongovernmental—have been established to promote the effectiveness of regime components and activities. An example of such a TSN, the OECD-sponsored Anti-Corruption Network for Transition Economies, established in 1999, brings civil society, business, and trade union groups together with governmental entities committed to fighting corruption and improving good governance practices in accordance with the OECD's Convention Combating Bribery of Foreign Public Officials in International Business Transactions. Encompassing the countries of Central and Eastern Europe and the former Soviet Union, the network meets on a regular basis, conducts workshops to build capacity and share information across sectors and countries, and maintains a website to disseminate new laws, new approaches, and lessons learned from past experience. Similar anticorruption networks have been formed in Asia and in subregions, such as the Stability Pact Anti-Corruption Initiative in the Balkans.

The need for regime strengthening is unquestioned, and the focus on implementation is critical. There may be alternative ways to bring it about. However, repeated negotiation on the domestic and international levels, rather than one-time legislation, is the nature of both the process and the product known as a regime. To expect more would be to see regimes as an exercise in hard law, by which count regimes in general would be wanting. An appropriate understanding of regimes as they are is the prerequisite for effective action to make a regime what one would like it to be. In regime building (as in many other aspects of international relations) negotiation matters. The active and official participation of stakeholder communities transnationally and of public policy networks globally is critical to a more effective interaction of the two levels on which regime negotiations take place.

Stability in Prospect

Much of the discussion of regime creation returns to the evaluative question: How far have we come? Have negotiations for international regimes been a success or not? Unfortunately, the full form of the question has not yet been asked. It is impossible to judge how far we have come when we have not yet spelled out how far we expect to go. If we travel from New York to Newark, our measure of the trip's success depends on whether Newark was our final destination or whether we want to end up in San Francisco. Newark versus San Francisco has not yet been posed in the literature on regime building, leaving an insufficient basis for rendering judgment.

The form that this question needs to take refers to the requirements for accomplishing the purposes of regime negotiations. What is the appropriate form of regime governance? What does it take to control the situation that is being managed through regime-building negotiations? What is the stable outcome that is expected when the problem is in hand? What form of governance is required to resolve the issue? These are questions that must be addressed if we are to be able to evaluate how far we have come. It should be emphasized that these questions are neither an exercise in prediction nor a demand for prescription. Rather, they have a double nature. They seek to make explicit the expectations that are inherent in the minds of analysts and practitioners as they go about their work. And they seek to establish verifiable and continually correctable estimates of the target at which negotiators are aiming. Thus, they fit importantly into understandings of aims and adjustments that form the basis of negotiation (Coddington 1968, chaps. 1 and 3) and that must be made explicit in order to be correctable, and correctable in order to be useful for negotiators.

These conclusions highlight a number of possible endpoints of governance that underlie various types of regime-building negotiations. Such endpoints are not mutually exclusive; they can coexist or one can lead to the other. Their existence does not suggest that efforts—or history—should end once we are "there," but they are important as targets that negotiators expect to achieve at the end of a process. Thus they may also be points for negotiators to avoid as they adjust course during negotiations.

State Coordination: This endpoint is a continuation of the continual negotiations among states. An effective agreement evolves when problems of coordination and control are worked out among sovereign states, for example, as with the agreement on chemical weapons. There is no supranational authority, no effective secretariat, and the "endpoint" is marked by repeated course changes negotiated by various changing forces and power among the states; treaty law is binding on state law, but implementation depends on national legislatures.

Corporate Directorate: In this case, attempts at issue-area regulation are taken over by the private agencies that are affected. The result is a business cartel self-regulating its own production, changes, and quotas. Unlike a narrow cartel, such an organization should involve both producers and organized consumers, both of which would take part in the regulation of supply and demand regarding regime activities.

The Market: This is a nonregulated supply-and-demand mechanism. Supply is affected by changes in costs, and demand is affected by changes in tastes and prices. The elements of change, therefore, are exogenous to the process; there is no external funding, and states are essentially the targets and subjects of autonomous control mechanisms. As in a free market, there are no players, only forces. (This seems to be one of the least likely outcomes and would be a problem to be controlled rather than a source of regulation.)

Subnational Coordination: This outcome foresees coordination among various internal agencies, such as sporadic or regular congresses of municipalities, local environmental agencies, college and university associations, or other subnational authorities that coordinate their efforts. These efforts are closer to grassroots consumers and take over the mechanisms of state control themselves.

Knowledge and Consciousness-Raising (Epistemic) Communities: Consensus on education and information is both the mechanism of control and the stable endpoint. Systematically spreading information creates the basis of voluntary consensus and compliance. The course changes as new discoveries appear. The epistemic community affects tastes and habits of consumers, which in turn affect both market and attempts at market control. Since world public opinion and scientific information are still inchoate, some kind of formal regulation would still be required but would be ancillary to the creation of an informational consensus on things to do and things not to do. Such ideas as the Geneva Convention on gas warfare or treatment of war prisoners may approximate this model.

The "Soap-Box" Moral Authority: An international advocacy organization working on a multitude of agencies coordinates awareness of regime issues, not as a legislative authority, but rather as an idealistic exponent of concern. Conscience essentially operates against state authority, building pressure at various rates in various countries at various times, producing regulatory effects that are uneven across time and within various states. Greenpeace is a current example, with its rises and falls in effectiveness and audience. Regulation is characteristically unstable.

Regime Network: This image foresees a cocoon of interstate negotiated agreements much like the GATT/WTO agreement. The regulatory mechanism then becomes a periodic negotiating session at which the members negotiate interlocking agreements. In this case, the secretariat is the procedural venue for such negotiations and for their enforcement through continued interstate negotiations, including grievance procedures. The secretariat has no financial authority, and financial incentives come from the negotiated agreements among states.

UN Agency: This model envisages an effective specialized UN agency such as the United Nations Environment Programme or the World Health Organization. Such a body would derive its powers from the United Nations and its budget would be part of the UN budget. It would serve as a mediator and secretariat for negotiations and for regulatory control, but only as a nonsovereign player in state-negotiated regulatory activities. It would function as a monitor and standard-bearer, with enforcement handled by the membership.

International Issue-Area Institution: This model would be a broad functional authority similar to the World Bank, governing a broad issue-area regime (such as health, the environment, or human rights). It would be an interstate agency established with states as members and endowed with its own funds, paid as membership fees by state members. It would also have its own bureaucracy and would be empowered by its position as a funding agency, enforcing the health of the states in the particular functional area. Incentives and funding would no longer depend on sporadic negotiations but would be the domain of the authority itself.

Transnational Regulatory Authority: This image identifies the endpoint as the result of steps leading to a self-sustained institutionalization. A transnational regulatory commission governs the issue and is sovereign over state legislators, much like the European Union at the end of the twentieth century. In this case, states come together to set up the regulatory commission in its basic area of competence; the commission sets further regulations, sanctions, and punishments. It develops financial resources through a taxation or licensing system where it meets other such international regulatory commissions. There is negotiation and coordination where their issue-areas overlap.

World Democracy: This most "extreme" image of an outcome foresees global legislation conducted by a functionalist dream. It sees problem-area regulation pushed by the requirements of its consumers and producers to the point at which a global legislative authority would be established through a spillover process of regime formation, and this authority would pass laws applicable throughout the world. Its effectiveness would depend upon the same kind of executive and implementing authorities that are now characteristic of states. This picture resolves contradictions between bureaucratic rationalism and democratic selection and—as in normal internal legislative processes—develops a working tension between technicians and politicians in the establishment of global regulations.

Some of these endpoints constitute a stable institutional framework in which workable rules, regulations, and procedures can be elaborated, although the process of doing so continues to involve negotiations, as does the preparation of bills for any legislative process. Others are characteristically soft and fluid, continually negotiated, all voice and little exit or loyalty. In the early twenty-first century, reality tends to lie at the softer end of the spectrum. But, as we have seen, where negotiators are able to translate their parties' interests and power into a common definition of a problem and its solution, that formula can stand as a stable frame for minor adjustments and effective governance. Even where major exogenous inputs challenge the ensuing course of the regime, a well-crafted formula can resist their shocks and provide guidelines for continued problem solving or bases for a new tack. But an equally important lesson that emerges from this study is the need to conduct that negotiation in depth and assure the diplomats and technicians on the upper level of support and communication at the bottom and intermediate levels.

References

Auer, Matthew R. 1998. "Colleagues or Combatants? Experts as Environmental Diplomats." *International Negotiation* 3 (2): 267–287.

Barrett, Scott. 1998. "On the Theory and Diplomacy of Environmental Treaty-Making." *Environmental and Resource Economics* 11 (3–4): 317–333.

Benedick, Richard Elliot. 1991. *Ozone Diplomacy: New Directions in Safeguarding the Planet.* Cambridge, Mass.: Harvard University Press.

Coddington, Alan. 1968. *Theories of the Bargaining Process.* Chicago: Aldine.

Deng, Francis, and I. William Zartman. 2002. *Strategic Vision for Africa.* Washington, D.C.: Brookings Institution.

Kuhn, Thomas. 1962. *The Structure of Scientific Revolutions.* Chicago: University of Chicago Press.

Reinecke, Wolfgang. 1999. "Global Public Policy Networks." Report to the Secretary-General of the United Nations.

Susskind, Lawrence. 1994. "Regime-Building Accomplishments." In *Negotiating International Regimes: Lessons Learned from UNCED,* ed. Bertram I. Spector, Gunnar Sjöstedt, and I. William Zartman. London: Graham and Trotman.

Zartman, I. William, ed. 2001. *Preventive Negotiation.* Lanham, Md.: Rowman and Littlefield.

Zartman, I. William, and Maureen Berman. 1982. *The Practical Negotiator.* New Haven, Conn.: Yale University Press.

Index

United States Institute of Peace

The United States Institute of Peace is an independent, nonpartisan federal institution created by Congress to promote the prevention, management, and peaceful resolution of international conflicts. Established in 1984, the Institute meets its congressional mandate through an array of programs, including research grants, fellowships, professional training, education programs from high school through graduate school, conferences and workshops, library services, and publications. The Institute's Board of Directors is appointed by the President of the United States and confirmed by the Senate.

Chairman of the Board: Chester A. Crocker
Vice Chairman: Seymour Martin Lipset
President: Richard H. Solomon
Executive Vice President: Harriet Hentges
Vice President: Charles E. Nelson

Board of Directors

Chester A. Crocker (Chairman), James R. Schlesinger Professor of Strategic Studies, School of Foreign Service, Georgetown University

Seymour Martin Lipset (Vice Chairman), Hazel Professor of Public Policy, George Mason University

Betty F. Bumpers, Founder and former President, Peace Links, Washington, D.C.

Holly J. Burkhalter, Advocacy Director, Physicians for Human Rights, Washington, D.C.

Marc E. Leland, Esq., President, Marc E. Leland & Associates, Arlington, Va.

Mora L. McLean, Esq., President, Africa-America Institute, New York, N.Y.

María Otero, President, ACCION International, Boston, Mass.

Barbara W. Snelling, former State Senator and former Lieutenant Governor, Shelburne, Vt.

Harriet Zimmerman, Vice President, American Israel Public Affairs Committee, Washington, D.C.

Members ex officio

Lorne W. Craner, Assistant Secretary of State for Democracy, Human Rights, and Labor

Douglas J. Feith, Under Secretary of Defense for Policy

Paul G. Gaffney II, Vice Admiral, U.S. Navy; President, National Defense University

Richard H. Solomon, President, United States Institute of Peace (nonvoting)

Getting It Done

This book is set in American Caslon; the display type is Giovanni. The Creative Shop designed the book's cover; Mike Chase designed the interior. Helene Y. Redmond made up the pages. Steven Hiatt copyedited the text, which was proofread by Karen Stough. The index was prepared by Sonsie Conroy. The book's editor was Nigel Quinney.